555

DATE DUE

MUSIC
AND
BIBLIOGRAPHY

Essays in honour of Alec Hyatt King

MUSIC
AND
BIBLIOGRAPHY

Essays in honour of Alec Hyatt King

Gerald Abraham □ Barry S Brook □ Winton Dean □ Rudolf Elvers
D W Krummel □ Margaret Laurie □ Richard Macnutt □ Miriam Miller
David Paisey □ John A Parkinson □ H Edmund Poole □ Brian Redfern
Albi Rosenthal □ Watkins Shaw □ Alan Tyson

Edited by Oliver Neighbour

K · G · Saur  Clive Bingley

New York · London · München · Paris

First published 1980
by Clive Bingley Ltd, a member of
the K G Saur International Publishing Group.
Copyright © Oliver Wray Neighbour
All rights reserved.
Set in 12/14 point Aldine Roman by Allset.
Printed and bound in the UK by
Redwood Burn Ltd of Trowbridge and Esher.
Bingley (UK) ISBN: 0-85157-296-0
Saur (US) ISBN: 0-89664-425-1

British Library Cataloguing in Publication Data
Music and bibliography.
    1. Music — Bibliography — Addresses, essays,
      lectures
    I. King, Alexander Hyatt
    II. Neighbour, Oliver Wray
    025.3'4'8   ML111

    ISBN 0-85157-296-0

CONTENTS

ACKNOWLEDGEMENTS

The editor wishes to thank the authorities listed below for permission to reproduce illustrations.

All plates in the articles by Margaret Laurie and David Paisey, as well as plate 2 in the article by H Edmund Poole, are reproduced by permission of the British Library.

Plate 3 in the article by H Edmund Poole is reproduced by permission of the Cultural Committee of the City of Manchester.

FOREWORD

OLIVER NEIGHBOUR

The specialist who enjoys a wide circle of friends within his chosen sphere is likely to have acquired them in one of two ways. He may have involved himself in the running of organizations concerned with his discipline, or he may have cultivated a broad range of interests. Alec King is one who has succeeded in doing both. In the first category he was involved in the preparation of the *British union-catalogue of early music* and the *International repertory of musical sources* (RISM), and he has held office as president of both the International Association of Music Libraries (IAML) and the Royal Musical Association. Many of the friends who have contributed to this book have been associated with him in one or other of these contexts—indeed, the happy idea for a volume in his honour originated with the United Kingdom branch of IAML. Other contributors have been his colleagues in the British Museum (and latterly in the British Library), where he spent the last thirty-two of his years of service in charge of the printed music collection and the Royal Music Library; it was the present editor's great good fortune to work with him day by day for a quarter of a century.

As for the second category, Alec King's interests have played a decisive part in shaping this volume, which reflects the main concerns of his own writings (bibliographies of which will be found in *MGG* and *The New Grove*): the history and documentation of the printing and publication of music; collections—particularly those now in the British Library —and collectors; the life and music of Mozart. If none of the byways into which his lively curiosity has led him—the glass harmonica, for instance, or Victorian illustrated titlepages—is pursued here, there are contributions in the fields of cataloguing and librarianship where he has for the most part been content to remain a highly respected practitioner rather than come forward as theorist. And two operatic interludes will serve to remind those who know his habits of another enthusiasm which has too rarely found expression in print, for whenever a revival of Handel or Mozart, Verdi or Strauss, or a rarity of any country or complexion is mounted, the hour when stumps are drawn will find him forsaking the cricket ground for the opera house. The excursion into the complexities of Meyerbeer's Italian operas will certainly make him impatient to sample their effect in performance.

The importance of this book lies primarily, of course, in the very substantial contributions made by the various authors to their chosen subjects. The reader need only study the list of contents and follow his fancy to discover that for himself. But despite their diversity the essays also complement one another, for most of them explore in some way the stages by which music reaches its audience, whether in the composer's lifetime or later. There are two aspects to this common theme. One relates to the stages themselves: the autograph score, manuscript copies intended for practical use or for the printer, the preparation and distribution of printed editions, and, at a further remove, the preservation of musical sources and the means of making them available. The other aspect is historical rather than technical, concerned with changes in the processes of publication brought about by constantly increasing demand. Although there is no reason why these two connecting threads should run parallel, they happen to do so to a considerable extent in the present volume.

For instance, two essays from the earliest period covered here, bridging the late seventeenth and early eighteenth centuries, also exemplify very forcibly problems which arise when music remains in manuscript. The manuscripts themselves, as the Chapel Royal part-books show, may be so confused as to make the task of evaluating their varying textual authority an extremely complex one; or the scribes, like those of John Blow's keyboard pieces, may take extraordinary pains to obscure the composer's intentions and muddle the ascriptions.   Similarly, two mid-eighteenth-century studies introduce techniques of printing: one publisher (Fougt) comes to grief through attempting to make use of the wrong technical process in the wrong place at the wrong time, while the working methods of a much more successful one (Forster) illustrate the vicissitudes through which music may pass on its way from copyist's manuscript to engraved plate.   The nineteenth century provides the context for studies of publishing in its wider aspects, in Berlin and in the London firm of Novello.   At this point, however, the logic that would have placed the middleman after the publisher conflicts with chronological considerations, for the middleman is represented here by Robert Martin, who sold Venetian music in seventeenth-century London and seems more at home at the beginning of the volume.   In the same way, Mozart has been allowed to take his natural place after Haydn, even though the demonstration that the composition of the 'Hunt' Quartet took much longer than has hitherto been supposed rests on a study of the autograph, and so might have stood in first place.

What the roughly chronological sequence adopted here serves to throw into especially sharp relief is the enormous expansion in publishing activity during the eighteenth and nineteenth centuries. The description of opera at the Dresden court points to the reason, for the townsfolk—however ridiculous their social and cultural pretensions may appear in the comic verses of J C Trömer—were helping to swell the vast new public for music that was emerging throughout Europe at the time.   Thus, whereas so few copies of the editions advertised by Robert Martin a hundred years earlier were printed that in many cases none has survived, Forster and his London and Paris contemporaries could operate on a previously unimagined scale. The rate of growth affected every aspect of production—the number of publications, their variety, the size of printings—and continued to increase phenomenally up to the end of the nineteenth century. Novello's octavo editions exemplify how a large-scale cheap music venture might be launched to meet a particular demand, in this case from choral societies in the growing industrial cities. But as the account of publishing in Berlin shows, such developments were eventually overtaken in their turn by the invention of a mechanical press which enabled music to be mass-produced at such low cost as to reach, and no doubt in part to create, still larger markets.

The literature of music, especially periodicals, formed an essential accompaniment to this great crescendo. If the public was not to be overwhelmed it needed guidance to help it keep its bearings, and periodicals, which had provided commentary on current musical matters since the eighteenth century, increased steadily in size and number. Russian periodicals, emerging relatively late, give ample evidence of the positive aspects of this development; the paranoid proposals of Chélard draw attention to a less happy but unfortunately perennial one. Not that musical literature owed an exclusive allegiance to the present: on the contrary, it catered simultaneously for a quite different feature of the time, the growing interest in music of earlier centuries. One important outcome of this interest was the realization that evidence about the past was disappearing at an alarming rate. In response to the needs of musical historians, institutions began adding to their antiquarian collections with fresh urgency, and the essay on Alfred Cortot's collection brings out very clearly the extent to which private collectors too were influenced by prevailing patterns of scholarly thought.

Although Cortot collected on a scale that would no longer be possible, certain types of musical sources have now become accessible in quantities that far exceed the legacy of nineteenth and twentieth-century collecting. Many musical archives belonging to great families or long-established foundations, both sacred and secular, have opened their doors to readers or passed into public ownership. Mere title and composer listing will not solve the resulting problems of co-ordination; only consistent thematic cataloguing, as the essay on that subject argues, will enable researchers to make full use of these resources. That is only one example of the new responsibilities which fall to bibliography and librarianship with the ever increasing accumulation of musical documentation—including new kinds of documentation such as sound recordings. Moreover the material itself constantly suggests new lines of study. The old divisions between the antiquarian and the modern, the academic and the practical, the serious and the ephemeral, broke down long ago; history embraces every kind of music right down to the present, along with its manner of performance and social function. It is therefore not surprising that the training of music librarians should generate endless discussion. The ideal list of specialist qualifications is formidable, as is the range of enquiry that they must meet. It is fitting that a volume devoted to the bibliography of music should close with a consideration of this all-important subject.

VENETIAN BAROQUE MUSIC
IN A LONDON BOOKSHOP:
the Robert Martin catalogues, 1633-50

D W KRUMMEL

Robert Martin was a London bookseller who specialized in the importation of foreign books. Following the practice of Maunsell and Fetherstone[1] he also issued catalogues of the books which he sold. Five of these catalogues are devoted to Italian books, arranged by subject; and each of these includes a section of music. The essential facts are shown in Table I.

TABLE 1

MARTIN'S ITALIAN CATALOGUES

1. Date of catalogue	1633	1635	1639	1640	1650
2. STC or Wing number	17512	17513 17513.5	17514	17515	M-849
3. Location of the music section (folios or pages)	$F4^r$-$G1^v$	57-61	63-67	$H1^v$-2^r	28-31
4. Number of music entries	131	129	141	107	77
5. Personal name used for alphabetization	Last	First	Last	First	Last
6. Are entries dated?	Dated	Dated	Often dated	Not dated	Not dated

It is always difficult to speculate how musical editions, music publishers, and music dealers may have influenced the musical tastes of the societies of which they were a part. In Martin's case there is some evidence—reasonably convincing insofar as it can be presented statistically—for suggesting that he was instrumental in placing in English libraries a good deal of Italian music which would otherwise have been lost, and so perhaps in influencing English musical taste in favour of an Italianate repertory.

Martin's cataloguing practices are typical for their day; that is to say, bad by current standards. In the list of citations at the end of this essay, Martin's entries for unidentified works are quoted exactly. They provide typical examples of the kind of information he gives. Often his statements present an insoluble but none the less diverting puzzle—entry 160, for instance. Martin re-catalogued his stock for each of the five catalogues, entries in the first four being about equal in detail, those in 1650 somewhat shorter. The information can vary considerably—see entry 200, for instance. With the help of modern citations of extant copies, two divergent citations can often be seen to refer to the same edition, though sometimes the opposite may be suggested—entry 145, for instance.

Thus while the five catalogues contain a total of 585 entries, many titles appear several times, a few in all five catalogues. There are altogether probably 232 different editions involved, of which 172 are extant. Of these, only seventeen appear to bear any imprint other than that of the great Venetian printing firm of Gardano (see Table II, item 9). This firm was far and away the largest music publisher in Europe between 1560 and 1620.[3] It declined in the seventeenth century, along with most other Venetian firms. On the death of Angelo Gardano in 1611 the business was taken over by his son-in-law Bartolomeo Magni, so that our count includes editions which mention either name or both. Martin presumably got his stock directly from Venice. Of the seventeen editions by publishers other than Gardano or Magni, only five come from other cities.[4] Of some significance is the absence of Rome, whose music publishers during the 1630s were challenging the trouble-ridden Venetians, and whose music was generally more in the spirit of the Counter-Reformation concerted style than that of the more open, secular, and dramatic Venetians.

TABLE II

NEW MUSIC IN THE MARTIN CATALOGUES

	1633	1635	1639	1640	1650	Total
1. Number of music entries	131	129	141	107	77	585
2. Titles seen for the first time	131	37	59	5	0	232
3. Of these, titles not extant	31	7	19	3	0	60
4. Gardano editions, pre-1600	7	1	2	0	0	10
5. – , 1600-1609[2]	14	1	7	0	0	22
6. – , 1610-1619	15	6	1	0	0	22
7. – , 1620-1629	47	9	0	0	0	56
8. – , 1630-1640	5	9	29	2	0	45
9. Other publishers' editions	12	4	1	0	0	17

It is hard to detect any kinds of Gardano edition which are conspicuously avoided or emphasized in the Martin catalogues. Instrumental, secular vocal and sacred vocal music are all represented. For a time during the mid-1630s Martin seems to have taken everything Gardano published. Of eight Gardano editions I know dated 1635, all are in the Martin catalogues; eight of twelve from 1636 are represented, and all ten from 1637. The holdings from the 1620s are far less complete. The Gardano firm was issuing upwards of twenty new editions during almost every one of these years, of which no more than five are likely to turn up in the Martin catalogues. By the mid-1630s, in other words, and presumably as a result of his 1633 catalogue, Martin's commerce in Italian music was apparently successful enough to encourage him to invest even more heavily in Gardano editions.   By 1640, however, things had changed. What?   The answer might have been political and religious (an obvious possibility, which would have been even more attractive if the 1640 catalogue had borne the date 1642), or musical (a possibility which is hard to establish but should not be neglected), or personal (having to do with Gardano, Martin, or Martin's customers or musical advisors, none of whom we know much about). Such important questions will continue to fascinate us.

What exactly do the catalogues tell us about Italian musical taste in England, and Robert Martin's role in fostering it? Alas, as little or as much as we want them to, and whatever we want them to.   Presumably Martin did have some role in whatever happened. Historians of printing have come to assume that whatever happened, happened to a greater degree when printing was involved. But what did happen? For instance, was the dramatic oratorio *Maddalena* (entry 230), with some music by Monteverdi, ever heard by an English audience, perhaps in some unrecorded private performance?   Did English musicians come to comprehend the dissonances of Gesualdo through having sung the madrigals from any of the five part-book editions which Martin imported?   Was Marenzio more popular than Palestrina in England because Martin imported twelve editions of the former and only a few of the latter?   More likely this particular preference was formed back in the days of Thomas Morley; but how much did Martin's imports serve to maintain it?   Were editions listed in successive catalogues because they sold well and Martin replenished his stock; or were they repeated because they failed to sell?   Did Martin lose interest in music after 1650 because his purchasers were no longer interested, or because he was no longer willing or able to supply their needs?   On such matters we can only speculate.

An examination of Martin's impact on present-day British

library holdings may throw some light on these questions. Of the 232 editions which Martin cites, it will be remembered, 172 are extant. Following an old rule among librarians and scholars, one expects the best collection of anything in the country itself, and the second best at the British Library. So it is here—almost. There is one surprise for us, in the library of Christ Church, Oxford. Table III shows it running neck and neck with the great library of Padre Martini, now

TABLE III

HOLDINGS OF COPIES OF EDITIONS CITED BY MARTIN

	Total number of copies held	Only known copies held
1. Oxford, Christ Church	70	21
2. Bologna, Civico Museo Bibliografico Musicale	72	10
3. London, British Library	49	5
4. Wrocłav Biblioteka Uniwersytecka	33	9
5. Other British libraries	35	1
6. Other libraries elsewhere	312	10
7. Total	571	56

housed in the conservatory in Bologna and known as the Civico Museo Bibliografico Musicale. Behind these fall the holdings which were assembled at the British Museum (now the British Library), while the great university library at Wrocław in Poland (formerly Breslau in Silesia) comes in fourth. I have not determined which library comes in fifth place, but it would probably not have any more than ten copies from our list.

British libraries in general seem to rank higher than would be expected (items 5 and 6 in Table III). The catalogue of the personal collection of Edward, Lord Herbert of Cherbury

(1583-1648), now in Jesus College, Oxford, lists eight music titles, of which three are on the Martin lists.[5] It may also be mentioned that Christ Church has a much higher proportion of complete part-book sets than any of the other four collections (Wrocław ranking second), though for present purposes the question of completeness has no bearing on the statistical evidence. What seems clear is that the similarity between the Martin catalogue listings and the Christ Church holdings is, as statisticians would say, 'more than could be accounted for by coincidence'.

One possible inference, then, is that the Christ Church collector got his music from Martin. In that case he may either have taken what Martin offered, or commissioned him to obtain his own selection of Italian music so that Martin acquired in the process a small extra stock to sell to other customers. Or the collector could conceivably have acquired his own copies in Italy, and then called the titles to Martin's attention. Such a possibility may seem far-fetched, until one looks at the manuscript holdings at Christ Church, which include music by a large number of Italian composers of the 1630s—ie, Faccho, Gaspare Filippi, Fontei, Gagliano, Gallerano, Alessandro Grandi, Gratiani, India, Francesco Maria Marini, Merula, Nenna, Pallavicino, Tomasso Pecci, Rovetta, Sances, Tomasi, and Trabattoni.[6] But the reasoning of historical causality, when printing and publishing are involved, is always treacherous in its reversability. We can equally well imagine the Christ Church collector, having acquired his music from Martin and enjoying what he got, later arranging for an Italian copyist to send him more music from his list of newly-discovered composers. It is also possible that we are not dealing here with a true collector at all—that is, a man who knew his collection, studied it, and used it as a means to expand his understanding of a subject to which he was passionately committed. He may instead have been speculating on an accumulation of music books which Martin failed to sell. The condition of the Christ Church books provides very few clues here. They have not been sumptuously bound, but neither do they show signs of neglect; in general they appear to have received some use, but not very much.

Finally, it is even possible that Dean Aldrich (1648-1710), who bequeathed the books to Christ Church[7], came upon the remnants of Martin's enterprise in London, and bought them up. Such a discovery made early in life could have led to Aldrich's continuing interest in Italian music, which is clearly reflected in his love for the music of slightly later Italian composers like Carissimi, and also in the style of his own compositions and those of his associates. Such a suggestion may seem far-fetched; but it is speculation of this kind that inspires the labours of music librarians, dealers and antiquarians.[8]

Nothing more is known about Martin as a person or as a man of business, except for a 1640 catalogue of French books which includes three music items. Martin's Italian catalogue for this same year also cites several French books,[9] in a separate section at the end.[10]

REFERENCES

1 G Pollard and A Ehrman *The distribution of books by catalogue* Cambridge, 1965, 91, where Martin is mentioned as being Fetherstone's successor. For general background see also p99. Also S Jayne *Library catalogues of the English Rennaissance* Berkeley, 1956 and J L Lievsay *The Englishman's Italian books, 1550-1700* Philadelphia, 1960.

2 This total incudes editions with the imprint of Raverio, active between 1606 and 1609, who was related to the Gardanos in business and through marriage.

3 C Sartori 'Una dinastia di editori musicali; documenti inediti sui Gardano e i loro congiunti Stefano Bindoni e Alessandro Raverii' *La bibliofilia* lviii 1956, 176-208.

4 These include Franck in Augsburg (entry 18, the only non-Italian imprint), Marescotti in Florence (66), an unidentified Milan printer (195), and Viotti in Parma (114-15). Other Venetian firms include Amadino (196), Dulcius (34), Franceschi (224), Marcolini (1), Polo (223), Salvatori (182), and Vincenti (81-2, 121, 123-4, and 183).

5 See C J Fordyce and T M Knox 'The Library of Jesus College, Oxford' *Oxford Bibliographical Society, Proceedings and papers* V 1936-9, 96. The Grandi, Piazza, and Polidori works cited there can be recognized on the list below as entries 82, 156, and 164, respectively. The Simonetti work cited there seems not to be the same as our entry 194, however, while the Monteverdi is an Antwerp edition, as incidentally is the one at Christ Church.

6 See G E P Arkwright *Catalogue of music in the library of Christ Church, Oxford* Oxford, 1915.

7 W G Hiscock *Henry Aldrich of Christ Church, 1648-1710* Oxford, 1960; see also the *Calendar of state papers, domestic series*, 1673, lxiv.

8 While the Wrocław holdings are also surprisingly strong, suggesting that another Martin may have been active in that part of the world, I think this unlikely to have been the case. These holdings become in fact even stronger in the latter half of the seventeenth century, and for the first half include many more imprints by other publishers, notably Vincenti, who was Gardano's main competitor.

9 The French editions are cited as 'Airs de Cour a 4 & parties', ie probably the Boësset series (RISM B-3272-86); 'Chansons pour dancer & boire', presumably the Ballard series beginning in 1627 (RISM 1627[5-6], 1628[10], 1631[4], 1632[8], 1633[3], 1634[5], 1637[4], 1638[6], and 1639[3]; see also the Huys catalogue of the Bibliothèque Royale, Brussels, items 261-5 and 368); and 'Vecchi Canzonette a 6 voci' (and if this is indeed a French edition I have not found it; for the Italian edition see RISM V-1026). It is interesting that no British libraries are known to hold any of these particular editions.

10 The author wishes to express special indebtedness and gratitude to the late Harris Fletcher in Urbana, for help in locating his films of the Cambridge copies of the catalogues; to H J R Wing at Christ Church, for excellent and most helpful assistance with the books there; and to Claudio Sartori in Milan and Iain Fenlon in Cambridge for special help involving their extensive knowledge of Italian baroque music.

MUSICAL EDITIONS CITED IN THE MARTIN CATALOGUES

In the citations which follow, three imprint abbreviations are used: V for Venice, G for Gardano, and M for Magni. The bibliographical reference works cited below are as follows:

Bohn: *Bibliographie der Musik-Druckwerke bis 1700 welche in der Stadtbibliothek, der Bibliothek des Acad. Inst. für Kirchenmusik, und der K. und Universitäts-Bibliothek zu Breslau aufbewahrt werden*, ed E Bohn, Berlin, 1883.

BUC: *The British union-catalogue of early music printed before the year 1801*, ed E Schnapper, London, 1957.

Eitner: R Eitner, *Biographisch-bibliographische Quellen-Lexikon der Musiker und Musikgeschichte* Leipzig, 1898-1904. (For purposes of tracing provenance and identifying lost copies—in the present list, at least ten from Berlin alone, along with many from Wrocław, such as entries 81, 99, and 175, and a number of others such as entry 124—Eitner remains quite indispensable.)

Gaspari: *Catalogo della biblioteca del Liceo Musicale di Bologna*, ed G Gaspari, Bologna, 1890-1943.

Hiff: *Catalogue of printed music published prior to 1801, now in the library of Christ Church, Oxford*, ed A Hiff, London, 1919.

RISM: *Répertoire international des sources musicales.* Three series in this inventory are distinguished according to the citation forms:

Year and superscript number: *Recueils imprimés XVIe-XVIIe siècles*, ed F Lesure, Munich, Duisburg, 1960.

Letter and number: *Einzeldrucke vor 1800*, ed K Schlager, Kassel, 1971-   (Numbers from vols 7 and 8, not yet published at the time of preparation of this study, have been kindly supplied by Otto Albrecht in Philadelphia and Frau Windisch in Kassel.)

'Ecr' and page number: *Écrits imprimés concernant la musique,* ed F Lesure, Munich, Duisburg, 1971.

Sartori: C Sartori *Bibliografia della musica strumentale italiana stampata in Italia fino al 1700* Florence, 1952, 1968.

1. Pietro AARON, *Toscanello in musica*
    (V: Marcolini, 1562)   Eitner 1:22.   RISM-Ecr 98.   Bohn 1.
    Gaspari 1:186
    1633 1635 1639
2. Giovanni Battista ALOISI, *Contextus musicarum, op.4*
    (V:M, 1637)   Eitner 1:116.   RISM A-876.   BUC 23.   Bohn 43.
    Gaspari 2:337.   Hiff 2
    1639

3. — , *Corona stellarum, op.5*
    (V:G, 1637) Eitner 1:116. RISM A-877. BUC 23. Bohn 42.
    Hiff 2
    1639 1640
4. — , *Harmonicum coelum*
    (V:M, 1628) Eitner 1:116. RISM A-875. Gaspari 2:21
    1635
5. Giovanni Battista ANDREINI, *Musiche de alcuni eccellentissimi
    musici*
    (V:G, 1617) Eitner 1:143.   RISM 1617³.   Sartori 1617h.
    Gaspari 3:7
    1633 1635 1639 1640 1650
6. Jacob ARCADELT, *Madrigali a 4 voci, libro 1*
    (V 1622) This edition not located; for others see RISM A-1314-67
    1633 1635 1639 1640 1650
7. Giovanni Giacomo ARRIGONI, *Concerti di camera*
    (V:G, 1635) Eitner 1:211. RISM A-2490. BUC 56. Bohn 50
    1635 1639
8. — , [unlocated edition]
    1633: 'Arigoni [sic] Motetti a voce sola con la partitura per
    l'Organo &c.'
9. Adriano BANCHIERI, *Vivezze di flora e primavera, op.44*
    (V:M, 1622) Eitner 1:327. RISM B-833. BUC 82
    1635 1639
10. — , *Barca di Venetia per Padova; Dilettevoli madrigali, op.12*
    (V:G, 1623) Eitner 1:325. RISM B-829. Gaspari 3:287
    1633 1635 1639 1640 1650
11. — , *Dialoghi, concerti, sinfonie, op.48*
    (V:G, 1625)   Eitner 1:326.   RISM B-811a.   Sartori 1625a.
    BUC 82
    1633
12. — , *La pazzia senile*
    (V 1627) This edition not located; for others see RISM B-816-23
    (1607 or 1621?)
    1633 ('Banchieri a 3 voci. Venetia 1627') 1635 1639 1640 1650
13. — , ('Dissonante Academico Filomuso Bolognese'), *Saviezza
    giovenile, op.1*
    (V:M, 1628) Eitner 1:327. RISM B-831. Gaspari 3:288
    1635 1639 1640 1650
14. — , [unlocated edition]
    1633: 'Filomuso a 3 voci 4. Venetia. 1627.' [Same as 12 above?]

15. Rodiano BARERA, [unlocated edition]
     1633 1635 1639 1640 1650: 'Madrigali a 4 voci, libro 1. 4. Ven.
     1624.'
16. – , [unlocated edition; mentioned by Fétis: see Eitner 1:341]
     1639 1640 1650: 'Madrigali a 5 voci, libro 2, Ven. 1615.'
17. Dionisio BELLANTE, *Concerti accademici, op.1*
     (V:M, 1629) Eitner 1:421. RISM B-1712. BUC 98. Hiff 6
     1633 1635
18. Joannes Baptista BESARDUS, *Concertationes musicae*
     (Augsburg: David Franck, 1617) Eitner 2:16. RISM 1617[26]
     1633 1635
19. Giovanni Pietro BIANDRA, [unlocated edition]
     1633   1635: 'Libro 3° madrigali a 5.4.3.2. voci con Basso
     Continuo. 4.'
20. . . . BONA [unlocated edition]
     1639: 'Bona. Stellario Musicale a 2 voci. 4. Ven. 1638.'
21. Johann BRANDSTETTER, *Nymphae duplicum aquarum incolae*
     (V:M, 1630) Eitner 2:173. RISM B-4256
     1633 1635 1639
22. Johann Martin CAESAR, *Concerti ecclesiastici*
     (V:M, 1614) RISM C-1751. BUC 177. Hiff 15
     1633 1635 1639
23. Serafino CANTONE, *Motetti concertati, libro 4*
     (V:M, 1625) Eitner 2:312. RISM C-887. Bohn 83
     1633 1635 1639 1640
24. Girolamo dalla CASA, *Il vero modo di diminuir . . .*
     (V:G, 1584) Eitner 2:351   RISM-Ecr 249. Sartori 1584d,e.
     Gaspari 1:331
     1635 1639
25. Dario CASTELLO, *Sonate concertate, libro 1*
     (V:M, 1629)   Eitner 2:361.   RISM C-1459.   Sartori 1629f.
     Bohn 90
     1633
26. Federigo CAUDA, *Catena cantionum sacrarum*
     (V:G, 1626) RISM C-1539. BUC 173. Hiff 14
     1633 1635 1639
27. Nicolo CHERUBINO, *Sacrae cantiones, liber 1*
     (V:M, 1629) Eitner 2:421. RISM C-2029. Bohn 98
     1633
     – , cf. 216 below (unlocated *Arie* by Cherubino Vesich [sic?])
28. Alessandro CIAIA, *Madrigali a 5 voci, op.1*
     (V:M, 1636) Eitner 2:439. RISM D-1394. BUC 262. Hiff 15
     1639 1640 1650

29. Antonio CIFRA, [unlocated edition]
     1633: 'Scherzi et Arie a 1.2.3. voci. fol. Ven. 1628.'
     For two other editions (V: Vincenti, 1614; Rome: Soldi, 1623)
     see Eitner 2:444, RISM C-2216-17, BUC 191
30. Giovanni Paolo COSTA, *Madrigali a 4 voci, libro 1*
     (V:G, 1613) RISM C-4223
     1633 1635 1639 1640 1650
31. Fabio CONSTANTINI, *Motetti a 1-5 voci, libro 4, op.12*
     (V:M, 1634) RISM 1634[1]
     1639 1640
32. Ambrosio CREMONESE, *Madrigali concertati, libro 1, op.1*
     (V:M, 1636) Eitner 1:126. RISM A-933. BUC 25. Hiff 18
     1639 1640 1650
33. Michele DELIPARI, *I baci; Madrigali, libro 1*
     (V:M, 1630) Eitner 3:168. RISM 1630[4], D-1393. BUC 262.
     Hiff 20
     1633 1635
34. Muzio EFFREM, *Censure sopra il 6. libro de madrigali di* . .
     Gagliano
     (V: A. Dulcius, 1623) Eitner 3:319. RISM-Ecr 289. Gaspari
     1:76. Fétis 7291
     1633 1635 1640 1650
35. Agostino FACCHO, *Madrigali, libro 2*
     (V:M, 1636) Eitner 3:379. RISM F-45. BUC 323. Hiff 24
     1639
36. − , *Motetti, libro 2*
     (V:M, 1637) Eitner 3:379. RISM F-44. BUC 323. Hiff 24
     1639
37. Benedetto FERRARI, *Musiche varie e voce sola*
     (V:M, 1633) Eitner 3:422. RISM F-265. BUC 332. Hiff 26
     1635 1639
38. − , − , *libro 2*
     (V:M, 1637) Eitner 3:422. RISM F-266. Bohn 128
     1639
39. Giovanni FERRARI, *Madrigali, libro 1, op.2*
     (V:M, 1628) Eitner 3:424. RISM F-295. BUC 332
     1635
40. Gaspare FILIPPI, *Concerti ecclesiastici, libro 1*
     (V:M, 1637) Eitner 3:444. RISM F-733. BUC 334. Bohn 131.
     Hiff 26
     1639 1640 1650
     − , [unlocated editions]
41.   1633: 'Filippi madrigali a 2.3.4. voci. 4. Venetia. 1632.'

42. 1640 1650: 'Gaspar Filippi Libro secondo a 1. & 2. voci. Ven.'
43. 1635 1639 1640: 'Gaspare Fillipi Faville Amorose a voce sola.
     4. Venet. 1633.'
     FILOMUSO = Banchieri
44. Giacomo FINETTI, *Motecta a 2 voci, libro 2*
     (V:G, 1621) Eitner 3:452. RISM F-817. Gaspari 2:421
     1633
45. — , *Sacrarum cantionum ternis vocib. . . . libro 4*
     (V:M, 1621) Eitner 3:453. RISM F-824
     1633
46. — , *Sacrae cantiones 2 voc. . . . , liber 3*
     (V:M, 1620) Eitner 3:453. RISM F-821. Gaspari 2:421
     1633
47. Cristoforo FLORIANI, [unlocated edition]
     1633 1635: 'Florani [sic] motecta a 2.3.4. voci cum basso 4.
     Ven. 1623.'
48. [Alfonso FONTANELLI], *Madrigali senza nome a 5 voci, libro 1*
     (V:G, 1616) RISM F-1480
     1633 1635 1639 1640 1650
49. — , — , *libro 2*
     (V:G, 1619) Eitner 4:24. BUC 642. RISM F-1483
     1633 1635 1639 1640 1650
50. Nicolò FONTEI, *Bizzarrie poetiche*
     (V:M, 1635) Eitner 4:24. RISM F-1485. BUC 343. Hiff 28
     1635 1639 1640 1650
51. — , — , *libro 2*
     (V:M, 1636) Eitner 4:24. RISM F-1486. BUC 343. Hiff 28
     1640 1650
52. — , *Melodiae sacrae*
     (V:M, 1638) Eitner 4:24. RISM F-1487. BUC 343. Hiff 28
     1639
53. Andrea GABRIELI, *Cantionum ecclesiasticarum 4 vocum . . .
     liber 1*
     (V:G, 1589) Eitner 4:112. RISM G-55
     1639 1640 1650
54. — , *Madrigali a 3 voci, libro 1*
     Eitner 4:112 and RISM G-68-71 cite four Venetian editions
         (V:G, 1575, 1782, 1590, and V:Raverio, 1607).   See also
         BUC 356, Gaspari 3:73
     1639 (date of 1602 specified) 1640 1650
55. — , *Madrigali et ricercari . . . a 4 voci*
     (V:G, 1589) Eitner 4:113. RISM G-77. BUC 356. Gaspari 3:73
     1633 1635 1639 1640 1650

56. — , *Mascherate . . . à 3, 4, 5, 6, et 8 voci*
    (V:G, 1601) Eitner 4:113. RISM 1601[11], G-79
    1635 1639 1640 1650

57. Giovanni GABRIELI, *Canzoni et sonate . . . à 3-22 voci*
    (V:M, 1615) Eitner 4:115. RISM G-88. Sartori 1615f
    1633 1635 1639 1640 1650

58. — , *Symphoniae sacrae . . . à 6-19 vocis*
    (V:M, 1615) Eitner 4:115. RISM G-87. BUC 356. Gaspari
    2:424
    1633 1635 1639 1640

59. Marco da GAGLIANO, *Musiche a 1-3 voci*
    (V: Amadino, 1615) Eitner 4:124. RISM G-115. BUC 357
    1633

60. — , *Madrigali a 5 voci, libro 6*
    (V:M, 1620) Eitner 4:124. RISM 1620[17], G-117
    1633 1640 1650

61. — , *Sacrarum cantionum . . . liber 2*
    (V:M, 1622) Eitner 4:124. RISM G-106. BUC 357
    1635
    — , [unlocated editions]

62. 1633: 'Bassus generalis a unis ad 6. fol. Ven. 1622.'

63. 1639: 'Bassus universalis de unis ad 6. voci. fol.'

64. 1633: 'Bassus generalis a 6 vocibus lib. secundus. fol. Ven.
    1622.'

65. 1633 1639: 'Madrigali a 5 voci. 4. Venetia. 1620.'

66. Vincenzo GALILEI, *Dialogo della musica*
    (Florence: Marescotti, 1581) Eitner 4:128. RISM-Ecr 344
    1633

67. Leandro GALLERANO, *Ecclesiastica armonica, libro 1, op.6*
    (V:M, 1624) RISM G-156. BUC 357. Hiff 29
    1633 1635

68. Pietro Francesco GARZI, *Madrigali e canzonette, op.3*
    (V:M, 1629) Eitner 4:160. RISM G-448. BUC 362
    1633 1635 1639 1640 1650

69. Jhan GERO, *Madrigali a 2 voci, libro 1*
    (V:G, 1629) RISM G-1640
    1633 1635 1640 1650

70. Carlo GESUALDO, Prince of Venosa, *Madrigali a 5 voci*
    (V:M, 1616) Eitner 4:219. RISM G-1724. BUC 372. Gaspari
    3:77. Hiff 70
    1633 1635 (dated 1617) 1639 1640 1650

71.　−, −, *libro 2*
　　(V:M, 1617)　Eitner 4:219.　RISM G-1729.　BUC 372.　Gaspari
　　　3:77.　Hiff 70
　　1635 (dated 1616)　1639　1640　1650
72.　−, −, *libro 3*
　　(V:G, 1619)　Eitner 4:219.　RISM G-1734.　BUC 372.　Gaspari
　　　3:77.　Hiff 70
　　1635　1639　1640　1650
73.　−, −, *libro 4*
　　(V:G, 1616)　Eitner 4:219.　RISM G-1738.　BUC 372.　Gaspari
　　　3:77.　Hiff 70
　　1635　1639　1640　1650
74.　−, −, *libro 6*
　　(V:G, 1616)　Eitner 4:220.　RISM G-1742.　BUC 372.　Gaspari
　　　3:77.　Hiff 70
　　1635　1639
75.　Marco GHIRLANDI, *Madrigaletti a 3 voci, libro 1*
　　(V:G, 1627)　Eitner 4:226 (lost Berlin copy only, not in RISM)
　　1633
76.　Ruggiero GIOVANELLI, *Villanelle et arie, libro 1*
　　(V:M, 1624)　Eitner 4:261.　RISM G-2472.　Gaspari 3:234
　　1633　1635
77.　... (Francesco?) GIULIANI, [unlocated edition]
　　1633: 'Giuliano Concerti a voce sola con basso continuo per
　　　l'Organo. 4. 1632.'
78.　Alessandro GRANDI, *Celesti fiori; Concerti, libro 5*
　　(V:G, 1638)　Eitner 4:334.　RISM G-3441.　BUC 394.　Gaspari
　　　2:433.　Hiff 32
　　1633　1640
79.　−, −, (The same work.)
　　(V:G, 1638)　Eitner 4:334.　RISM G-3442.　BUC 394.　Bohn
　　　162.　Hiff 32
　　1639　1650
80.　−, *Messa et salmi* [i.e., 'Raccolti'] *a 2, 3, et 4 voci*
　　(V:G, 1636-37)　Eitner 4:334.　RISM 1636^1, G-3461.　Bohn 160
　　1639
81.　−, *Cantade et arie a voce sola*
　　(V:Vincenti, 1620)　Eitner 4:335.　Bohn 158　(Copy lost; not
　　　in RISM)
　　1633
82.　−, [Motets, various books in various editions]
　　(V:Vincenti, 1610-30)　Eitner 4:335.　RISM G-3417-57.　BUC 394
　　1633: 'Grandi il 1.2.4.5.6. Libro de Motetti.'

83. — , *Motetti a voce sola*
    (V:M, 1628) Eitner 4:334. RISM G-3444. BUC 394.   Bohn
    160. Hiff 31
    1633 1639 1640
84. . . . GRATIANI, [unlocated edition]
    1633: 'Gratiani Motetti concertati a 2 voce. 4. Ven. 1630.'
85. Annibale GREGORI, *Sacrarum cantionum, op.8*
    (V:M, 1635) RISM G-3813 (Glasgow copy, not in BUC)
    1639
86. — , *Ariosi concenti, op.9*
    (V:M, 1635) Eitner 4:362. RISM G-3815
    1640
87. Antonio GUALTIERI, *Motetti a 1-4 voci, libro 3, op.10*
    (V:M, 1630) RISM G-4793. BUC 407. Hiff 34
    1633 (dated 1632)
88. — , [unidentified edition]
    1633   1635: 'Gualtieri Madrigali a 2.3.4.5. voci. 4. Venetia.
    1628.'
    1639 1640: 'Ant. Gualtieri Concertati a 2.3.4.5. voci.'
    Gualtieri's op 8 is the *Madrigali concertati a 1, 2, et 3 voci* of
    1625 (RISM G-4796), making the lost book a likely candidate
    for op 9
89. Cesario GUSSAGO, [unlocated edition]
    1633 1635 1639 1640 1650: 'Gussachius Solatium spirituale
    in Psal. Davidis a 2. 3. & 5. [or: 2. 3. & 4.] voci. Venetia. 1619.'
90. Sigismondo d'INDIA, *Madrigali a 5 voci, libro 1*
    (V:G, 1610) Eitner 9:169. RISM I-21. BUC 543. Hiff 36
    1633   1636   1639   (1639 specifies an edition of 1615, not
    located)
91. — , — , *libro 2*
    (V:G, 1611) Eitner 9:169. RISM I-25. BUC 543. Hiff 36
    1633 1635 1639
92. — , — , *libro 3*
    (V:M, 1615) Eitner 9:169. RISM I-27. BUC 543. Hiff 36
    1633 1635 1639
93. Stefano LANDI, *La morte d'Orfeo: Tragi-comedia pastorale*
    (V:M, 1619) Eitner 6:34. RISM L-528. BUC 593
    1635 1639 1640
94. — , *Arie da cantarsi ad una voce, libro 5*
    (V:M, 1637) Eitner 6:34. RISM L-535. Bohn 232
    1639 1640

95. Orlando di LASSO, *Motetti a 3 voci . . . , libro 1*
(V:G, 1592) RISM L-1001. Bötticher 1592e.
1633 1635

96. Alberto LAZARI, *Armonie spirituali concertate, libro 2, op.2*
(V:M, 1637) Eitner 6:88. RISM L-1182. BUC 604. Bohn 242.
Gaspari 2:447
1639 1640 1650
— , [unlocated editions]

97. 1639 1640 1650: 'Madrigali a 3 voci. 4. Venetia. 1637.'

98. 1639 1640: 'Glorie de Venetia cantado, a 2 voce [or: a 1.2.
voci]. fol.'

99. Madalena (i.e. Francesco) MANNELLI, *Musiche varie, libro 4, op.4*
(V:G, 1636) Eitner 6:303. Bohn 271 (Copy lost; not in RISM)
1639 1640 1650

100. Antonio MARASTONI, *Madrigali concertati, op.6*
(V:G, 1628) Eitner 6:308. RISM M-407. BUC 647. Hiff 40
1633 1635 1639 1640

101. Luca MARENZIO, *Madrigali a 5 voci, libro 2*
(V:G, 1606) Eitner 6:321. RISM M-543. BUC 652
1633 1635 1639 1640 1650

102. — , — , *libro 4*
(V:G, 1607) Eitner 6:322. RISM M-552. Gaspari 3:103
1633 1635 1639 1640 1650

103. — , — , *libro 5*
(V:G, 1605) Eitner 6:322. RISM M-556. Gaspari 3:103
1633 1635 1639 1640 1650

104. — , — , *libro 6*
(V:M, 1614) Eitner 6:324. RISM M-559. BUC 652
1633 1635 1639 1640 1650

105. — , — , *libro 7*
(V:G, 1609) Eitner 6:324. RISM M-562. Gaspari 3:104
1633 1635 1639 1640 1650

106. — , — , *libro 9*
(V:G, 1609) Eitner 6:324. RISM M-570. Gaspari 3:104
1633 1635 1639 1640 1650

107. — , *Madrigali a 6 voci, libro 1*
(V:G, 1603) Eitner 6:321. RISM M-503. BUC 652
1633 1635 1639 1640 1650

108. — , — , *libro 2*
(V:G, [1600?]) Eitner 6:322. RISM M-506. BUC 652. Gaspari
3:103
1639 1640 1650

109. − , − , *libro 4*
      (V:G, 1605) Eitner 6:323. RISM M-514. BUC 652
      1633 1635 1639 1640 1650
110. − , − , *libro 5*
      (V:G, 1610) Eitner 6:323. RISM M-518. BUC 652
      1633 1635 1639 1640 1650
111. − , − , *libro 6*
      (V:G, 1609) Eitner 6:324. RISM M-520. BUC 652. Gaspari
      3:103
      1633 1635 1639 1640 1650
112. − , *Motecta festorum totius anni, liber 1*
      (V:G, 1606) Eitner 4:322. RISM M-498
      1633 1635
113. Biagio MARINI, *Arie, madrigali, et corenti, op.3*
      (V:M, 1620) Eitner 6:333. RISM M-659. Gaspari 3:104
      1633
114. − , *Scherzi et canzonette, op.5*
      (Parma: A. Viotti, 1622) Eitner 6:333. RISM M-660. Gaspari
      3:242
      1635 1639
115. − , *Le lagrime d'Erminia, op.6*
      (Parma: A. Viotti, 1623) Eitner 6:333. RISM M-661. Gaspari
      3:104
      1635
116. − , *Musiche di camera; concerti, op.7*
      (V:M, 1634) Eitner 6:333. RISM M-662. BUC 654. Hiff 43
      1635
117. − , *Sonate concertate symphonie, op.8*
      (V:M, 1626) Eitner 6:333. RISM M-663. Sartori 1629g (also
      vol.2, 1629m). Bohn 272
      1633 1635 1639
118. − , *Madrigaletti, libro 5, op.9*
      (V:M, 1635) Eitner 6:333. RISM M-664. BUC 654. Hiff 44
      1635
119. Francesco Maria MARINI, *Concerti spirituali, libro 1*
      (V:M, 1637) RISM M-672. BUC 654. Bohn 274. Hiff 44
      1639
120. Giovanni Battista MECCHI, *Motecta 5 et 8 vocum, liber 1*
      (V:G, 1611) Eitner 6:414. RISM M-1690. BUC 667. Gaspari
      2:458
      1633 1635 1639 (cites 'Madrigali a 5. & 8. voci') 1640 1650

121. Pietro MELLI, *Intavolatura di liuto*
     (V:Vincenti, 1616) Eitner 6:432. RISM M-2221-3. BUC 669
     1633

122. Tarquinio MERULA, *Musiche concertate, libro 2*
     (V:M, 1635) Eitner 6:445. RISM M-2349. BUC 671. Hiff 45
     1639

123. − , *Motetti . . . a 2, 3, 4, e 5 voci, op.6*
     (V:Vincenti, 1624)   Eitner 6:445.   RISM M-2338.   Gaspari
       2:460
     1633

124. − , *Satiro, e Corisca; Dialogo musicale*
     (V:Vincenti, 1626) Eitner 6:445 (Berlin and Paris copies only).
       RISM M-2347 (Venice copy only)
     1633

125. − , *Curtio precipitato et altri capricii*
     (V:M, 1638) Eitner 6:445. RISM M-2351. BUC 671
     1639

126. Grammatico METALLO, *Ricercari a 2 voci*
     (V:M, 1626) RISM M-2450. Gaspari 4:213
     1633 1635 1639 1640 1650

127. Girolamo MONTE DELL'OLMO, *Applausi ecclesiastici, libro 1*
     (V:M, 1636, 1637) Eitner 4:267. RISM 1636³, 1637¹,
       G-2516-17. BUC 687. Bohn 156. Gaspari 3:428. Hiff 47
     1639 1640 1650

128. − , *Sacri affeti; Motetti a voce sola, libro 2*
     (V:M, 1637) Eitner 4:268. RISM G-2518. BUC 687. Hiff 47
     1640

129. Claudio MONTEVERDI, *Lamento d'Ariana*
     (V:M, 1623) Eitner 7:45. RISM M-3451
     1633 1635 1639

130. − , *Madrigali a 5 voci, libro 1*
     (V:M, 1621) Eitner 7:45. RISM M-3455. BUC 687. Hiff 48
     1633 1635 1639 1640

131. − , − , *libro 2*
     (V:M, 1621) Eitner 7:45. RISM M-3458. BUC 687. Gaspari
       3:129. Hiff 48
     1633 1635 1639 1640

132. − , − , *libro 3*
     (V:M, 1621) Eitner 7:45. RISM M-3466. BUC 687. Gaspari
       3:129
     1633 1635 1639 1640

133. − , − , *libro 4*
      (V:M, 1622) Eitner 7:45. RISM M-3473. BUC 688. Gaspari
      3:129
      1633 1635 1639
134. − , −, *libro 5*
      (V:M, 1620)   Eitner 7:46. RISM M-3483. BUC 688. Gaspari
      3:129
      1633 1639
135. − , − , *libro 6*
      (V:M, 1620) Eitner 7:46. RISM M-3492. BUC 688. Gaspari
      3:129. Hiff 48
      1633 1635 1639
136. − , *Madrigali a 1-6 voci, libro 7*
      (V:M, 1628) Eitner 7:46. RISM M-3497. BUC 688. Gaspari
      3:130. Hiff 48
      1633 1635
137. − , *Scherzi musicali a 3 voci*
      (V:M, 1628) Eitner 7:46. RISM M-3489. BUC 688
      1633 (specifies a 1632 edition) 1635   1639 (specifies a 1638
      edition)
138. − , *Scherzi musicali a 1 & 2 voci*
      (V:M, 1632) Eitner 7:46. RISM M-3499
      1633 1635 1639 (specifies a 1638 edition)
139. − , [unlocated edition]
      1633: 'Monteverdi Motetti a 2.3.4. & 6 voci. 4. Venet. 1630'
      (the date is hard to read; it could be 1620).
      − , *Musica della Maddalena.* See no. 230 below
140. Pomponeo NENNA, *Madrigali a 5 voci, libro 1*
      (V:M, 1617) Eitner 7:170. RISM 1617[18], N-383. BUC 727.
      Gaspari 3:136. Hiff 50
      1633 1635 1639 1640 1650 (?)
141. − , − , *libro 4*
      (V:M, 1617)   Eitner 7:171.   RISM N-385.   Gaspari 3:136.
      BUC 727. Hiff 50
      1633 1635 1639 1640 1650 (?)
142. − , − , *libro 7*
      (V:M, 1624) Eitner 7:171. RISM N-396. BUC 727. Gaspari
      3:137. Hiff 50
      1633 1635 1639
143. Simpliciano OLIVO, [unlocated edition; cf. Eitner 7:236]
      1633   1635   1639   1640   1650: 'Olivo la carcerata minsa
      (i.e., "Ninfa"). favola Boscareccia. fol. Venetia 1618.'

144. Giovanni Pierluigi da PALESTRINA, *Madrigali a 4 voci, libro 1*
(V:G, 1605) Eitner 7:299. RISM P-760. Gaspari 3:141
1633 1635 1639 1640 1650

145. — , *Madrigali a 5 voci, libro 1*
(V:G, 1604) Eitner 7:299. RISM P-762. Gaspari 3:141
There are two citation forms in the Martin catalogues:
    1633 1639: 'Aloysio il primo libro de Madrigali a 5 voci. 4.
    Ven. 1604.'
    1635 1640 1650: 'Gio. Pietro al Praeneste primo libro de
    Madrig. a 5 voci con Basso Contin.'
The latter form presumably identifies another edition with an
added continuo, not now extant

146. Benedetto PALLAVICINO, *Madrigali a 5 voci, libro 1*
(V:G or Raverio, 1606) Eitner 7:302. RISM P-774-5. BUC
760. Hiff 53
1639 1640 1650

147. — , — , *libro 2*
(V: Raverio, 1606 or G, 1607) Eitner 7:302. RISM M-777-8.
BUC 760. Hiff 53
1639 1640 1650

148. — , — , *libro 3*
(V: Raverio, 1606 or G, 1607) Eitner 7:302. RISM M-780-1.
BUC 760. Hiff 53. Gaspari 4:143.
1639 1640 1650

149. — , — , *libro 4*
(V:G, 1607) Eitner 7:302. RISM 1607[22], P-788. BUC 760.
Gaspari 3:143. Hiff 54
1639 1640 1650

150. — , — , *libro 5*
(V:G, 1609) Eitner 7:302. RISM P-792. BUC 760. Gaspari
3:143. Hiff 53
1639 1640 1650

151. — , — , *libro 6*
(V:G, 1611) Eitner 7:302. RISM P-794. BUC 760. Gaspari
3:143. Hiff 54
1639 1640 1650

152. — , [unlocated edition]
1633 1635 1639 1640 1650: 'Madrigali [in 1640: "Madrigaletti"] a 4 voci. 4. Venet. 1607.'

153. Desiderio PECCI, *Sacri modulatus, op.3*
(V:G, 1629) RISM P-1100. BUC 766. Hiff 56
1633

154. ... (Tomasso or Desiderio?) PECCI, [unlocated edition]
        1633: 'Pecci le Musiche sopra l'Adone di Malvezzi. fol. Venet.
        1619.'
155. Diego PERSONI, [unlocated edition]
        1639 1640 1650: 'Diego Persone madrigali a 4 voci. 4. Ven.
        1622.'
156. Giovanni Battista PIAZZA, *Canzonette a voce sola* [*libro 1*
        and/or 2]
        (V:M, 1633) Eitner 7:429. RISM P-2037-8. Gaspari 3:248.
        BUC 782. Hiff 58
        1635
        − , − , [unlocated editions]
157. 1639 1640: 'Piazza Canzonette a voce sola, libro 3. 4. Ven.
        1636.'
158. 1639 1640 1650: 'Gio. Bapt. Piazza, Lib. quarto a voce sola.'
159. 1639 1640 1650: 'Corrente alla Frencese. fol. Ven. 1637.'
        [Cf Eitner 7:429; Sartori, vol 2, 1628o]
160. Antonio PICCOLO (?), [unidentified edition]
        1640 1650: 'Anto. Piccolo à Pula [in 1640: "Pulic"] à 5. vocis.'
161. Francesco PIOVESANA, *Misure harmoniche regolate*
        (V:M, 1627) Eitner 7:454. RISM -Ecr 655. Gaspari 1:242
        1633 1635 1639
162. Atanesio da PISTICCI, *Motetti a 2 & 3 voci, libro 3, op.6*
        (V:M, 1633) Eitner 7:459. RISM P-2454. BUC 786. Bohn 310.
        Hiff 58(?)
        1639 1640 1650
163. − , *Motetti a 2 voci, libro 4, op.7*
        (V:M, 1637) RISM P-2455. BUC 786. Hiff 58
        1639 1640
164. Ortensio POLIDORI, *Motetti a voce sola, op.13*
        (V:M, 1636) RISM P-5024. BUC 801. Hiff 59
        1639
        Massimo POLLETTI, [unlocated editions]
165. 1635: 'Massimo Polletti Canzoni Spirituali 4. Venet. 1627.'
166. 1633: 'Polletti da cantarsi nell'Organo a 2 & 3 voci col Basso
        Generale.'
167. Giovanni Battista PORTA, *Madrigali a 5 voci*
        (V:M, 1616) Eitner 8:31. RISM P-5208. Gaspari 3:153
        1635 1640 1650
168. Allegro PORTO, *Madrigali a 5 voci, libro 1*
        (V: [M?], 1622) RISM P-5239. Upsala 357
        1635

169. – , *Madrigali a 5 voci* [different from the above]
    (V:M, 1625) Eitner 8:33. RISM P-5240. Upsala 357
    1635 1639

170. Pellegrino POSSENTI, *Canora sampogna a 2 & 3 voci*
    (V:M, 1628)   Eitner 8:35.   RISM P-5248.   Gaspari 3:154.
    Bohn 313
    1635 1639 1640 1650

171. – , *Concentus armonici*
    (V:M, 1628)   Eitner 8:35.   RISM P-5250.   Gaspari 4:140.
    Bohn 313
    1633 1635 1639 1640 1650

172. Giovanni PRIULI, *Delicie musicali*
    (V:G, 1625) Eitner 8:72
    1635 1639

173. Gabriello PULITI, [unlocated edition]
    1633   1635   1639   1640: 'Gab. de Pulitis motecta [in 1635:
    "Sacrae Modulationes"] a una voce. 4. Ven. 1629.'

174. Francesco RASI, [unlocated edition]
    1633: 'Rasi Musiche per una voce sola. . . . Venet. 1613.'

175. Giovanni Antonio RIGATI, *Musiche concertate, libro 1, op.2*
    (V:M, 1636)   Eitner 8:233.   Bohn 333 (Copy lost; not in
    RISM)
    1639 1640

176. Cipriano de RORE & Annibale Padovano, *Madrigali a 4 voci*
    (V 1599) This edition not located
    1633 1635 1639 1640 1650

177. Cristoforo ROSSI, [unlocated edition]
    1640 1650: 'Cristof. de Rossi. Motetti a 4 voci.'

178. Giovanni Battista ROSSI, *Organo de cantori* . . .
    (V:M, 1618) Eitner 8:322. RISM-Ecr 717, R-2740. BUC 903.
    Gaspari 1:250
    1633 1635 1639

179. Salomone ROSSI, [unlocated edition]
    1635: 'Salomon Rossi Musiche varie a Voce sola. fol. Venet.
    1628.'

180. . . . ROSSI, [unidentified edition]
    1639: 'Rossi a 3. & 4. voci. 4. Ven. 1636.'

181. Giovanni ROVETTA, *Madrigali concertati, libro 1, op.2*
    (V:M, 1629) Eitner 8:341. RISM R-2981. BUC 905. Hiff 63
    1633   1635   1639 (specifies a 1636 ed: Eitner 8:341.   RISM
    R-2982 including a Glasgow copy not in BUC.   Bohn 342)
    1640

182. Galeazzo SABBATINI, *Regole facile e breve per sonare . . .*
     (V: Salvatori, 1628) Eitner 8:373. RISM-Ecr 742. Gaspari
     1:288-9
     1635 1639

183. Giovanni Felice SANCES, *Cantade et arie a voce sola* [*libro 2,
     parte 1*]
     (V: Vincenti, 1633) Eitner 8:413. RISM S-765. Gaspari 3:255
     1639 (date of 1635 specified) 1640

184. − , *Cantade . . . a 2 voci* [*libro 2, parte 2*]
     (V:M, 1633) Eitner 8:412. RISM S-766. BUC 917. Gaspari
     3:255. Hiff 63
     1635 1639

185. − , *Motetti a 1, 2, 3, & 4 voci*
     (V:M, 1638) Eitner 8:412. RISM S-768. BUC 917. Bohn 374.
     Gaspari 2:493. Hiff 63
     1639 (date of 1637 specified)

186. − , [unlocated edition]
     1639 1640: 'Felice Sances Cantate & Arie a voce Sola lib. 3.'

187. Claudio SARACINI, *Le quinte musiche*
     (V:M, 1624) Eitner 8:425. RISM S-913. BUC 921. Bohn 376.
     Hiff 64
     1633 1635 1639 (Mis-entered under Scarani)

188. − , *Le seste musiche*
     (V:M, 1624) Eitner 8:425. RISM S-914. BUC 921. Bohn 377.
     Hiff 64
     1633 1635 1639 (Mis-entered under Scarani)

189. . . . (Giovanni Vincenzo?) SARTI, [unlocated edition]
     1633: 'Sarti Concerti a 2. 3. & 4. voci. 4. Venetia. 1629.'

190. Marco SCACCHI, *Madrigali a 5 voci*
     (V:M, 1634)   Eitner 8:444 (including Ambrosiana copy).
     RISM S-1131
     1635 1639 1640 1650

191. Giuseppe SCARANI, *Concerti ecclesiastici, libro 1, op.2*
     (V:M, 1641 [sic]) Eitner 8:450. RISM S-1168 (1630 ed!).
     Gaspari 2:496. Bohn 380
     1639 (date of 1635 specified) 1640 (The interrelationship
     between the various dates of imprints and of citations calls for
     more thorough study than can be attempted here.)

192. − , *Sonate concertate, op.1*
     (V:M, 1630) Eitner 8:450. RISM S-1167. Sartori 1630b.
     Bohn 380
     1633 1635 1639

193. Heinrich SCHÜTZ, *Symphoniae sacrae*
     (V:M, 1629) Eitner 9:86. RISM S-2287. BUC 934. Bohn 392.
     Hiff 63
     1633 1635 1639
194. Leonhardo SIMONETTI, [unlocated edition]
     1633 1639: 'Simonetti Motetti a voce sola. 4. Venetia. 1631.'
195. Giovanni STEFANI, [unlocated edition]
     1633: 'Stefani Canzonette a una voce sola. 4. Milano. 1621.'
196. Antonio TARONI, *Madrigali a 5 voci, libro 1*
     (V: Amadino, 1612) Eitner 9:355. RISM T-227. Gaspari
     3:175
     1633 1635 1639 1640 1650 (Dates of 1622 are specified,
     however)
     – , [unlocated editions]
197. 1633 1635 1650: 'Il 2. libro de Madrigali a 5 voci. 4. Venetia.
     1622.'
198. 1639: '[Madrigali] a 1. 2. & 3. voci il secundo libro.'
199. Biasio TOMASI, *Motecta 2, 3, 4 vocibus, op.6*
     (V:M, 1635) Eitner 9:421. RISM T-922. BUC 1015. Bohn
     409. Hiff 67
     1639
200. Girolamo TORRE, [unlocated edition]
     1633: 'Torre lib. 1° a 2.3.4. & 5 voci con Basso continuo 4.
     Veneti. 1623.'
     1635: 'Girolamo Torre Sacra Girlanda a 2.3.4. & 5. voci con
     Basso Contin.'
201. Egidio TRABATTONI, *Concerto a 2, 3, & 4 voci, libro 2, op.4*
     (V:M, 1629) RISM T-1070. BUC 1017. Hiff 67
     1633 1635
202. Francesco TURINI, *Madrigali a 1, 2, & 3 voci, libro 1*
     (V:M, 1624) Eitner 9:475. RISM T-1389. BUC 1023. Gaspari
     3:179. Bohn 411. Hiff 67
     1633 1635 1639 (dated 1634) 1640
203. ... (Giovanni?) VALENTINI (?), [unlocated edition]
     1633 1635 1639: 'Jo. Valenini [sic] motecta 4.5. & 6. vocum
     4. Venetiis. 1611.'
204. Lazaro VALVASENSI, *Secondo giardino d'amorosi fiori, op.8*
     (V:M, 1634) Eitner 6:89. RISM V-185. BUC 1033. Hiff 68
     1635 1639
     – , [unlocated editions]
205. 1639 1640: 'L'Amante secreto a voce sola. 4. Ven. 1637.'
206. 1639 1640 1650: 'Amorosi fiori arie a una & due voci. 4.
     Ven. 1635.'

207.   1635 1640: 'Arie a voce sola &c. 4. Venet. 1635.'

208.   1633   1635: 'Concerti ecclesiastici a una & due voce. fol. Venet. 1627.'

209.   1635: 'Giardino primo ... lib. a voce sola. Venet. 1634.'

210.   1639 1640: 'Laberinto d'Amore a voce sola. 4. Ven. 1634.'

211.   1639: 'Madrigali a voce sola. 4.'

212.   1633: 'A 1 voci Cantarsi nel Clavicembato [sic] Chitarone overo Organo.'

213.   Orazio VECCHI, *Canzonette a 6 voci, libro 1*
       (V:G, 1587) Eitner 10:41. RISM V-1026. BUC 1035. Gaspari 3:261
       1633 1635 1639 1640

214.   — , *Le veglie di Siene overo i varii humores*
       (V:G, 1604) Eitner 10:42. RISM V-1053. Gaspari 3:181
       1633 1635 1639

215.   Giovanni Maria VERATO, *Il verrato insegna* ...
       (V:M, 1623) Eitner 10:56. RISM-Ecr 860. Gaspari 1:272
       1633

216.   Cherubino VESICH, [unlocated edition]
       1633 1635 1639 1640 1650: 'Cherubino Vesich. Arie a 1.2.3. voci. 4. Venetia. 1628.'

217.   ... VILLELMO, [unlocated edition]
       1633: 'Villelmo il libro 5. de Madrigali a 1.2.3.4. voci. 4. Venet. 1625.'

218.   Filippo VITALI, *Arie a 1, 2, et 3 voci*
       (V:G, 1622) Eitner 10:108. RISM V-2131. BUC 1046. Bohn 423
       1633 1635 1639 1640 1650

219.   — , *Concerto di madrigali, libro 1*
       (V:M, 1629) Eitner 10:108. RISM V-2136. BUC 1046. Bohn 424. Gaspari 3:187. Hiff 73
       1635 1639

220.   — , *Varie musiche, libro 5*
       (V:M, 1625) Eitner 10:108. RISM V-2134. Bohn 424
       1633 1635 1639

221.   — , [unlocated edition]
       1635 1639 1640: 'Filippo Vitale Musiche a 3 voci folio Venet. 1626.'

222.   Giaches de WERT, *Madrigali a 4 voci, libro 1*
       (V:G 1599) This edition not located. For earlier ones see Eitner 10:237. RISM W-870.
       1633 1635 1639 1640 1650

223. Lodovico ZACCONI, *Prattica de musica*
     (V:Girolamo Polo, 1622)   Eitner 10:317.   RISM-Ecr 904.
     Gaspari 1:265
     1633 1635

224. Gioseffo ZARLINO, *Institutioni et dimonstrationi di musica*
     (V: Franceschi, 1602) Eitner 10:332. RISM-Ecr 907. Gaspari
     1:268
     1635 1639 1640

225. Paolo ZASA, *Selva spirituale armonico*
     (V:M, [163-?], 1640; V:G, 1645) *Libro 1*: not extant. *Libro 2*:
     Eitner 10:333. RISM Z-101. Bohn 435. *Libro 3*: RISM Z-102.
     1639 1640 1650 (In 1639 and 1640 Martin is presumably
     citing *Libro 1*.)

226. Cesare ZOILO, *Madrigali a 5 voci*
     (V:M, 1628) Eitner 10:359. RISM Z-371.
     1633 1635 1639 1640 1650

227. *Canzoni a 2 voci, libro 1*
     (V:G, 1586) Eitner 4:150. RISM 1586⁶
     1633 1635 1639

228. *Leggiadre nimphe a 3 voci*
     (V:G, 1606)   Eitner 4:155.   RISM 1606⁸.   Gaspari 3:201.
     BUC 608
     1639 1640 1650

229. *Musica di 13 autori illustri a 5 voci*
     (V:G, 1576)   Eitner 4:154.   RISM 1576⁵.   Gaspari 3:57; *or*
     (V:G, 1589)   Eitner 4:154.   RISM 1589⁶.   Gaspari 3:37.
     BUC 361
     1633 1635 1639 1640 1650

230. *Musiche . . . composte per la Maddalena*
     (V:M, 1617) RISM 1617³. Gaspari 3:7. Eitner 7:45
     1635

[Unlocated editions by unspecified composers]

231. 1639: 'Intavolatura per la Chitarra. 4. Ven. 1633.'

232. 1639: 'Piccolo [*sic*] Littania a 5 voci. 4. Ven. 1635.'

THE CHAPEL ROYAL PART-BOOKS

MARGARET LAURIE

Among the treasures of the Royal Music Library (now in the Music Library of the British Library Reference Division) are the surviving Chapel Royal part-books, running from c 1675 to c 1850. The English Chapel Royal was at that time the most important ecclesiastical establishment in the country, and its books are clearly a prime source of sacred music of the period, especially since many of the principal composers, such as Purcell, Blow, Croft, Greene, Boyce, Nares, Dupuis and Arnold, were actually Gentlemen of the Chapel Royal, often its official composers, and most of their works were copied into the books during their period of office. It is perhaps disappointing that Handel is represented only by a few unauthentic arrangements, mainly from *Messiah* and *Israel in Egypt*, but, although he was appointed a Composer to the Chapel Royal on February 25 1722/3, this was a supernumerary appointment and his role seems to have been confined to the provision of ceremonial works for special occasions which were always copied and paid for separately.[1] In addition to contemporary material, the books also include a fair number of sixteenth and early seventeenth-century works, demonstrating considerable stability of tradition. Their make-up and chronology, however, are not always easy to grasp, and the following is an attempt to elucidate some of the problems involved.[2]

There are 102 volumes in all, most of which have been arranged in six overlapping sets with the shelf-marks R.M. 27.a.1-15–R.M. 27.f.1-9; a set of Sanctus and Commandments settings (R.M. 27.g.1-4), a book of chants (R.M. 27.g.5), and ten treble books largely making good earlier material (R.M. 27.h.1-10), all of which date from the first half of the nineteenth century, complete the collection. Each book seems to have been bound before copying started, and most of the earlier ones, judging by the way in which they have been trimmed, have been rebound at least once since.

The earliest set of books (R.M. 27.a. 1-15) consists of countertenor, tenor and bass decani books, all four cantoris[3] books and a bass fragment on vellum; countertenor verse, lute and two violoncello books on paper, and three organ books, the first two again on vellum. The six men's choir books were given their present form in c 1705 by a scribe who can be identified as John Church, since his works are regularly signed John (or J) Church and the hand agrees with examples of Church's hand found elsewhere, for instance in the Chapel Royal Subscription book.[4] Incorporated into these books, however, as Watkins Shaw has established,[5] are a considerable number of pages from earlier books. The pagination of these earlier books was preserved where possible, rejected pages being replaced by new, blank ones, and extra pages were added at the end.

Shaw identifies two main groups of earlier pages. The first, containing twenty-four items (five only fragmentarily), is in the hand of William Tucker[6] (see Plate 1) aided by two other scribes who provide words only. Shaw notes that the relationship between the contents of this section and the list of items given in the Lord Chamberlain's records as 'transcribed into the books of his Majesty's Chappell Royall since anno 1670 to Midsummer, 1676'[7] is sufficiently close to suggest that most of it was copied towards the end of the period covered by the list.[8] It must, in any case, have been copied before Tucker's death on February 28 1678/9,[9] and probably before Blow received his doctorate on December 10 1677, since he is designated 'Mr' throughout. Thus this

Plate 1. Hand of William Tucker. R.M.27.a.8, fol 30v.

section was probably copied in the years 1675-77.

The bass fragment (R.M. 27.a.7), consisting of pages 9-38 of a larger volume, is entirely in the hands of Tucker and his assistants. It contains chorus sections only. Although these copyists worked also for Westminster Abbey, this fragment must surely belong to the Chapel Royal set, not the contemporary Westminster one, for it is on vellum of the same size (allowing for trimming) as the Chapel Royal books, while the Westminster ones are on paper of smaller format, and it contains the same repertory in the same order as the Chapel Royal books, which the Westminster books do not. It presumably comes, therefore, from an extra chorus book for the Chapel Royal set. It bridges an apparent gap after Blow's *Service in G* in the other books, for it contains not only the commonly used canticles of this service but also the Commandments and Creed, Sanctus and Gloria, with two anthems (by Amner and Hutchinson) between the two pairs of movements.

Two bass books in the same three hands have also survived. One (formerly belonging to Richard Border) is now British Library Add. MS 50860; the other is in the Ohki Collection, Nanki Music Library, Tokyo (N-5/10).[10] Although the Nanki book is smaller than Add. MS 50860, it contains almost the same repertory in the same order (allowing for missing pages and some inversion in pairs), and where the bass part splits the two books have complementary parts, so presumably they are the cantoris and decani books respectively of the same set. Since Add. MS 50860 bears the arms of Charles II on its binding they must be Chapel Royal books. They again predate the conferral of Blow's doctorate and thus must be almost contemporary with the Royal Music set, though the presence of three Purcell anthems of a rather more developed kind than 'Lord, who can tell' in the latter suggests that they are marginally later. The Nanki book contains, in addition, twelve more works in several somewhat later hands, the first being a Purcell autograph of 'Sing unto the Lord'—a variant of 'Sing unto God' dated 1687 in the Gostling score-book now in the Humanities Research Centre of the University of Texas in Austin.[11]

Shaw's second group falls into two distinct sections, separated from each other by a varying number of new pages. Four copyists contributed to the first section, and about seventeen to the second. Some of the latter hands are very similar; several seem immature and may be those of choir-boys. Though most contribute to only one item, sometimes providing words alone, there is clearly one principal scribe whose very distinctive hand (see Plate 2) is found in at least one part of nearly every work. This hand can be identified from the 'old' Cheque book of the Chapel Royal as that of Edward Braddock, since he was Clerk of the Cheque (responsible for keeping the records) from November 1688 until his death in June 1708.[12] Braddock was probably also the last copyist of the first section, for although a few of the letter forms are different—particularly 'p' and 'y', which have exuberantly curved tails in the first section and the bare minimum of tail in the second—most of the letter forms are the same, notably the oddly kinked 'l', and the differences could be due to a considerable lapse of time between the two sections. Although the identification is not absolutely certain, these sections, for convenience, will be referred to as first and second Braddock sections respectively.

The first Braddock section consists of Purcell's *Service in B*♭ with four anthems between its movements. It is complete in the countertenor decani book and almost so in the countertenor cantoris, but the tenor decani book contains only two double leaves of the original (in the wrong order embedded in make-good with changed pagination), while the other books have no original pages at all. It seems likely that the original

Plate 2. Hand of Edward Braddock. R.M.27.a.3, fol 69v.

pages of this section came from the same set of books as the Tucker section, and followed it after only a short gap containing two anthems (present, in part at least, in the countertenor cantoris and tenor decani books respectively at the end of the Tucker section) and Aldrich's *Service in A* (the end of which immediately precedes the Purcell *Service* in the countertenor decani book), for this material would just about fill the number of original pages missing. As Shaw points out, Aldrich is still called 'Mr' here, so the beginning of this section probably dates from before, or at least not long after, he received his DD in 1682.[13] The Purcell *Service* was certainly in existence by September 1682 when payment was made for copying it into the Westminster books.[14]   Thus c1681-82 seems a likely date for this section.

The second Braddock section, present not only in all six men's books but also in the treble cantoris book (which Church kept in its original state), appears to have come from an entirely different set of books from the earlier sections, for the original pagination in four of the books has even numbers on *recto* pages and so could not have been a continuation of the more usual pagination found earlier. Church was forced to change at least some of the pagination in all of the men's books except the countertenor cantoris, though he tried to keep as closely as possible to the original in the tenor cantoris and both bass books as well.

The last three items copied under Braddock's supervision are preceded by one in a hand which, despite minor differences, is almost certainly Church's, and followed by thirteen anthems definitely in his hand, which are still on old vellum with altered page numbers and in virtually the same order in all seven books. These fill the old vellum in the countertenor and tenor decani books; indeed, the last work is squeezed into the tenor book, while in the countertenor book, despite efforts at compression, it runs for one and a half lines on to new vellum; although there is no appreciable difference in the hand, this is probably not the original ending. The other five books all have the same anthem after this one, still on old vellum, and most have a further one as well. In view of the apparent disorder of Church's subsequent work it seems likely that this part of his contribution was entered at the end of the earlier books before they were dismantled.

Four of the first seven items of this section are dated 1687, Christmas 1687, 1693 and April 1696 respectively in the Gostling score-book.[15] Gostling notes that the last of these, Blow's 'We will rejoice', was composed for a Thanksgiving Day for 'ye discovery of ye plot against King William' and adds that it was 'Composed. . . Ap: 9th 1696. Perform'd ye 16th following at Whitehall [ie the Chapel Royal]'; it was thus presumably entered into the Chapel Royal books during the week April 9-16 1696, and the preceding items were probably copied within the previous two or three years. Shaw's dating of c1680-87 is certainly too early.[16] Only one more item of the combined second Braddock/first Church section bears a later date: Church's ninth item, Blow's 'I will call', written for the Fast Day on January 19 1704. Church was sworn Gentleman Extraordinary of the Chapel Royal on January 31 1697, and advanced into a full place the following August.[17] He could have taken over from Braddock at any time after this; the spacing suggests that he did not finally do so until at least 1700, possibly a year or two later.

Both Tucker and Braddock had included verse (ie solo) parts where necessary, the former distributing them between both sides of the choir, the latter giving them almost entirely to the decani side. Church, with a few exceptions, omitted them altogether. He must, therefore, have either made separate verse books or used this set as chorus books to another. The extant countertenor verse book does actually contain most of the anthems of Church's first section but out of order among somewhat later works, so it cannot be contemporary. The original disposition of verse parts, however, must soon have proved unsatisfactory.

After Church had selected the old pages required and interspersed them with new, he was faced with a considerable amount of making good, for he had to copy not only beginnings and ends where they ran over into rejected pages but in many cases one or more complete parts as well. Missing parts of the Tucker section (where still wanted) were recopied more or less in order at the beginning of each book, but the Braddock sections were less systematically treated. Only two new anthems seem definitely to have been added during this process; one of them, Clarke's 'Bow down thine ear', is said to have been written for a Fast on April 4 1705.[18]

At this point, several blocks of blank pages still remained between the filled ones in each of the men's books. Church proceeded to fill them in what appears to be higgledy-piggledy fashion. Items were usually copied in batches; shorter works were fitted in according to space, worked mainly forward, but occasionally back, from any of the filled pages (or utilizing odd blank corners within them), while longer works were normally started on a *verso* page to reduce page-turning, the preceding page (or pages) sometimes being left blank and filled later. As a result, the order and position of the items is different in each book, and a chronological order can be established only for groups of works, not for individual items.

I have been able to distinguish three main groups (each with sub-groups) before Croft changes from 'Mr' to 'Dr' in July 1713. The first contains nineteen anthems (six very incomplete), five of which were written for special occasions (mostly at St Paul's Cathedral) dating from September 7 1704 to December 31 1706. They are not, however, in chronological order, the latest appearing in the middle of the group. Thus, although it seems likely that this group was copied in c1706-07, it may date from slightly later. The middle group contains two services and eleven anthems, mainly of sixteenth and seventeenth-century origin, while the last contains a service by Church himself and eighteen anthems, mostly new; it runs straight into the next, 'Dr Croft', section.

It is clear that several books in addition to the main choir books were started before 1713. The earliest extant ones are the countertenor verse and lute books (R.M. 27.a.9,12). There must also have been tenor and bass verse books, and possibly a treble verse book, though this is less likely since few treble verse parts are needed and in at least one case both the required treble parts are copied into the counter-tenor book. The lute book is figured and contains verse anthems only. From page 93 of the verse book and page 150 of the lute book they tie up with the last pre-1713 section of the choir books, the verse book being in the same order. The lute book's order, however, is somewhat jumbled—a charac-teristic of many of the instrumental books throughout the series. All except two of the preceding forty anthems in the verse book are also in the lute book (the majority in roughly the same order), interspersed with fifty-six other items. Much of this material relates to earlier sections of the extant set, but strangely, although the middle pre-1713 group must have been copied at much the same time, the verse parts of all four of its verse anthems are entered, contrary to usual practice, into the choir instead of the verse books. Fifteen items appear initially only in the verse and lute books and a further thirty in the lute book alone, though some of these were copied into a few of the other books later. Nine come from the main 'Nanki' repertory and four more from its additional section; on the other hand at least seven, and probably more, are new works. It would seem that the lute book, and to a lesser extent the verse book(s), were designed for use not only with the extant set, but also with other sets currently in use, including at least one other containing new material. The post of lutenist was not actually established until August 1715.[19] Since the lute book clearly predates this, the appointment must merely have confirmed previous practice, but presumably this was not of very long standing, and the book is probably the first lute book ever.

When Church made up the men's choir books, the treble cantoris book was no more than a third full. Yet it contains only five anthems from the main pre-1713 section together with four from the countertenor verse/lute material; presumably the rest were copied into another book, now lost. Instead, the surviving book contains a service section in the middle, probably contemporary with the last pre-1713 group, but possibly slightly earlier. This includes the three services of the pre-1713 section, one from the Tucker section and nine other earlier ones.

The first violoncello book (R.M. 27.a.10) was begun shortly before July 1713 (since it has only a little music attributed to 'Mr Croft).   It starts with a service section containing twelve of the thirteen services in the treble book (in a different order) plus seven more. Two of these were entered into the countertenor decani book, one of them into the countertenor cantoris as well, but none into the other books at this stage.   An anthem section, containing both contemporary and earlier material, was begun simultaneously in the middle of the book.

The first organ book (R.M. 27.a.13) is again divided into anthem and service sections; the former contains most of the last pre-1713 group and two works from the middle one, together with four from the countertenor verse/lute material, but very few earlier items. Five fragments in the Fitzwilliam

Museum[20] almost certainly come from earlier organ books, though they do not tie up exactly with the extant set. The service section contains eleven of the nineteen services in the violoncello book; four more were added to the next organ book in the 1720s.

Only nine complete items were entered into the books between July 1713 and the first pair of works by Greene, one of which, 'O Lord, give ear', dates from February 1720,[21] though the violoncello and organ books discussed above mostly date from this period. From the last complete work before the first Greene one, Church's hand-writing begins to change: his 'g' regularly takes on a form it had only occasionally shown earlier, and several of his capital letters become straight and thick, though in each case both forms co-exist for a little (see Plate 3).

The treble cantoris book was revived for the Greene section, and the countertenor verse and first organ books continued in use. Before the latter was finished, however, a second organ book (R.M. 27.a.14) was started, and as soon as the first was filled a third book (R.M. 27.a.15) was begun, so for most of this section two organ books were in use at once. The second violoncello book (R.M. 27.a.11) covers the whole of the Greene section but was not actually started until after Greene had received his doctorate in July 1730. Although called 'Violoncello', this book is figured throughout and therefore was probably at first meant to be a lute book; it must soon have been used as a violoncello book, however, since the first book copied by the next scribe was another lute book (R.M. 27.b.14) containing the same material.[22]

In addition to the complete items, Church entered fourteen services and thirty-one anthems of sixteenth and seventeenth-century origin into the bass decani book only. Another service and four full anthems of similar date are given among the first works of the Greene section in this book and were

Plate 3. Hand of John Church, c.1720; transitional form showing curly L's and D's in heading and ascription, straight ones in text. R.M.27.a.2, fol 72v.

probably copied before the others, for although these precede the Greene section in the book, the prevalence of straight letter forms suggests that they were copied later. The services include all those in the treble cantoris and violoncello books not already in the bass decani book, plus two more. Seventeen of the twenty-one verse anthems had already appeared in the lute book (ten of them in the countertenor verse book as well); all their verse parts are given. It looks as if Church had intended to gather together all the older works which the Chapel Royal wished to retain in its repertory, but never completed the work.

On April 3 1734, Church was paid £3.8.6 (+ office fees) for copying into the Chapel Royal books.[23] Two months earlier James Chelsum had been paid £12.7.8 for the same task.[24] Although payments for copying had been recorded at roughly two-year intervals from 1718 until July 1731,[25] these are the first entries to name the copyists. Evidently Chelsum took over from Church at some time between July 1731 and 1734. The relative amounts paid suggest early 1732, but the total seems rather little for two and a half years' work, and it is possible that a payment in 1733 has been omitted from the records. That Chelsum is indeed the next copyist is confirmed by his entries in the Chapel Royal Subscription book.

The countertenor and bass decani books were full before Church had finished his work, and he had started the corresponding books of the next set (R.M. 27.b.2,4).[26] Chelsum used the remaining four choir books of the first set for his initial eight items but then, although none was yet quite finished, also moved into new books (R.M. 27.b.3,6-8). At the same time he began four verse books: countertenor, tenor, bass and a general book called 'tenor bass' (R.M. 27.b.9-12). These are clearly all that there were, for treble solos are distributed among them. Both treble choir books of this set have also survived (R.M. 27.b.1,5), though in poor condition. The original first ten and twelve pages respectively are now missing, but the pagination suggests that they both contained a few Church items at the beginning.

The second violoncello book of the first set was continued into this one and on completion followed by R.M. 27.b.13. Chelsum's first lute book, as we have seen, contained mostly Church material; R.M. 27.b.15 again follows it immediately. Similarly, the last two organ books of the first set were continued into the second, but R.M. 27.a.14 was abandoned long before it was full and replaced by R.M. 27.b.16. R.M. 27.b.17 starts with the last two Chelsum items. These books seem to have been copied after the others, and seventeen (out of fifty-five) items are omitted. Possibly one organ book of the set has been lost.

Payments for copying were made regularly to Chelsum from 1734 until July 1741.[27] Smaller payments for miscellaneous sundries, including copying, were also made to the Sub-Dean from February 1737 until February 1742.[28] This apparent anomaly is explained by the books themselves, for although Chelsum copied all the vocal parts, six more scribes contributed to the instrumental books, and these presumably were paid through the Sub-Dean. They included the principal composers of the section, Greene and Boyce, who also occasionally corrected the other men's work.

The Chelsum section is followed by six Greene anthems in the hand of a new main copyist, assisted by yet another scribe in the violoncello and lute books, and Greene himself in the organ book. The violoncello book alone then has Greene's 'O God, thou hast cast us out', written for the Fast Day on December 18 1745[29] (mainly in the hand of Chelsum's successor but finished by Greene), followed by five more anthems, four of which are also in the lute book but not in any of the others. Since instrumental parts are unlikely to have been copied before vocal ones, it would seem that the remaining parts of these works were entered into another set of books.

The next two payments to specific copyists were £18.12.0 to Ellis Webster for copying from October 1743 to October 1744,[30] and £16.18.3 to Thomas Barrow for copying from June 1746 to December 1747.[31] A further payment of £4.16.0 was made to the Sub-Dean for copying 'for two Years & two Months ending Lady Day 1747 [ie February 1745 to March 25 1747]'.[32] The precision of the dating of these payments makes it clear that there are gaps for August 1741 to September 1743 and November 1744 to May 1746 in the main series, and March 1742 to January 1745 in the Sub-Dean's series, not covered by the recorded payments. There may have been no copying undertaken in the first gap, for although Chelsum did not die until August 3 1743,[33] he ceased to copy for Westminster in 1741[34] and may well have done so for the Chapel Royal at the same time. Both establishments seem to have had trouble in finding a member of their choirs willing (or judged competent) to replace him, for Ellis Webster did not belong to the Chapel Royal (and nothing further is known of him), while the next payment for copying at Westminster was also made to an outsider.[35] The presence of the Fast Anthem of December 1745 and the five succeeding anthems shows that some copying, however, was undertaken in the second gap, which the payment to the Sub-Dean in 1747 seems insufficient to cover.

An example of the hand of Chelsum's successor in Add. MS 17861 (fol 24) is identified by Samuel Arnold as being that of Samuel Porter. Porter, however, was born only in 1733. He was a chorister at St Paul's, not the Chapel Royal, and the admittedly scanty samples of his hand in the St Paul's Vicars choral book (where he several times during the years 1752-54 signed for Greene's dues) are not the same. Arnold's ascription therefore seems unlikely, and this hand probably is that of Ellis Webster, though in view of the gaps in the payments this is not absolutely proven.

As noted above, Thomas Barrow started copying in June 1746, two months after he had been appointed a Gentleman of the Chapel Royal,[36] and he continued this work until shortly before his death on August 13 1789,[37] adding almost 200 items during this period (see Plate 4 for an example of his early hand).

His first task was apparently to continue the work of consolidation begun by Church, for he started by entering thirty-eight sixteenth and seventeenth-century items, twenty-nine of which are among those entered by Church into the first bass decani book. Barrow copied this material into the cantoris books first, starting new books for the purpose (R.M. 27.c.3-6) although the men's books of the R.M. 27.b set were not yet full. Twelve of these works had already appeared in Church's treble cantoris book. Barrow's (started by an assistant) now contains only eight of the rest, together with other make-good material, but it is very imperfect and probably originally contained more, though whether it ever had the whole section is open to question. The make-good section was almost complete in these books by the time Barrow copied in his second group of new material. Since Boyce is here credited with his doctorate, this must date from after July 1749 but is probably considerably before 1756, for it is some time before works by Dr Nares appear.[38]

Barrow continued to use the countertenor and bass decani books of the R.M. 27.b set for his current material (doubling their size by adding extra paper), but started a new tenor book (R.M. 27.c.2). He did not, however, enter the make-good material immediately into the latter, but added it gradually among new works during the years 1765-73, and never completed the task, for twelve items (including eight of

Plate 4. Hand of Thomas Barrow. R.M.27.a.5, fol 100v.

the nine verse anthems) are missing. Little make-good was
needed in the bass decani part; what there is was again entered
later, in c1770-73. Barrow entered the make-good material
for the countertenor decani into a special (vellum) book
(R.M. 27.c.1). Two services by King, copied into the other
books in c1750, appear superfluously very early in this book,
and several items dating from c1773 come at the end, so
although it might have been copied with the cantoris books it
is far more likely to have been compiled concurrently with
the tenor decani, especially since it, too, lacks most of the
verse anthems.

Barrow also started a new set of verse books, this time containing first and second treble as well as countertenor, tenor,
bass and 'general' books (R.M. 27.c.7-12). Most of the
contents of the second treble book were recopied into R.M.
27.e.12 in c1793. These verse books between them contain,
in addition to current material, nearly forty items from the
first set, duplicating Church's countertenor verse book where
relevant, which suggests that this book and its companions
were no longer in use.

The lute part was apparently discontinued after 1763, but
the violoncello part was maintained until c1793. Barrow
copied a fair amount of his make-good section into a new
organ book (R.M. 27.c.15) at the beginning of his career,
but continued to use R.M. 27.b.17 as well. More make-good
was copied into the end of R.M. 27.a.14, probably fairly
early, but some remained for the start of R.M. 27.d.8 in
c1765, and most of the verse anthems were again never
entered at all. R.M. 27.c.16 overlaps R.M. 27.b.17, and
R.M. 27.d.8 was begun before the latter was quite full.
R.M. 27.a.15 was also sporadically used, mainly for earlier
material, so again at least two organ books were in use
simultaneously for much of Barrow's contribution.

As Barrow filled the countertenor and bass decani books

of the R.M. 27.b set and the treble and verse books of the
R.M. 27.c set he moved into new books (R.M. 27.d.1-7), but
when he had completed the tenor decani and men's cantoris
books of the R.M. 27.c set he went back to the unfilled
books of the R.M. 27.b set, again increasing their size by
adding new paper. These books are therefore lacking in the
R.M. 27.d set. When these books in turn were completed
they were replaced by those of R.M. 27.e. Each chorus book
of all these sets has a group of Sanctus and Commandments
settings at the end, obviously worked backwards.

For the most part, once the make-good sections were
completed, Barrow's order is quite straightforward, though
there is one group of sixteen anthems in a different order in
each book, and there are the usual quirks in the violoncello
and organ books.

Material continued to be added to the books after Barrow's
death on a fairly regular basis until c1808, and then much
more sporadically until 1849; dates of copying are usually
given from 1809 onwards. New books (R.M. 27.f.1-9) followed those of the R.M. 27.e set as needed. This final set,
however, contains no verse books since the verse parts were
once more copied into the choir books. None of this set was
ever filled.

With the books is a small index of apparently mid-
nineteenth-century origin, which gives page numbers to tenor
cantoris and verse books. By the time that it was compiled,
the R.M. 27.a set was no longer in use, having been superseded
by Boyce's *Cathedral music*. Books from the R.M. 27.b-f
sets are, however, duly indexed, together with five more, one
a printed collection of chants, the others containing works
by mid-nineteenth-century composers such as Mendelssohn
and Goss. These may well have been printed rather than
manuscript collections.

The amount of very incomplete material in the books

suggests that there were at times other Chapel Royal part-books which no longer survive. Warren's notes to his edition of Boyce's *Cathedral Music* provide further confirmation of this, for he lists thirteen Boyce anthems as being 'in the books of the Chapel Royal',[39] ten of which are not in the extant sets. The existing books have suffered, too, from the ravages of time and choir-boys. Nonetheless, they contain a valuable collection of music, much of it presumably copied under the composers' supervision.

REFERENCES

1 See D Burrows 'Handel and the 1727 Coronation' *Musical times* cxviii 1977, 469.

2 I should like to express my gratitude to the librarians of all the institutions which I have used during this study, especially to the staff of the Music Library of the British Library (Reference Division) —notably Alec King himself—who have given very generous assistance. I am indebted also to Benedict Beneditz, Hugh McLean, Peter Marr, Eric van Tassell, Canon Mansell (Sub-Dean of the Chapel Royal), Mr Tipman (of the Lord Chamberlain's Office) and, above all, to H Diack Johnstone, who worked with me in the early stages, identified most of the eighteenth-century hands and generally provided much help and encouragement.

3 Actually called 'Sub-Decani'.

4 Cambridge, Fitzwilliam Museum MU.MS.1011.

5 'A contemporary source of English music of the Purcellian period' *Acta musicologica* xxxi 1959, 38-44. These six books were at that time separate from the rest, and had the shelf-marks R.M. 23.m.1-6. The whole collection has since been re-arranged and given the present shelf-marks.

6 H W Shaw 'A Cambridge manuscript from the English Chapel Royal' *Music & letters* xlii 1961, 264.

7 H C de Lafontaine *The King's Musick* London, [1909], 305ff.

8 'A contemporary source. . .', *op cit*, 40.

9 *The old cheque-book. . . of the Chapel Royal* ed E F Rimbault, London, 1872, 16.

10 See H McLean 'Blow and Purcell in Japan' *Musical times* civ 1963, 702-5.

11 *The Gostling manuscript* [facsimile edition] Austin, 1977, Choral anthems 124.

12 Original manuscript (still in the Chapel Royal), fols 9v-12.

13 'A contemporary source. . .', *op cit*, 40-1.

14 *Treasurer's accounts*, Michaelmas 1682 (Westminster Abbey Muniments 33717), fol 5v. The Purcell *Service* is not identified in the accounts, but it is the B♮ *Service* which is present in the books.

15 *The Gostling manuscript* Orchestral anthems 123, 104; Choral anthems 78, 102-109.

16 The Gostling score-book was not available to Shaw when he wrote 'A contemporary source...' in 1959. Faced with conflicting evidence for the date of 'We will rejoice'–'For the Thanksgiving Day for the discovery of the plot against the King's life. Performed Thursday 16 of April, 1695' in Add. MS 31444 (fol 42) and 'For the thanksgiving of yᵉ Rye [House] plot [1683]' in Harley MS 7340 (fol 119)–Shaw dismissed Add. MS 31444's date in favour of the earlier one on the grounds that there seemed to be no occasion for such a thanksgiving in 1695 and April 16 that year was a Tuesday not a Thursday. Gostling confirms that Add. MS 31444 was more nearly correct, for April 16 *was* a Thursday in 1696, and there was just such a thanksgiving on that day (*cf* Luttrell *A brief historical relation of state affairs* Oxford, 1857 iv, 45).

17 *The old cheque-book. . . op cit*, 21f.

18 Add. MS 31821, fol 55. This is, however, an early nineteenth-century manuscript (though referring to an earlier source) and this Fast is not mentioned by Luttrell.

19 *The old cheque-book. . . op cit*, 28.

20 MU.MS.152; *cf* Shaw 'A Cambridge manuscript. . .'. Three further leaves continuing 'fragment A' are in Fitzwilliam Museum MU.MS.671 fols 100-102.

21 Add. MS 17853, fol 62.

22 The last lute book (R.M. 27.c.14) contains an index (without page numbers) in Church's hand listing many of the works of his Greene section, and has some Church bass clefs on its first page. This was probably intended to be the violoncello book corresponding to R.M. 27.a.11.

23 Public Record Office (Chancery Lane), Warrant book L.C. 5/19, 225.

24 *ibid*, 197.

25 L.C. 5/157, 134; L.C. 5/158, 17,387; L.C. 5/159, 12; L.C. 5/18, 117,266.

26 Both now lack their opening pages; p 5 of the bass begins in Church's hand. The first ten pages of the countertenor were early recopied by Barrow; those surviving start with Church material.

27 L.C. 5/20, 259; L.C. 5/21, 47, 146, 311.

28 L.C. 5/21, 94,234,321.

29 Add. MS 17861, fol 3.

30 L.C. 5/22, 139.

31 *ibid*, 389.

32 *ibid*, 334.

33 *The marriage, baptismal, and burial registers of the Collegiate Church or Abbey of St Peter, Westminster* ed J L Chester, London, 1876, 364.

34 The last payment to him is recorded in the *Treasurer's Accounts* Michaelmas 1741 (W.A.M. 33773), fol 5.

35 Robert Hiller (*Treasurer's accounts* 1746 (W.A.M. 33777), fol 5v).

36 On March 31 1746 (*'New' cheque book of the Chapel Royal* (unpublished MS), 33).

37 *The. . . registers of. . . Westminster, op cit*, 446.

38 Nares was appointed organist on January 13 1756, and gained his doctorate later in the same year.

39 W Boyce *Cathedral music* ed J Warren, London 1849, i, 11.

THE HARPSICHORD MUSIC OF JOHN BLOW:
a first catalogue

WATKINS SHAW

INTRODUCTION

The harpsichord music composed by John Blow and his pupils and colleagues forms a considerable body of music scattered over several contemporary publications and numerous manuscripts, the identification and documentation of which is a matter of some intricacy and confusion. There are, however, catalogues of all the music by Jeremiah Clarke[1] and Henry Purcell[2] giving information about sources, while the publication of the complete harpsichord music by Purcell,[3] likewise that of William Croft,[4] has helped to place the output of those composers on a sound footing, and incidentally has clarified a number of anonymous transcripts. But of the remaining composers (mainly lesser figures such as John Barrett, Francis Pigott or Robert King) it is noteworthy that Blow himself, the most senior composer of this group, has not been the subject of an essay towards a complete listing of his harpsichord music, although Howard Ferguson has dealt with a quantity of the dance movements.[5] Such an essay is now therefore attempted in this present catalogue. It cannot be expected that the result will be final, and one hopes that a provisional list such as this may facilitate the identification of mis-attributions, further early sources, and even, perhaps, additional works. There follows (1) a list of sources, (2) the catalogue itself, with an appendix of doubtful or wrong attributions, and (3) a table of the first few notes of each item for more precise identification.

In the list of sources, publications which appeared during the composer's lifetime stand first, and are given in chronological order. The manuscript sources are then cited in alphabetical order of the places in which the various collections are situated.

In the absence of any obviously self-determining principle, the catalogue is arranged as follows. First, suites, beginning with the six published in Blow's lifetime, numbered as in Howard Ferguson's edition, and followed by those derived from manuscript sources; next, single dance (and kindred) movements; third, abstract pieces of sectional construction, whether 'chacones' or grounds; and finally an overture and preludes. Except for Suites 1-6, where it has been thought well to maintain the numbering of Ferguson's edition, an alphabetical sequence of keys has been adopted within each of these four groups.

Thus arranged, the pieces have been serially numbered. Such numbers are obviously of no musical or chronological significance whatever, but simply afford a conventional means of reference. And because these numbers have no meaning divorced from my method of working, I have prefixed them with 'S', the initial letter of my surname, in token that they possess no intrinsic authority. It will be evident from what has been said that the sequence in which the sources are cited for each piece does not indicate any order, ascending or descending, of textual authority, which is not a matter that can be investigated here.

For purposes of listing in column 2 of the catalogue, titles have been standardized. For example, I see no reason to refer to one piece as a saraband in contrast to another as a sarabrand, as if those titles betokened something distinct, any more than one would refer to one anthem as by Pelham Humphrey and to another as by Pelham Humfrey, as if they were two different people. 'Sarabrand' therefore has been standardized as *Saraband*; 'Almond' and 'Almaine' as *Almand*; 'Gavatt' as *Gavott*; 'Grownd' as *Ground*; 'Preludium' as *Prelude*; etc. But column 3 of the catalogue carefully records the exact form used in any one of the sources.

The brief quotations from the beginning of each piece, collected at the end of the paper, are deliberately given without ornaments, and with two exceptions take no account of minor variants between one source and another. Once or twice a cancelling accidental in the modern convention has been introduced.

REFERENCES

1 T F Taylor *Thematic catalogue of the works of Jeremiah Clarke* Detroit, 1977.
2 F B Zimmerman *Henry Purcell, 1659-1695. An analytical catalogue of his music* London, 1963.
3 Henry Purcell *Eight suites* and *Miscellaneous keyboard pieces* ed H Ferguson, London, 1964, 2/1968.
4 William Croft *Complete harpsichord works* ed H Ferguson and C Hogwood, 2 vols London, 1974.
5 John Blow *Six suites* ed H Ferguson, London, 1965.
6 I am grateful to Malcolm Boyd, Margaret Crum, Howard Ferguson and the late Thurston Dart for drawing my attention respectively to manuscripts in Cardiff Public Library, the Bodleian Library, the Fitzwilliam Museum and the Brussels Conservatoire royal de Musique. Gwilym Beechey contributed an article on the manuscript in the National Library of Scotland to *Music & letters* l 1969, 178-89.

LIST OF SOURCES
(a) Published in Blow's lifetime.
   I. The Second Part of Musick's Hand-maid: containing The Newest Lessons, Grounds, Sarabands, Minuets, and Jiggs. Set for the Virginals, Harpsichord, and Spinet. London, Henry Playford, 1689.
  Ia. A Choice Collection of Lessons, being Excellently Sett to the Harpsichord, by ... Dr. John Blow And the late Mr. Henry Purcell. London, 1705. [A re-issue of I above.]
  II. A Choice Collection of Lessons for the Harpsichord, Spinnet, &c. Containing four Sett's ... By Dr. John Blow. [London], Henry Playford, [1698].

IIa. Another edition of II, issued by J Walsh and J Hare. London, [? 1704].

III. A Choice Collection of Ayres For the Harpsichord or Spinett ... Never Before Published Composed by ... Dr. John Blow ... Mr. Francis Piggot ... Mr. Jeremiah Clarke ... Mr. John Barrett ... & Mr. William Crofts. [London] J Young, 1700.

IV. The Second Book of the Harpsichord Master containing A Choice Collection of Lessons for the Harpsicord or spinnett ... By Dr. Blow, Mr. Courtivall, Mr. Clark, Mr. Barrett & Mr. Croffts. London, J Walsh, 1700.

(b) Manuscript.

Bentley, Hants. Gerald Coke's Collection.

    A   Un-numbered MS associated with William Walond of Chichester.

Brussels. Conservatoire royal de Musique.

    B   MS 15418.

Cambridge. Fitzwilliam Museum.

    C   Music MS 653 (52.B.7).

Cardiff. Public Library.

    D   Mackworth Collection, MS M.C.1.39(j).

Edinburgh. National Library of Scotland.

    E   Inglis 94, MS 3343.

Glasgow. University Library.

    F   Euing MS R.d.54.

London. British Library (Reference Division).

    G   Egerton MS 2959.

    H   Add. MS 22099.

    J   Add. MS 31403.

    K   Add. MS 31465.

    L   Add. MS 31468.

    M   Add. MS 34695.

    N   Add. MS 41205.

    O   Add. MS 52363.

London. Royal College of Music (Parry Room Library).

    P   MS 2093.

Oxford. Bodleian Library.

    Q   MS Mus.Sch.c.61.

Oxford. Christ Church.

    R   Music MS 47.

    S   Music MS 1003.

    T   Music MS 1177.

    U   Music MS 1179.

Paris. Bibliothèque nationale.

    V   MS Rés. 1186 *bis*, part 1.

Tokyo. Nanki Music Library.
W   Ohki Collection, N-3/35 (formerly r.1).

CATALOGUE
   Column 1: 'S' number.
   Column 2: Title, standardized as necessary, and Key (capital
              letter—major; lower-case letter—minor). Where no
              source provides a title, a suggestion is printed in
              square brackets.
   Column 3: Sources. Sigla as above.
   * Anonymous in this source.   † No title in this source.

Group 1. Suites

Suite No. 1 in d.

1.	2.	3.
1	Almand in d	II/IIa, item 1, *Almand*.
2	[Corant] in d	†II/IIa, item 2; †**G**, f.12v.
3	Tune in d	II/IIa, item 3, *Tune*; †**G**, f.11v.
4	Jigg in d	*†I/Ia, item 2; II/IIa, item 4, *Jigg*;***O**, p.66, *Jigg*.

Suite No. 2 in d.

1.	2.	3.
5	[Almand on a] Ground in d	II/IIa, item 5, *Ground*.
6	[Rondo] in d	†II/IIa, item 6; †**G**, f.12.
7	Minuet in d	II/IIa, item 7, *Minuet*; **G**, ff.12v-13, *Minuett*; **O**, p.65, *Minuet*.

Note on Suites 1 and 2. Source II/IIa speaks of 'four Sett's' (ie, four
suites) without giving a heading to each separately. The movements
therefore run without a break, beginning with seven in the key of D
minor; but the division of those seven into two suites, as shown above,
is obvious enough.

Suite No. 3 in a.

1.	2.	3.
8	Almand in a	II/IIa, item 8, *Almand*; †**J**, f.53v.
9	Corant in a	II/IIa, item 9, *Corant*; †**J** ff.53v-54.
10	Saraband in a	II/IIa, item 10, *Saraband*; †**J**, f.54.
11	Jigg in a	II/IIa, item 11, *Jigg*; **J**, f.54v, *Jigg*.

Note on Suite 3. In a narrowly limited sense, S8, S9, and S10 are anonymous in **J**; but the ascription 'Dr. Blow' at the end of S11 must surely be taken to refer to the whole group, notwithstanding that (perhaps to avoid an awkward page turn) the scribe left some staves blank at the foot of f.54 after S10 before turning to f.54v to transcribe S11. As Blow's authorship of them all is attested in II/IIa, this would not be worth mentioning, were it not that this method of ascribing a whole group becomes of account in relation to Suites 8-11.

Suite No. 4 in C.

1.	2.	3.
12	Almand in C	†II/IIa, item 12; *****D**, f.54v reversed, *Almane*; **O**, p.98, *Almand*; **U**, pp.22-23, *Almand*.
13	Corant in C	II/IIa, item 13, *Corant*; **O**, pp.98-99, *Corant*.
14	Saraband in C	I/Ia, item 8, *Saraband*; II/IIa, item 14, *Sarabrand*; **O**, p.99, *Saraband*; †**U**, p.20.
15	Gavott in C	†I/Ia, item 7; II/IIa, item 15, *Gavatt*; **O**, p.100, *Boree*; †**U**, p.18.

Suite No. 5 in d.

1.	2.	3.
16	Almand in d	III, p.1, *Almand*; **O**, pp.174-5, *Almand*.
17	Corant in d	III, p.2, *Corant*; **G**, ff.10v-11, *Corant*; **O**, pp.175-6, *Corant*.
18	Minuet in d	III, p.3 *Minuett*; **O**, p.177, *Minuet*.

Suite No. 6 in g.

1.	2.	3.
19	Almand in g	IV, item 1, *Almand*; ***C**, p.24, *Almand*; ***L**, ff.3v-4, *Almand*; †**U**, pp.26-27; ***V**, f.43v, *Almand*.
20	Saraband in g	IV, item 2, *Saraband*; *†**L**, f.4v.
21	Air in g	IV, item 3, *Aire*; *†**C**, p.24.

Note on Suite 6. These three pieces, though consecutive, are printed separately in IV, each beginning on a fresh page and separately attributed to Blow without any heading as a group. But Howard Ferguson's view of them as a suite is not likely to be controverted.

Suite [No. 7] in d.

1.	2.	3.
22	Almand in d	**G**, f.10, *Almand*.
----	Corant in d	See S17.
23	[Saraband] in d	†**G**, f.11 (an arrangement of 'The Grace's Dance' from 'Venus and Adonis').

Note on Suite [7]. S22, S17, and S23 stand first in a group of seven entered consecutively in **G**. All are in D minor, each is separately attributed to Blow, and at the end is written 'Finis Dr. Blow'. It is impossible to consider all seven as constituting a suite; but even though a title must be supplied to S23, when one plays the first three of them one has the clear impression of a suite. That the Corant, S17, does duty also in Suite No. 5 is not necessarily an objection. Some instability in the make up of suites is to be observed at this date, for example in the works of Croft.

Suite [No. 8] in d.

1.	2.	3.
24	[Almand] in d	†**S**, ff.24v-25.
25	[Gavott] in d	†**S**, f.25.
26	[Jigg] in d	†**S**, f.25v.

Note on Suite [8]. S26 is ascribed at the end to 'Mr Blow', and I treat all three pieces, S24, S25, and S26 as the suite they have every appearance of constituting, and regard the ascription as relating to the whole.

Suite [No. 9] in F.

1.	2.	3.
27	Almand in F	**E**, ff.1v-2, *Almond*; *****V**, f.40, *Almand*.
28	Corant in F	*****C**, f.48, *Corant*; **E**, ff.2v-3, *Corant*.
29	Saraband in F	*****C**, ff.48-49, *Sarabrand*; **E**, ff.3v-4, *Saraband*; **F**, ff.34v-35, *Saraband*; **H**, f.16, *Sarabrand*, attributed to William Croft.

Note on Suite [9]. S27, S28, and S29, though found independently elsewhere, are grouped as a suite in **E**, each item individually ascribed to Blow.

Suite [no. 10] in G.

1.	2.	3.
30	Hunting Almand in G	†**J**, f.56v; ***K**, ff.42v-43, *The Hunting Almand*; ***O**, pp.101-2, *Almand*; ***U**, p.41, *Hunting Almond* (incomplete); ***V**, f.37, *Hunting Almand in Gamut*#; **W**, f.15, *Hunting Almond*.
31	Corant in G	**J**, ff.56v-57, *Corant*;**T**, ff.38-37v reversed, *Corant*.
32	Gavott in G	**J**, f.57, *Gavott*;***V**, f.38, *Gavot*; **W**, f.15v, *Gavatt*.

Note on Suite [10]. In **J** no composer is named for S30 and S31, but at the end of S32 'Dr Blowe' is written, and the movements run continuously as a suite. I regard them as such and treat the ascription at the end of S32 as applying to them all. As noted, there are independent ascriptions to Blow for S 30 and S 31.

Suite [No. 11] in G.

1.	2.	3.
33	Almand in G	**K**, ff.53v-54, *Almand*; *†**T**, f.37 reversed (fragment only).
34	Corant in G	**K**, 54v, *Corant*; ***V**, f.37v, *Corant*.
35	Saraband in G	**K**, f.55, *Saraband*; ***V**, ff.37v-38, *Sarabrand*.

Note on Suite [11]. In **K** no composer is named for S33 and S34, but S35 is ascribed to 'Dr. Blow'. As all three run as a group without a break and have every appearance of constituting a suite, I have little hesitation in supposing that the attribution at the end of S35 governs them all. However, unlike S30 and S31 in Suite [10], no confirmatory attribution is available for S33 and S34, which are therefore included among Blow's works solely on the strength of this consideration.

Suite [No. 12] in G.

1.	2.	3.
– –	Hunting Almand in G	See S30.
– –	Corant in G	See S34.
– –	Saraband in G	See S35.
– –	Gavott in G	See S32.

Note on Suite [12]. Although the first and fourth, and the second and third of these pieces occur in Suites [10] and [11] respectively, they are found as a definite suite grouping (though without composer's name) in **V**.

Group 2. Single dance and kindred movements.

1.	2.	3.
36	[Air] in a	†**U**, p.36.
37	Air in C	**H**, f.5, *Air.*
38	[Air] in d	†**U**, p.25.
39	Almand in C	**U**, p.23, *Almand.*
40	Hunting Almand in C	**E**, ff.55v-56, *The Hunting Almand* (an arrangement from 'Venus and Adonis', not a version of S30).
41	Almand in D	**T**, ff.36-35v reversed, *Almaine.*
42	Almand in D	**N**, f.9, *Almand.*
43	Almand in d	*****K**, ff.44v-45, *Almand;* **T**, ff.34-33v reversed, *Almaine.*
44	Almand in g	**O**, pp.45-47, *Almand.*
45	Corant in C	**U**, p.24, *Corant.*
46	Gavott in g	I/Ia, item 10, *Gavott in Gamut.*
47	Minuet in a	*****C**, p.15, *Minuit;* †**O**, pp.31-32; †**U**, p.19.
48	Minuet in C	**H**, f.5v, *Minuet.*
49	Saraband in a	**D**, ff.57-56v reversed, *Saraband.*
50	Saraband in C	I/Ia, item 11, *Saraband in C fa ut;* **U**, p.22, *Saraband.*

51	[Saraband] in d	†S, ff.23v-24.
52	[Saraband] in G	†H, f.17.
53	Saraband in G	E, f.40v, *A Saraband.*
54	Theatre Tune in d	I/Ia, item 18, *Theatre Tune*;*'Apollo's Banquet' (1690, 1693), entitled *Mr Mountford's Delight.*

Group 3. Chacones and Grounds

1.	2.	3.
55	Chacone in C	E, ff.41v-45, *A Chacone*; W, ff.17v-18, *Chacone* (shorter version).
56	Chacone in F	C, pp.42-46, *Chacone*; N, ff.15v-18v, *Chacone*; version for strings a 4, Bodleian MSS Mus.Sch. e.443-5, and f.570.
57	Chacone in g	C, pp.22-23, *Chacone*;*L, ff.5v-7, *Chacone*; N, ff.13v-15, *Chacone*; U, p.27, *Chiacone* (short version); *W, ff.18v-19, *Chacone.*
58	Ground in C, 'The Hay's a Ground'	*A, unfoliated, *A Ground*; H, ff.10v-11, *The Hay's a Ground*; *†J, ff.49v-50.
59	Ground in C	†R, pp.58-62; U, pp.28-32, *Ground in C fa ut.*
60	Ground in C	D, ff.56v-54 reversed, *Ground.*
61	Ground in e	*B, p.141, *Grownd* (incomplete); C, pp.50-57, *Ground*; E, ff.7v-11, *A Ground* (short version); J, ff.46-49, *Dr Blow's Ground in E la mi*; N, ff. 1-5v, *A Ground.*
62	Ground in G, 'Morlake's Ground'	I/Ia, item 23 ('Mortlack's Ground' in pencil in Ia); J, ff.61v-62v, *Morelake Ground*; †K, ff.31v-33v (longer version); T, ff.22-20v reversed, *Morlake Ground* (longer version); †V, ff.38-39v (longer version).
63	Ground in G	N, ff.19-20v, *Ground.*
64	Ground in G, No.2	M, ff.23v-24v, *Second Ground in G#*; N, ff.24-25, *Ground*; U, pp.33-35, *A Ground in G#.*

| 65 | Ground in g | *C, pp.26-27, *Ground*; E, ff.50v-53, *A Ground* (shorter version); †Q, pp.7-6 reversed; T, ff.20-18v reversed, *Ground*; W, ff.16v-17. *A Ground in Gamut* ♮; version for strings a 3, British Library, Add. MS 33236, f.63v-64. |

Group 4.   Overture and Preludes

1.	2.	3.
66	Overture in g	C, p. 25, *Overture* (2 short movements).
67	Prelude in C	*C, p.18, *Prelude*; H, f.10, *A Prelude*; P, f.23v, *Dr Blow's Voluntary*; *T, f.16v, *Prelude*; W, f.15v, *Prelude*.
68	Prelude in C	M, ff.3v-4, *Preludium*.
69	Prelude in G	U, p.37, *Prelude G#*.
70	Prelude in G	M, ff.22v-23, *Preludium in G#*; *W, ff.19v-20, *Prelude*.

Appendix.   Uncertain or erroneous attributions

1.	2..	3.
App.1	Corant in d	*K, ff.45v-46, *Corant*.
App.2	Saraband in d	*K, f.46v, *Saraband*.

Note on S/App.1-2.   These two contiguous pieces are immediately preceded in **K** by the Almand, S43, here anonymous. As set out in this source, the three pieces seem fairly clearly to constitute a suite. Given that the Almand (S43), on the testimony of **T**, is by Blow, this raises a possibility that the whole suite may be by him.

1.	2.	3.
App.3	Almand in F	*C, p.47, *Almand.*
App.4	Minuet in F	*C, p.49, *Minuet.*

Note on S/App.3-4. Immediately between these two pieces in **C** are the Corant and Saraband, S28 and S29, here anonymous, the four pieces appearing as a suite. S28 is attributed to Blow in **E**, and S29, though ascribed to Croft in **H**, is attributed to Blow in both **E** and **F**. If those ascriptions be accepted, once again there is a possibility that in **C** we have a complete suite by him.

1.	2.	3.
App.5	Saraband in c	**L**, ff.19v-20, *Sarabrand.*
App.6	Almand in c	**L**, ff.20v-21, *Almond.*
App.7	Almand in e	**L**, f.1, *Almand.*

Notes on S/App.5-7. Source **L** clearly attributes each of these pieces to Blow. However, the weight of other evidence allots the second and third to Croft, each respectively occurring in suites attributed to him in British Library Add. MS 31467, though the other sources of each are anonymous, ie **C**, pp.71 and 67 respectively. Of the Saraband, S/App.5, no other text is known to me, but its exceptionally clear-cut style makes me strongly hesitant to accept its attribution to Blow. The opening bars, as well as the general character of its continuation, are struck from the same mould as Croft's Saraband in C minor, vol. 1, p. 8 of Ferguson and Hogwood's edition.

1.	2.	3.
App.8	Almand in D	**K**, ff.36v-37, *Almand in D#.*
App.9	Corant in D	**K**, ff.37v-38, *Corant.*
App.10	Saraband in D	**K**, ff.38v-39, *Saraband.*

Note on S/App.8-10. These three pieces, though firmly ascribed to 'Dr Blow' in **K**, are to be found, together with a 'Jigg Allmaine', ascribed to 'Albert Bryne' (Blow's predecessor as organist of Westminster Abbey), in Bodleian Library, MS Mus.Sch.d.219. Like B A R Cooper, who drew attention to this in *The Musical times* cxiii 1972, 142-3, I consider the attribution to Bryne to be the more reliable.

1.	2.	3.
App.11	Almand in A	*C, p.1, *Almand*; G, f.19, *Almand*, attr. to 'Mr King'; *N, f.8, *Almand*; *V, ff.45v-46, *Almand*; *W, f.26, *Almand*; Dulwich College MSS, 2nd series, 95D, *Almand*, attr. to 'Mr King'; †Oxford, Christ Church Music MS 46, f.74 rev., *Allmand*, attr. to 'R.K.'; Tenbury, St. Michael's College MS 1508, ff.65v-66, *Allemande*. '12me Suitte, King'.
App.12	Minuet in A	*K, f.34, *Minuet*; *†N, f.8v.
App.13	[Gavott] in A	*†N, f.8v.
App.14	Prelude in C	*D, f.35v reversed, *Almand*; *†N, f.8v. *Preludio*.
App.15	[Corant] in C	*†N, f.23.
App.16	Fugue in C	*D, f.35 reversed, *Fuga*; *N, f.23v, *Fuga*.

Notes on S/App.11-16. All these six pieces were printed as Blow's by Ernst Pauer in part 4 of his *Old English composers for the virginal and harpsichord* (Augener Ltd, 8300d) and some have passed into other anthologies under the same ascription. Note that Pauer presented the first three as a single item, which suggests that he was working from source N, where they occur in sequence. No other trace of any of them with Blow's name attached is known to me. I disregard the fact that at the end of the 'Fugue' (S/App. 16) in N someone has added 'Dr Blow' lightly in pencil. There seems no reason to doubt that S/App. 11 is the work of Robert King (fl. 1680-1730) as attested by several of the sources named.

A DRESDEN OPERA-GOER IN 1756:
Johann Christian Trömer, called 'Der Deutsch-Franzos'

DAVID PAISEY

Kehn Mensch von Million, die in kanss Welt kewess,
So was sie ahn keseh, so Oper wie ssu Dress.

There is a fascination in established cultural institutions whose apparent permanence seems to defy the laws of social dynamics, but with hindsight we can usually identify signs of the forces which have inevitably transformed even the most hallowed. Opera is no exception, nor is occasional verse, and some works in the latter genre by a Dresden opera fan, written on the eve of the Seven Years' War, that economic disaster for Saxony which marked the end of the Dresden baroque era, manifest the changes at work within the particular traditions of these byways of social history.

By 1756, the Dresden court opera had for years been famous throughout Europe for its magnificence. The opera-house designed by Pöppelmann and Mauro had been one of the largest on the continent when first opened in 1719, holding over 2000 spectators, and with a stage forty-three metres deep. It adjoined the south-west pavilion of the Zwinger (which was to house the royal library) and had a gently-pitched roof at that point so that, from the internal garden, its bulk would obtrude as little as possible on the marvellous harmony of one of the finest of all baroque architectural layouts (Plate 1). Just as the opera seria of this house often took its subjects from Roman history, so Pöppelmann's conception of the Zwinger sought consciously to create for the Saxon court an ensemble of publicly representative buildings for culture and entertainment as a sort of

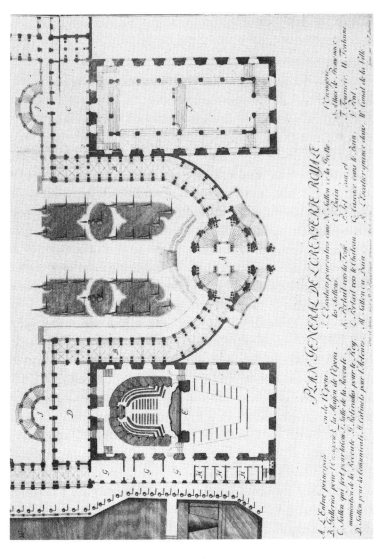

Plate 1. M. D. Pöppelmann: plan of the Zwinger at Dresden (southern end only).

forum on the Roman model, mediated by Vitruvius.[1] No expense was spared, despite Saxony's increasingly precarious financial state, to make the opera a by-word for artistic excellence and luxury. The orchestra set new standards, the best Italian singers were engaged, as were usually foreign designers. Winckelmann's criticism of Dresden as culturally 'a foreign colony' is often quoted and was largely justified where the opera was concerned, though we should recall that, from 1731, its presiding genius was a German, Johann Adolf Hasse,[2] albeit that he wrote in the Italian style.

Productions were often very spectacular. Thus in 1753, for Hasse's *Solimano*, to a libretto by the Dresden court poet G A Migliavacca, the stage held (apart from crowds) elephants, camels, horses and a stage band; the Hasse/Metastasio *Ezio* in 1755 had a parade of 400 men, 102 horses and five chariots, as well as camels and bandsmen, while during the concluding ballet there were 300 people on stage, 42 of them dancers. The annual cost of maintaining the opera in 1756 was over 100,000 Thalers,[3] and even after the Seven Years' War more than 23,000 Thalers were spent on a single production (*Siroe*, 1763).[4] During the war itself, when the court was in Warsaw, first minister Count Brühl apparently thought nothing of attempting to silence charges of extravagance with the untruth 'la dépense de la chasse et de la musique . . . est un mince objet'.[5] The court budget bore the whole expense of the opera, which did not charge for admission, as a piece of aristocratic self-advertisement. Moritz Fürstenau makes the excellent point that, with no need to meet the changing taste of a paying public, it was all too liable to stagnate in musico-dramatic terms, and manifest growing elaboration but not progress.[6] The taste expressed at Dresden for so long and, until the loss of Poland as a result of the Seven Years' War, at Warsaw, was the Italianate one of Friedrich August II, which replaced the mainly French preferences of his father.

As in Venice the principal opera season was at carnival time, whereas the bourgeois town theatre with its private impresarios[7] functioned also during the regular Saxon trade fairs. On gala nights at the opera the electoral family sat at the front of the stalls, the rest of the stalls being occupied by court ladies. On ordinary nights the electoral family sat in the stage boxes with gentlemen of the court in the stalls and ladies in the amphitheatre; the first tier of boxes was for top-ranking officials, ambassadors and foreign visitors, the second for the rest of the court, army officers and middle-ranking officials, and the top tier (the 'gods') for servants. Townsmen and women could be admitted to the amphitheatre on ordinary nights, and certain operas with great triumphal scenes even gave opportunities to provide spectacles for the general populace, when the hundreds of extras would process in costume through the Zwinger garden before vast crowds of people who were not opera-goers. Members of the audience were shown to their seats by court functionaries or soldiers, according to their rank, and soldiers were responsible for order inside and outside the theatre.[8] The conventions of operatic production, with characters deployed according to various degrees of precedence rather than dramatic verisimilitude, with musical opportunities to match, mirrored the strict divisions of the audience,[9] where, as in all such theatres, even the sight-lines were distributed by the architect in conformity with the social hierarchy.

How did these extravagant shows, these peaks of aristocratic culture, strike people who were not part of it themselves? We can attempt a few answers to the question from the testimony provided by an extraordinary Dresden literary figure, Johann Christian Trömer (c 1697-1756), who called himself 'der Deutsch-Franzos' (occasionally 'Jean Chrétien Toucement'), obviously a keen opera fan, and author of a number of occasional verse publications describing specific performances. His life (the best account is by Erich Schmidt in the *Allgemeine deutsche Biographie*) is scantily documented, and it is not clear how reliable is the autobiographical evidence of his works. He seems to have been attached to various noblemen and courts in a variety of capacities, probably including that of licensed comic, may have had experience of business, and held at least two possibly honorific posts: German agent of the Russian Academy, and Saxon post-commissar with some responsibility for road-building.[10] He is known to musical historians for describing how he came to be present at the student performance of Bach's lost cantata *Entfernt euch, ihr heitern Sterne* in Leipzig in 1727,[11] and to literary historians because the comic, strongly French-flavoured German in which he wrote provided one of the models for a character in Lessing's *Minna von Barnhelm* (1767). His neglect by scholars is unjustified, as he seems to me a real innovator, as well as a mine of sociological information. His *Schrifften* (1736; second edition, as *Avantures*, 1745), an anthology of his various occasional pieces with rhymed autobiographical framework, are at once a sort of culmination of the eighteenth-century development of occasional verse with a confessional element written by members of the bourgeoisie for the aristocracy,[12] and a radical new departure. Is there an earlier verse autobiography?

His products, while remaining occasional, were inevitably directed at a regular audience, the participants in the various court events being celebrated, who were happy to identify with his familiar[13] attitude to elevated society, and in particular to the Elector and his wife, whom he always termed 'Lanss-Papa' and 'Lanss-Mama'. His separate texts thus came to accommodate elements of continuity in the form of internal cross-references and, as their reprinting in the serial *Neu-eröffnete historische Correspondenz von Curiosis Saxonicis* (Dresden, from 1746) underlines, took on something

of the character of a gossipy court-column. Court entertainers of all kinds have always been allowed to give delight, and a little more, but hurt not: thus Haydn's 'Farewell' Symphony made a serious point as the musicians extinguished their candles, but the music's integrity of form was not broken. The Electors of Saxony seem to have liked satire as much as the next ruler,[14] as long as it amused without making them feel insecure, not touching the real power relationships, and so Trömer, a clown from a different class, in court circles but not of them, satirised all but the aristocracy. His motto 'Ridendo verum dicere' overstates matters: he had no reform effect. His works' usual folio format and occasional illustration by engravings rather than the cheaper woodcuts also indicates a rich readership. The 1745 *Avantures*, in particular, published by J C Lochner of Nürnberg, is a charming piece of rococo book-production for the upper-class market.[15]

One of his most astonishing works, the *Parentation uff ehne Paucker-Mohr* (1729),[16] is a part parodic, part affectionate elegy for a real black drummer,[17] which must be among the earliest literary tributes to a black member of European society, and which, further, decades before the revival of interest amongst intellectual circles in folk-literature, embodies an entire folk-tale in verse, that of the Jüterbog smith who outwits both the devil and death.[18]

As ever, in this man's works comedy and parody prove fertile fields for experiment, but Trömer's predilection for them has denied him the attentions of more serious-minded scholars in Germany, combined as it is with his concentration on occasional verse, particularly since the Romantic eclipse of this staple of the poetry of the preceding two centuries by the 'new' confessional genres, and of the urbane amateur by the professional poet.

His language is his most obvious distinguishing feature. As he tells us himself, it was first tried as a *jeu d'esprit* in verses for a wedding, but proved such a success that he adopted it as a permanent gimmick, never in fact using his real name in his publications, only the pseudonym 'der Deutsch-Franzos'. The style, whose features are soon told— many French loan-words and neologisms from French roots, mixed genders, missing initial h, k for g, ck for ch, ss(sz) for tz(z)—was imitated both during his lifetime, by students at Leipzig as a joke, for example when talking to their girl-friends, or by an unknown plagiarist in 1729, and immediately after his death in two publications describing the current war.[19]

This is not the place to detail Germany's love-hate relation-ship with French culture, manifested from the so-called *à la mode*-period in the 1620s in overlapping waves now of imitation of aspects of metropolitan French aristocratic manners and fashions by the almost entirely provincial German aristocracy and upper bourgeoisie, now of reaction, usually motivated by political antagonism to a dangerously powerful neighbour and adversary. The particular aspect of large-scale linguistic borrowing, with opposing campaigns for 'purification' of the German language, is an obvious indicator of nationalism most familiar to us from its twentieth-century manifestations, but was a rising feature of the social and literary scene from the seventeenth century.[20] It is the aspect of class antagonism, however, which is most important amongst the history-reflecting facets of our author's 'German-French' pseudonym. As early as 1637, in a popular song called *Die Teütsch Frantzösin*,[21] the adoption of French costume by ordinary townsfolk had been castigated because it threatened the clarity of the social hierarchy:

Es ist ein Schandt man kan kein Standt/
Mehr vor dem andern kennen.

In the eighteenth century, the language of the Saxon court was French, not German, clearly marking the division between the ruling class and the rest of society. This was not a state of affairs peculiar to Saxony;[22] the Prussian court too, for example, spoke French. Nor was it new. In *Der Teutsch-Französische Moden-Geist*, published in 1689 with the false imprint 'Geyersbergk', the anonymous author had complained:

> Wer nicht Frantzösisch kann/
> Der kömmt zu Hoff nicht an.

So the rising bourgeoisie, in particular, needed to assert the strength of its own language, and that Trömer's language was received as comic seems to me a sign of this fast-growing force. The court, his principal audience, was amused by his clumsy aping of its culture, the middle class by his pretensions. The language was funny to both, in reality irreconcilable, elements of the class mésalliance, having the prestige of neither, and his borrowings from French, though easy to imitate, could not in such circumstances hope to establish themselves in general usage. At the most basic linguistic level, therefore, he is a terminal phenomenon of absolutist court culture, though simultaneously a portent of the confidently rising culture of his own class which also produced in his work the notable innovations mentioned above.

We should perhaps try to identify more closely the social stratum in question. The academic sector of the bourgeoisie had begun its cultural rise much earlier on the groundwork laid by Reformation schoolmen, still according Latin an important, though diminishing, place, and institutionalizing the occasional genres which Trömer adopted and parodied. But in Saxony by the late seventeenth century bourgeois lawyers were being replaced in the state administration by aristocrats. In the eighteenth century, as the country sank deeper into debt, it was the turn of the traders and manu-facturers, whose vital role in economic recovery became obvious, to establish their ideological and cultural influence and, most importantly, to win appropriate administrative reforms.[23]

We can see these general characteristics taking on more precise form in relation to the court opera from a closer look at two of Trömer's last products (he died on May 1). They were written (in verse, like all his works) at the end of the carnival season of 1756 and describe events in it. Dated respectively March 5 and 19, they were entitled *Ehn Drey mal Friedrick-Fest werd Euthe celebrir* and *Ehn Freud uff ander komm, denn Euth iss arrivir die kross Josepha-Tagk*,[24] and printed by the court printer, Stösselin's widow. The operas performed this year were Metastasio and Hasse's *Il re pastore, Ezio* (the block-buster from the previous year with its vast triumph-scene), and the new *Olimpiade*, while the greatest popular success was a ballet, *Don Quichotte*, arranged by the ballet-master Antoine Pitrot, presumably to music by the resident composer of ballet-music, Johann Adam. Trömer is at pains to single out the German per-formers, artists and craftsmen who played a part in these dazzling spectacles.[25] The pastoral opera had sets by one Dresden native, a painter named Müller, while the machinery activating the transformation in the second act of *Ezio*, with its hundreds of ropes and pulleys, changing a garden with many fountains into a palace gallery, was designed by another, Gottlob Reuss:[26]

Er ath uns woll lass seh, dass uff Stadt-Krab[27] logir,
Ock Leut, die was versteh und die koenn was praestir
. . .
O! bey die liebe Deusch, à part bey ehrligk Sackss,
Die Kunst und die Merittes sie thu wie Bilsse[28] wacks.

Apart from the two foreign ballet-masters, one of the other dancers, an unnamed German, is also praised, and Trömer even expresses the hope that a school of ballet might be established in Dresden.   He thinks it wrong for German artists and craftsmen to Latinise their 'honourable German' names (as of course many did, as a sign of the greater prestige of foreign culture), and wishes they would proclaim their nationality to the rest of the world.

He relates how he saw *Ezio*, by invitation, from a box where, extraordinarily, his neighbour was 'ehn kelehrt Bauermann' (an educated peasant, or more probably farmer), without Latin, but with knowledge of mathematics and astronomy, who had never seen an opera before.   In his exchanges with Trömer, which are presented in dialogue form, he speaks in Saxon dialect.   It was not new to have dialect, and peasant characters speaking it, in occasional verse, especially epithalamia, but it goes without saying that the audience for such works were never peasants.   It is noteworthy that, whenever Trömer is dealing with peasant characters, his otherwise habitual persona of naive clown takes on a conscious intellectual superiority.   Thus in his description of the parade through the Zwinger garden, thronged with thousands of townspeople and peasants, associated with the Shrove Tuesday performance of *Ezio* in the previous year,[29] he had made fun of ordinary people's uncomprehending responses to historical costume.   Our farmer of 1756 is amazed by the appearance on stage of horses and camels, by the transformation-scene, by the ballet, and by a soprano display aria with oboe obbligato.   His ignorance of such things is presented as comic, though he is allowed to remark, on the transformation, ' . . . ey wos dos kost fer Kald!' Trömer's rather coy explanation of the nature of castrati makes plain to him that the phenomenon is Italian, not German, and perhaps even, by implication, un-German.

Plate 2. The crush outside the opera-house. The figure on horseback is Trömer.

The extraordinary demand by town women to get in to the ballet performances led to riotous scenes at the entrance to the opera-house, which Trömer illustrates in an engraving in the verses for March 5 (Plate 2). Since seats not taken up by those on the court lists were as usual allocated to townsfolk without tickets on a 'first-come-first-served' basis, all fans were in competition with each other for admission. The soldiers guarding the entrance were so besieged that for the first time they had to erect a barrier to control the crowd. Two pregnant women were caught in the crush, a woman had the sleeve of her coat torn off, while another, dressed in blue taffeta, tried unsuccessfully to crawl through the legs of a guardsman, an incident illustrated in the verses for March 19:

Die Schelm (sans flatterie)
er drück sein Beine ssu,
Er ätth sie bald erwürgk
die arme blinde Kuh. (Plate 3)

Plate 3. No
way in to the
opera-house.

The amphitheatre was full, and women took over many of the seats reserved for men, one of whom took revenge by stitching together two girls' dresses, which tore when they got up to leave:

Vielleicht sie ahn keborgk die Kleid die arm Marmott;
In dies schwehr Zeit das sess sie schon in krosse Noth.

Correct dress was officially required for opera-going at that time (the tradition lives on today in some German houses), and Trömer had an eye for its importance. He makes fun of a court kitchen-servant, dressed in cheap cloth, with a large cap covering her too homely face, who, in the throng outside the entrance, had a dispute with a woman she thought had pushed her, in which she swore and slapped her opponent, thus drawing attention to her station which disqualified her from admission. At the previous year's *Ezio* too,[30] where some women had fought 'like dragons' to get in, one had fallen foul of the authorities because she was hatless, whereas the fashion prescribed a little ruched black satin cap. Similarly, Trömer's verses for March 5 and 19 1754[31] had taken some Dresden women to task for wearing dresses with trains to the opera, and hoods in summer while going bare-headed in winter.

Inside the opera-house, there could be other breaches of the strict code of etiquette. Back at the 1756 *Don Quichotte*, Trömer is shocked at the unseemly (in the royal house, that is) conduct of an NCO, who persuades his colleagues to stitch his coat to the dress of a girl he wants to get to know. But we can appreciate this example of natural ebullience on the part of someone not there by choice, whose lack of interest in the culture of a different class led him to make some entertainment of his own. In this respect he was like the servants whose unruly behaviour in the part of the house set aside for them had provoked repeated court decrees limiting their numbers and seeking to regulate their conduct from the very opening of the theatre in 1719.[32]

For those townspeople who wanted to get in, however, the ultimate stratagem to jump the disorderly queue was tried, if all in vain, by some foolhardy women who climbed the wooden ladder kept beside the opera-house as a fire-escape. Judging from Bellotto's 1758 engraving of the Zwinger, after his own painting of 1754 (Plate 4), this ladder must have been a permanent feature of the precautions against fire instituted after the private, short-lived (1746-48),

Plate 4. Bellotto, the northern half of the Zwinger from the park. The engraved inscription to the right informs

wooden Mingotti theatre, built in the middle of the Zwinger garden, had burned down. Theatres were particularly vulnerable to fire, of course, and few had the built-in water-supply for scenic effects and fire-fighting of Frederick the Great's Berlin opera-house of 1742. In Dresden, the life of the opera-houses had a crude correspondence to periods of social history. Society gets the opera it deserves, like everything else, but in Dresden's case the very buildings seem to rise and fall with ideologies. Our Zwinger house, after the hiatus of the war years 1756-63, in the course of which it served the Prussians for a time as a sort of arsenal, had only a few years' more active life for opera, and had covered the period of absolutism. Its successor was the much smaller Moretti theatre somewhat to the east of the Zwinger (1755-1840), with paying audiences and an increasingly German repertory, and which covered the early moves towards a constitutional monarchy. The Zwinger opera was deliberately burned down on May 6 1849 during the bourgeois revolution, watched from his look-out post by Wagner, who had recently conducted some epoch-making performances of the Choral Symphony in that former scene of Hasse's triumphs. Then the successive Semper opera-houses (1841-69 and 1878-1945) served Dresden's bourgeois era: time alone will tell whether the current restoration of the second has a more than architectural significance.

Trömer's admiration for Hasse was boundless. Of *Olimpiade* he writes:

> Die schoen Music die war von die Mann componir,
> Von die bey Ewigkeit ihr Ruhm iss inscribir.

Burney had the greatest regard for him all his life, and called him the Raphael to Gluck's Michelangelo of then living composers,[33] and Hans Schnoor quotes another characterization of him as 'the Correggio of church-music'.[34] It

is a pity we have so little opportunity to judge him in performance ourselves.[35]   But I have deliberately omitted music
from my remarks, partly because I am no musicologist and
am unqualified to consider changes in Hasse's style during his
years at Dresden, and partly because of the fundamental
difficulty of writing about musical invention historically in
relation to social change.   Although its externals are irrefu-
tably historically conditioned, intrinsically music has no
precise verbal meaning.   I forbear to enter these deep aesthetic waters, where knowledge of a stroke or two cannot make
up for ignorance of the currents.   And a study of Hasse's
libretti, mainly by Metastasio (again, according to Burney,[36]
composer and poet constituting the two halves of a Platonic
Androgyne), though it would no doubt help us to understand
the self-image of eighteenth-century absolutism, would only
rarely be specific to the Saxon court.

The language of the libretti is significant, however, since,
like the French language spoken and written at court, it was a
cultural barrier erected around the mainly aristocratic audiences.[37]   This may partly explain the exceptional demand
by social-climbing Dresden townspeople to see the ballet,
where they experienced no language problem.   The story of
the rise of German opera has often been told.   It suffices
merely to recall again the commonplace that cultural nationalism was a result of the demand of the bourgeoisie, as it grew
ever more emancipated, for its own culture.   Another result
was its earlier, and equally familiar, take-over of the dramatic
stage in the *bürgerliches Trauerspiel* on the English model,
social developments here having led the way: Lessing's *Miss
Sara Sampson* was first performed at Frankfurt on the Oder
in 1755.   So Trömer's pride in German achievements was
symptomatic, and if linguistic nationalism is not one of his
explicit themes, the very fabric of his language is a constant
reminder of its importance.

Even today, the language in which opera is sung can tell us as much about its intended audience as seat-prices. The recent account by a former chairman of the Royal Opera in London of his board's defence in the early 1970's of opera in the original language[38] makes quite clear that house's lack of interest in fundamental popularisation: with its jet-setting stars, it serves an increasingly international elite. The English National Opera, on the other hand, keeps the metropolitan middle class happy with its own language, though the new English National Opera North, in November 1978, mounted its first production ominously in French.

It is salutary for those who, like me, have a weakness for opera, to try occasionally to assess its social function, in the twentieth no less than the eighteenth century, where Trömer, with his useful concentration on the audience, has enabled us to see many signs of social and cultural mobility within the framework of a frozen convention.[39]

REFERENCES

1 'Thermae, Circus, Palestra, Theatrum, Colossaeum, Amphitheatrum, Basilicum, Xystus, Peristylum, Atrium, Oecus, Arcus, Porticus, Pinacotheca, Bibliotheca,&c.' M D Pöppelmann *Vorstellung und Beschriebung des von Sr.Königl. Majestät in Pohlen, und Churfl. Durchl. zu Sachssen, erbauten so genannten Zwinger-Gartens Gebäuden* Dresden, 1729, introduction. Fig. 1, from this book, shows the southern end of Pöppelmann's plan of the Zwinger, with the operahouse at the left and, at the right, the balancing but short-lived Redoutensaal (it was gone by 1722). J L Sponsel, in his *Der Zwinger, die Hoffeste und die Schlossbaupläne zu Dresden* Dresden, 1924 says (p207) that Pöppelmann sometimes represents what he wanted to build, rather than what he actually built, but excepts the opera-house from the stricture. It was remodelled several times before 1756.

2 Apart from a slight flicker in 1747-52, when it seemed for a moment that Porpora's star might eclipse his ever-increasing brilliance.

3 M Fürstenau *Zur Geschichte der Musik und des Theaters am Hofe zu Dresden*, Teil 2 Dresden, 1862, 294-296.

4 *ibid*, 230.

5 Letter of August 21 1762, printed in H Schlechte *Die Staatsreform in Kursachsen 1762-1763* Berlin, 1958, 290. Court festivities, it seemed, had always to go on at all costs. There had been a race to finish the building of the opera-house on time through the severe winter of 1718/19. Work went on by day and by night, and the 150 workmen who revolted on February 24 1719 because one had been beaten by a foreman were forced to work for four days in chains (Fürstenau, *op cit*, 129). Some small craftsmen were made to wait for their payment because the court was temporarily short of cash (Sponsel, *op cit*, 234). The first performances in the new house were for the wedding of the Prince, subsequently Friedrich August II, and the Archduchess Maria Josepha of Austria, celebrated with exceptional splendour though parts of Saxony were suffering severe food-shortages. In January 1728, during a visit to Dresden by King Friedrich Wilhelm of Prussia, a ceremonial sleigh-ride by the court ladies, threatened by the melting of lying snow in the town, was saved by the importation of hundreds of cart-loads from the surrounding countryside.

6 Fürstenau, *op cit*, 199, 243.

7 This method of financing opera, with some official subsidy and paying audiences, only established itself in Dresden after the Seven Years' War.

8 Fürstenau, *op cit*, 139f.

9 M Hammitzsch *Der moderne Theaterbau. Der höfische Theaterbau* Berlin, 1906, 139, remarks on the number of mid-eighteenth century drawings in the Dresden Sammlung für Baukunst showing the allocation of seats according to strict etiquette.

10 He is credited with having the Ostraallee in Dresden laid out, in 1747 according to C Goedeke (*Grundriss zur Geschichte der deutschen Dichtung aus den Quellen*, Band 4, 2nd ed Dresden 1889-91, 39), while A Hantzsch (*Namenbuch der Strassen und Plätze Dresdens* Dresden 1905, 104) says the avenue dates from 1744.

11 The relevant extract was reprinted privately, Vienna 1954, by Isolde Ahlgrimm and Erich Fiala.

12 I have written elsewhere on this phenomenon: 'The first fruits of Johann Friedrich Hager, printer at Göttingen, in 1729: poems for King George II of England' in *Gutenberg-Jahrbuch* 1977, 170-182, especially 173.

13 Fürstenau (*op cit*, 276) calls it 'meist fuchsschwänzerisch' (syco-phantic).

14 A 'gazette comique' had been written for Friedrich August I (after 1708) by Angelo Constantini, satirising courtiers and court affairs, and in 1748 the court had enjoyed a three-act farce by Giovanni Casanova, with music by Salvatore Apollini, parodying the operas of Metastasio (Fürstenau, *op cit*, 26, 258).

15 Ahlgrimm & Fiala, *loc cit*, remark that the copy they used for their edition was in a much worn noble binding. The British Library's copy (11521.f.20), acquired in 1870, is similarly in a nice, if now battered, eighteenth-century gold-tooled calf binding.

16 This date is given in Trömer's *Avantures*. Goedeke (*op cit*) has 1731.

17 Presumably employed at the court of Johann Adolf, Duke of Saxe-Weissenfels, as Trömer had been himself.

18 This part alone of the text was republished in the nineteenth century with a new, possibly pseudonymous, verse famework in imitation of Trömer's style: Ernst Fréderic Le Mang, *Avantures von sswe kute Freund ... Keschrieb uff die Manier von Deutsch-Franzoss*, s.l.& a. Goedeke's date for this new, undated, edition is 1857, but since the British Library's copy (11526.e.68(1)) was acquired in 1846, this can be amended to ca 1845.

19 One of these, *Relation vom Kriek in kute Deutscheland* Dresden, 1757, though poor verse, is of much interest for its picture of the Prussian occupation of Saxony and its economic consequences.

20 Cf the introduction to W J Jones *A lexicon of French borrowings in the German vocabulary (1575-1648)* Berlin & New York, 1976.

21 British Library copy, printed at Innsbruck, 11517.aa.35. This has a companion-piece, *Teutscher Franzoss* (11517.aa.34), printed 'zu Nutz vnnd Warnung aller frommen Teutschen Patrioten'.

22 Both in the Seven Years' War and the Napoleonic period, however, Saxony's Francophilia had an important political dimension.

23 H Schlechte, *op cit, passim*.

24 British Library copies 11501.k.14(9 & 10).

25 There is a list of the singers and orchestral players employed at the Dresden court in 1756 in F W Marpurg's *Historisch-kritische Beyträge zur Aufnahme der Musik* Band 2, Stück 5 Berlin, 1756, 475-477. Amongst the singers, Italians outnumber Germans, but the situation is reversed in the orchestra. Fürstenau (*op cit*, 294-296) adds details of their salaries.

26 Thus the Industrial Revolution touched the Dresden opera, though it seems doubtful whether it reduced the work-force which only the previous year had had to push the flats for this scene. Fürstenau (*op cit*, 283) says the machines took 250 men to work them.

27 Stadt-Graben (ie in Dresden).

28 Pilze (mushrooms).

29 *Was Jn die kansse Welt es iss nock nit kescheh* Dresden, 1755 (British Library copy Hirsch IV 1351). My epigraph comes from this text.

30 *ibid.*

31 British Library copies 11501.k.14(6 & 7). The latter also includes the sad tale of a bald old woman who went to the opera in a wig, only to have it blown off in the Zwinger garden.

32 eg Fürstenau, *op cit*, 140, 257.

33 *The present state of music in Germany, the Netherlands, and United Provinces*, 2nd ed London, 1775, i, 281, 353.

34 *Dresden. Vierhundert Jahre deutsche Musikkultur* Dresden, 1948, 97.

35 Perhaps the ever-enterprising Camden Festival in London could mount an opera (without elephants)—there is even one, *Euristeo* (1732), dedicated to the English nation. A German Hasse revival in 1883 (*Alcide al bivio*) seems to have been a flop.

36 *op cit*, i, 240.

37 There were some signs of movement, however. For Hasse's first Dresden opera *Cleofide* in 1731 the libretto-book had included a translation into French, but from 1738 translations into German replaced French in the printed libretti, starting with a performance of *La clemenza di Tito* (Fürstenau, *op cit*, 172, 226).

38 Lord Drogheda: *Double harness*, London 1978, p.332ff.

39 Since this article went to press, the British Library has acquired a further eleven occasional publications by Trömer, dating from 1742 to 1753 (pressmark C.13.h.15), one from the earliest year including the folk-tale of Him, Ham and Hum, and the latest providing more highly interesting material on opera audiences. Even more recently, the British Library has acquired an anthology of Trömer's later occasional pieces, which was published in Nürnberg in 1772 as *Schrifften*, Bd.2.

HENRIC FOUGT, TYPOGRAPHER EXTRAORDINARY

JOHN A PARKINSON

In *Four hundred years of music printing* Alec King draws attention to the work of Henric Fougt, the London music printer whose career, although brief, caused something of a stir among his contemporaries. Little information about Fougt has so far been published in English and many references to him still derive from a passage in Sir John Hawkins' *History of Music*. Writing in 1776, Hawkins describes him in these words:

> About ten years ago one Fougt, a native of Lapland, arrived here, and taking a shop in St Martin's Lane, obtained a patent for the sole printing of music on letter-press types of his own founding, which were very neat. This patent, had it been contested at law, would undoubtedly have been adjudged void, as the invention was not a new one. He published several collections of lessons and sonatas under it, but the music-sellers in London copied his publications on pewter plates, and by underselling, drove him out of the kingdom.

In *Music engraving and printing* (London, 1923) William Gamble devotes some attention to Fougt, whom he describes as a German, and his patent music types. The most comprehensive account of Fougt's work as a printer is, however, to be found in the article 'New Music Types: invention in the eighteenth century' by Edmund Poole.[1] Like Mr Poole, I am indebted for many biographical details to the researches of Dr Sten G Lindberg, contained in his important article

'John Baskerville och Henric Fougt'.[2]   Further valuable information is provided by an article 'Henric Fougts engelska musiktryck' by Åke Vretblad.[3]   My own researches have uncovered further particulars to complete the picture.

Henric Fougt was born at Lövånger in Sweden in 1720 and was entered as a student at Uppsala in 1734.   He was already known as an engraver in 1749 when he provided the illustrations for Linné's *Amoenitates academicae.*   Later he turned his attention to music printing, following the example of J G I Breitkopf, whose invention of music types was made public in 1755.   On November 7 1763 Fougt applied to the Swedish government for the exclusive privilege of printing music and books for the term of forty-five years.   Despite the opposition of the printers' guild he was granted a license on March 9 1764 empowering him to print music with 'loose cast types, in looks and device similar to notes engraved in copper'.   In addition to this license, valid for twenty-five years, he was granted the same rights to print and publish books as other printers.   However his application to the Riksdag for financial support for a scheme to improve the quality of printing throughout Sweden was refused, as was his application for the post of printer to the King and Queen.

Disillusioned, he resigned his official position in the Board of Mining on November 12 1766 and in December deposited at the Bank of Sweden a specimen of his type-printed music.[4]   In March 1767 he informed the Bank of Sweden of his intention to seek his living abroad.   On July 6 the King gave him leave to travel to England, where his safe arrival, complete with music types, was reported by the Swedish embassy on November 10 1767.

On arrival in England Fougt promptly applied for a patent to print music.   His application, No 888, was granted on December 24 1767 for a term of fourteen years.   The specification attached to his application, quoted by both Gamble and Poole, refers to 'certain new and curious types by me invented for the printing of music as neatly and as well in every respect as hath been usually done by engraving'. His music types differed from the 'choral' types used in earlier music, in which each note was cast complete with the five lines of the stave. Instead Fougt built up each note and each line of the stave on which it stood from separate elements, much in the same way that printers' 'flowers' are built up by the regular arrangement of small constituent parts. Although his method required five times as many characters as the earlier method, Fougt claimed that the results were far superior. His specification was accompanied by a hand-drawn diagram representing the characters he proposed to use, numbering 166 in all. Poole and Gamble both reproduce this diagram; the latter comments on the similarity between Fougt's characters and the elements used in modern music founts.

From his premises in St Martin's Lane, at the sign of the Lyre and Owl, Fougt produced a succession of distinctively printed publications. In some cases the titlepage is ornamented with a woodcut of an owl, perched somewhat precariously upon a pair of scales at the entrance to a rocky cave, illuminated by a burning torch. The lyre, however, is conspicuous by its absence. Clearly Fougt pictured himself as a wise old bird, casting the light of knowledge in dark places, but dependent upon the scales of justice (and English fair play?) for acceptance of his novel ideas.

One of Fougt's early publications was a set of trio-sonatas by Francesco Uttini. According to a letter printed on the flyleaf of this publication, his invention was submitted to the Society for the Encouragement of the Arts, Manufactures and Commerce of Great Britain. On the fly-leaf of a later publication, Croce's sonatas, Fougt proudly quotes their verdict, in a resolution passed on December 28 1768, to the effect that 'Mr Fougt's method of printing music is an improvement superior to any before in use in Great Britain; and that it appears to answer all the purposes of engraving in wood, tin or copper, for that end and can be performed with much less expense'.

The established music printers can hardly have been expected to welcome this upstart foreigner with any display of enthusiasm. The music publishing scene had long been dominated by Walsh, but since his death in 1766 the firms of Bremner and Welcker had disputed the supremacy in the quality field, with others such as Thompson not far behind. Type-printing, although in general use until the end of the seventeenth century, had long since gone out of favour, except for the crudest of publications, such as the song-supplements to magazines. All these publishers used the standard method of printing from engraved pewter plates and in many cases produced work of high quality. The opinion, quoted by Gamble from an unnamed authority, that 'Fougt was the only printer in his day who produced any good music work' must surely refer to type-printers only. The London printers must have been outraged at the suggestion that type-printed music could challenge the quality of their engraved productions.

Between 1767 and 1770 Fougt published the following works at his own expense:

> Giovanni Andrea Sabatini: *6 sonatas for two violins and bass*, Op1 (1767)
> Bartolomeo Menesini: *6 sonatas for two violins and bass* (1767)
> Francesco Uttini: *6 sonatas for two violins and bass*, Op1 (1768)
> Benedetto Leoni: *6 lessons for the harpsichord* (1768)
> Giuseppe Sarti: *Three sonatas for the harpsichord* (1769)

Pietro Nardini: *Six solos for the violin*, Op5 (1769)
Giacomo Croce: *6 sonatas for the harpsichord* (1769)

Of these composers, only Nardini, Sarti and Uttini are known. The others are not listed in any biographical dictionary, nor are any other works by them extant. Uttini was an Italian from Bologna, who had been appointed court musical director at Stockholm in 1755, remaining there until his death in 1795. His main claim to fame is that he was the first to compose operas to a Swedish libretto, but his reputation at that time was hardly widespread. Possibly the other unknown composers were, like him, Italians in the employ of the court of Stockholm, and since Fougt was under the necessity of publishing music as cheaply as possible he took the risk of promoting these totally unknown characters. Otherwise one is tempted to imagine that they are either pseudonyms for Fougt himself or even pirated publications of other composers.

The harpsichord sonatas by Sarti cannot be verified from any other source. Indeed if they are by him then they are the first of his instrumental works to be published and his only works for solo keyboard. On the other hand Burney does mention[5] that the young Sarti, on his way back to Italy from Copenhagen, passed through England and published some sonatas for harpsichord. The Nardini sonatas, although not printed elsewhere, are accepted as genuine by Clara Pfäfflin in her doctoral thesis *Pietro Nardini; seine Werke und sein Leben* (Stuttgart, 1930). The first sonata is found in MS in the Berlin Staatsbibliothek, listed as Tartini, arr Nardini. The last sonata is evidently genuine, since the composer is shown holding a copy of it in the engraved portrait by G B Cecci after M Vestri which forms the frontispiece to Nardini's *Sei sonate per violino solo e basso*.[6]

Fougt also published some works at the author's expense,

eg Dibdin's *First collection of ballads sung at Ranelagh* and Pietro Guglielmi's *Six divertimentos for the harpsichord and violin*. On July 17 1769 he advertised 'Twelve of the most famous French songs collected from the operas. . .adapted for the guitar'. I have been unable to trace any extant copy of this work. He also published a large number of smaller items—some eighty-two songs and short instrumental pieces are listed by Vretblad, only a few of which are to be found in British libraries. Clearly Fougt found it difficult to sell his wares, particularly substantial works by unknown composers. Moreover he soon ran into opposition from the other London music publishers. There is no proof of Hawkins' assertion that Fougt was undersold by the other publishers. Indeed, it would have been difficult for them to do so, since Fougt's single songs were priced at a penny a page, or eighteen for one shilling, considerably less than the regular price of engraved music. However Hawkins is correct in stating that other publishers 'copied his publications on pewter plates'. A direct challenge in this way came from the firm of Longman & Co, of 26 Cheapside, who issued a rival edition of Sarti's sonatas which bore the following 'Advertisement to the Public':

> On comparing Mr Henry Fougt's new invented type printed music with the specimen of plate printed music here offer'd to the public; we doubt whether their approbation in general will coincide with the opinion of all the eminent musicians in the cities of London and Westminster. Which is, that the following method of plate printed music is greatly superior to type printing, in neatness, clearness to the sight, cheapness and in every other respect.

Longman's edition is indeed more legible than Fougt's, if less characteristic, and by compressing into nineteen pages of engraved music the twenty-three pages which Fougt had allowed himself, Longmans were able to sell it at the same price of two shillings.

More trouble was in store for Fougt. On July 20 1769 the *Public advertiser* carried this advertisement:

> Some of the songs in the comic opera of the Padlock having been pirated in a collection of vocal music, a bill was last week filed against the publisher, who has paid the costs and entered into a bond to offend no more; and the proprietor has given orders to prosecute one FOUGHT, a foreign printer, in what he calls musical types, for an offence of the like nature.

A later advertisement, on September 23, announced that:

> The proprietor of the music of the Padlock has commenced a suit against one Henry FOUGHT, a foreign music-printer, for pirating some of the songs of that opera, and against Samuel Fores, stationer, for vending the same.

The composer of *The Padlock* was, of course, Dibdin, and it seems curious that he should have been involved in a prosecution of the person who had published his own Ranelagh ballads. Either they had fallen out, or the action was brought at the instigation of John Johnson, who published the opera on Dibdin's behalf. The result of the legal proceedings is not known, but it may well have had the effect of bringing Fougt's London career to an abrupt end. He was still advertising his publications in January 1770 when Guglielmi's *Six sonatas for harpsichord with accompaniments* was announced. No copy of such a work has survived—possibly the advertisement refers to the six divertimentos previously published.

By the end of 1770 it was clear to Fougt that the streets of London were not paved with gold, and sadder, but no doubt wiser, he packed up his stock-in-trade and returned to Sweden. He sold his patent music types to Robert Falkener, who employed them with some success to produce single sheet songs by Handel and others which, like Fougt's publications, were sold at a penny a page. Many of Fougt's own publications remained unsold. The inventory of his effects after his death in 1782 revealed[7] that he was still in possession of 110-180 copies of each of his major publications, apart from the works by Menesini and Leoni.

On his return to Stockholm Fougt resumed his interrupted career as engraver and printer. His later work shows the influence of John Baskerville's English type-faces. He did not venture to repeat his unsuccessful attempt to revolutionize the art of music-printing, although his own interest in music remained undiminished, as the contents of his library reveal.[8] In addition to many unpublished musical MSS he owned vocal collections in French and English, sonatas by Bach, Haydn and Schobert[9] and was also the proud possessor of a harpsichord by Hasch of Hamburg, a piano by Broman and an Amati violin. As a keen amateur musician perhaps he found solace in music for the failure of his expedition to England. But one tantalising question remains unsolved. Did Sabatini, Croce, Menesini and Leoni actually exist or were they merely figments of Fougt's imagination?

REFERENCES

1 *Journal of the Printing Historical Society* i 1965, 21-38; ii 1966, 23-44.
2 *Biblis* 1958, 67-134.
3 *ibid*, 135-145.
4 Reproduced in Poole, *op cit*, ii, 36.

5 In his article on Sarti in A Rees, *The Cyclopaedia* London, 1819.
6 Reproduced in the article on Nardini in MGG.
7 See Vretblad, *op cit*, 144.
8 See Lindberg, *op cit*, 128.
9 But surely not Schubert, as Lindberg would have us believe!

MUSIC ENGRAVING PRACTICE
IN EIGHTEENTH-CENTURY LONDON:
a study of some Forster editions of Haydn
and their manuscript sources

H EDMUND POOLE

In 1699 William Pearson published *Twelve new songs* by as many leading composers of the day 'chiefly to encourage' a music type that he called his 'New London Character'. In the preliminary pages he printed an address 'To all Masters and Encouragers of Musick'. He shared his puffs between his types and the reputation of English music, in the hope that each might well serve the other:

> What I have to say to the rest of the world is this: that the charge of this New Character, will be much easier, than what is possible to be done on copper; and I leave the Note next to the Masters Opinion, so to speak for itself. And as the Noble Art is now more flourishing than ever, and spreads itself into Foreign Parts from our Nation; yet by the general false Writing, and the Dearness of Engraving, with the mean collections of some others; the Honour of our *English* Composers is darkened; But in you, Gentlemen, I hope, the Reputation of *English* compositions, may, at least, give place, to none, except *Italy*.

His final paragraph does not shine with quite the same lustre:

> *Gentlemen,* Tho' I have not had the opportunity to Communicate to each of you your several Proofs, to Examine before they were work'd off; yet the Care I have taken, and having had your own Copies to go by, I make no doubt, but this Collection of your Songs, will be as correct as any yet Extant.

And he remained their 'Humble Servant William Pearson'.

This description of Pearson's offering reveals sound commercial imperatives. They were: to obtain authentic copy, to publish it as economically as was practicable—having one eye on the market and the other on the output of his competitors—and to print it as accurately as these considerations and his own conscience permitted.

He was venturing into a fiercely competitive market-place where one or other of these unexceptionable principles was likely to be much bruised. From the earliest days in France and Italy printers and publishers of music had never been averse to putting their 'sickle into another man's corne'. The accuracy of the Attaignant and Gardano editions quickly attracted the distinction of widespread piracy. In Pearson's own day printers did not always wait for a by-your-leave before offering Purcell and other eminent composers to the Town, and by the eighteenth century there was throughout Europe a flourishing music trade sustained as much by chicanery and the unauthorised publication of manuscripts, and once- and twice-printed editions, as by legitimate business transacted between publisher and composer.

Copy was not difficult to come by in this ramshackle world. It could be stolen from a composer via an unscrupulous copyist; it could be stolen by engraving an edition already published (preferably by a colleague in some other country); it could be manufactured by attributing to a well-known composer a few movements thrown together by a musical hack (just as a wine very *ordinaire* might be given vintage worth merely by the judicious application of a prestigious label). Finally it could be acquired honestly by purchase, either directly from the composer or from his authorised agent, and published bearing the cachet 'with authority'.

Despite the very large amount of music that was in circulation during the period, very few manuscripts of works published with the approval of the composer have survived from the eighteenth century. This is one of the circumstances that makes two collections in the British Library of such special interest. Egerton 2379 contains symphonies, trios, quartets and other works by Joseph Haydn authenticated by the composer. Two more of his symphonies are in Egerton 2335. Supporting material is collected in Egerton 2380, which contains letters from Haydn relating to the music, and a contract between Haydn and William Forster of London who acquired publishing rights in all the works.

The first mention of Haydn's name in the English newspapers occurred in the *St James's chronicle* for June 25/27 1765 where an edition of his Quartets Op1 'Printed at Amsterdam and sold by R Bremner opposite Somerset House in the Strand' was announced.[1] His music became much sought after, and not only in London. It found great favour in Oxford where, as early as the 1770s it was introduced into the repertory of the concerts held in the Music Room 'and gained such a hold over the concert-going public that by the end of the 1780s he stood second only to Handel in their affections'.[2] By this time his music was being enjoyed in other provincial towns too. It continued to maintain its high vogue among the conoscitori in the metropolis.

The market was strong, therefore, and publishers issued more and more of Haydn's music—very little of it 'authorized', some of it roughly in the form that the composer might have acknowledged had he seen it, a great deal of it in a mishmash of arrangements and adaptations.

William Forster was the first English publisher with whom Haydn entered into direct relationships. Widely known as 'Old Forster', or William Forster II (his father was William Forster I), he was the founder of a distinguished line of stringed instrument makers and was regarded as one of the two or three most skilful luthiers of his time. There is no evidence to explain why he diversified into publishing. His son, William III, was also an accomplished craftsman though not in the same class as his father. He seems, however, to have had 'all the music part of the business with liberty to work in his own behalf' from July 1787 onwards.[3]

Although a small flurry of single sheet songs bear his imprint, Forster's main output was music for strings either alone or in consort with other instruments. The music of Joseph Haydn is particularly well represented: indeed, apart from Artaria, Haydn's 'official' publisher in Vienna, Forster was the most considerable publisher of Haydn's music throughout Europe in the 1780s. One tally of his compositions published by the Forsters, father and son, credits them with 'one hundred and twenty-nine pieces besides a few others of lesser importance'.[4] Some of these works have been found to be spurious, or taken from sources which cannot be identified. The music in the Egerton collections, on the other hand, was copied by two or more of Haydn's most trusted copyists (some of the parts are signed by Johann Radnitzky, others carry his initials). The manuscripts bear autograph corrections by Haydn, many parts are signed by him with a form of words 'per me giuseppe Haydn' as authentication. The compositions were sent to London under Haydn's own seal. These circumstances give the Forster editions of the Egerton music, whatever their shortcomings, the status of authentic prints, and an important place in the corpus of the composer's published works.

Contact between Haydn and Forster seems to have been established through General Charles Jerningham, British Ambassador in Vienna, though nothing is known of the preliminaries that led to the first approach. According to one of William Forster's account books for 1786, it was on August 22 1781 that he received authentic manuscript copy for the first of the Haydn works for which he had contracted.

Other manuscripts followed during 1782, 1784, 1785 and 1787.[5] With the exception of the parts for Overtures 1 and 2 (Hob. I 74 and I 70) all this music has survived in Egerton 2335 and Egerton 2379. There is next to no information about the financial investment that music publishing called for in the 1770s and 1780s but estimates of the cost of producing the 'Passione' (the *Seven last words*) in 1786-7 suggest that risks were high and rewards meagre.[6]

65 Pewter plates at 1s 6d per plate	4	17	6
Engraving the same at 4s 6d do	14	12	6
Copper title and engraving	1	11	6
66 quires of perfect paper for 75 copies, at 1s	3	6	0
*Printing 75 copies, at 1s 2d	4	7	6
	28	15	0
Cost of the manuscript	10	10	0
Making in aggregate	39	5	0

*Only 50 copies were printed in 1787; the remainder (25) were printed 'about the year 1817-18'.

Income was calculated at £45 and 'several copies of those last printed were disposed of as waste paper, therefore no very profitable trade speculation'. The publisher of works in greater demand where hundreds, rather than tens, of copies might be ventured, could expect larger profits, but there was imperative need to keep costs down.

The attitude of diverse publishers to the same material may be illustrated from the editions of Haydn's Quartets Op33 (Hob.III 37-42) issued by Artaria, Hummel, Guera and Forster. It is noticeable that as between editions plates vary in size, the number of stave systems is not the same, neither is the number of characters punched on one system. Hummel varies the intervals between his stave systems to accommodate high and low notes on ledger lines: the other publishers retain standard distances, and crowding between low notes and high notes on successive staves is, therefore, inevitable.

The detail summarized in a reference below[7] shows that Artaria, using the largest plates, needed ninety-eight text pages (1,240 staves) to accommodate the same music that Hummel skilfully and legibly brought within fifty-nine pages (845 staves). Guera and Forster chose similarly economic solutions. These differences, suggesting as they do wide variations in the total amount of money required for investment in metal (for plates), paper and printing, must have been reflected in the production costs, and in the eventual selling price too. It is clear that Hummel, Guera and Forster worked according to criteria very different from those chosen by Artaria, whose spacious treatment may in part have been adopted to accord with Haydn's expressed wishes. Whatever the criteria were they derived from publishing experience in which the technology of engraving and printing played a part.

As far as the present writer is aware the only account of the procedures of music engraving current in Haydn's day appears in Volume 5 of the *Recueil des planches* (1767) of *L'Encyclopédie* (Paris, 1751-80). It was written by Madame de Lusse, a professional engraver, who was clearly more at home with her burin and punches than she was with her pen. After a short introduction in which she refers to the history of music engraving so far as it was then known, she turns to the methods which had reached 'the point of perfection' current in her own day. She continues:

> The way to perform this mode of engraving is to imitate the manuscript copy exactly either on a copper or pewter plate free hand, without using any of the methods of reduction which engravers in general avail themselves of.
>
> First the plate is worked over with dividers to establish a rectangle, which is then traced in lightly with a point

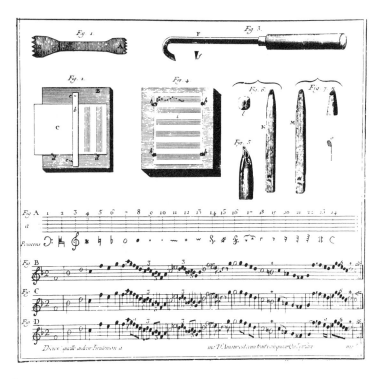

Plate 1.

Fig. 1. *Griffes* or five point markers used to fix the extremities of the stave lines. (The tool can be used for marking points to produce stave lines at alternative intervals. A and *a* draw attention to this possibility.) Fig. 2. The ruling board (B), the ruler (b) and a plate in position under it (C), fixed pegs aligned to hold the plate square with the rule (*dd*), and pins to control the position of the ruler (*ee*). Fig. 3. The scriber seen in profile (F), with the bevel shown in a section through the cutting edge (f). Fig. 4. The striking stone (G), fitted with adjustable clips (*hhhh*), and the plate (*i*). Fig. 5. Punch for the G clef, seen from above. Fig. 6. Punch for a white note head shown full length (K), and (*l*) in plan. Fig. 7. Punch for a black note head, three .inches long (the customary length for all punches) shown upright, with the guide marks on which the engraver places his thumb when striking to ensure that the aspect of the note is always the same (*m*). Hatching cut on the face (*n*): when struck into the plate this takes up the ink and holds it ready for printing. The head of a black note head with a stem attached (*o*): it will appear in the correct sense—turned right to left—when printed.

and a ruler. The proper intervals between the stave line systems are taken off from these lines: the number of these systems is determined only by the size of the plate. The distances fixed in this way are marked at their extremities with a *griffe*, a tool finished at each end by five equidistant points. The plate is then passed under an iron ruler fixed to a ruling board: the plate is controlled with one hand and the other is free to start cutting lines with a scriber in the positions marked by the *griffe*. The engraver draws the scriber across the plate towards himself: it being understood that the design of the tool permits this (Plate 1 Fig. 3). This is done in succession to the bottom of the plate: a scraper is then used to smooth the surface and remove the burrs which the scriber leaves in passing.

According to Madame de Lusse the illustrations suffice to give a general idea of dimensions of all the other punches.

Fig. A. A repertory of 24 punches displayed (the suite does not include the figures 0 to 9 which are used to number pages and the like and to figure the bass line of the music.) Sets of two, three and four times 24 punches are required to meet the need for characters of different sizes—larger or smaller.

Madame de Lusse comments:

'The basic equipment of the music engraver is usually made up of the 24 punches shown. If some engravers carry more than this it is due to ancient custom and practice rather than reason, for the bar lines, slurs, ties and other features which they still strike can be done equally well with burins; so can single and combined tails to notes, as has been mentioned already. The burins are the same as those used by the lettering engraver.'

Fig. B. A stave system on which the notes have been punched in previously marked positions: the bar lines are shown sketched in.

Fig. C. The same stave system showing note stems and bar lines engraved with a burin.

Fig. D. The same stave system, finished. The notes have their stems and tails, their ties, etc, in short everything that is likely to be called for in a similar piece of music. Words have been added to present a complete, though concise, example.

All that appears in the manuscript is then lightly sketched in with a point in the reverse order to which it occurs, so that the image appears in the correct direction (left to right) when printed.

The plate is supported on a stone of appropriate size and fitted with small moveable clips that serve to hold the plate steady. The stone must be thick enough to resist the blows of the hammer and sustain the plate as the punches are struck. After the punching is finished the plate is planished on an anvil using a hammer with a slightly convex face. To achieve the neatest result this planishing should be done on the under side of a pewter plate and on the upper surface of a copper plate. This done, a burin is used to cut the necessary stems to all the notes which need them, and to distinguish such notes that require tails in various combinations. A burin is employed for single tails and an *échoppe*, a graver with a flat cutting edge, in those cases where single, double and other multiple tails are linked (as at *a* in Plate 1 Fig. D).

When all is finished a burnisher is passed from one end of the plate to the other to polish the surface and give the plate the final touch of perfection. Some people use horsetail (scouring rush) to achieve this result on pewter but apart from the fact that it takes longer, it has the additional disadvantage that it bites too actively in the engraved areas of the plate. When it is necessary to make corrections or changes, the underside of the plate is beaten on the anvil with light strokes from the small end of a hammer in those places where adjustments are necessary. The surface of the plate is then smoothed with a scraper to remove the protuberances raised by the hammer blows and so restore the affected surface and leave it prepared to receive the impressions of new characters.

Words are engraved with a burin according to the methods used by letter engravers. Letters may be engraved either before striking the notes or afterwards: the first alternative is usually preferred.

Although Madame de Lusse describes the preparation of the copper or pewter plate and the placing of the stave systems, she is not informative about the preliminaries to the engraving of the notation. She says that everything appearing in the manuscript should first be scratched in with a point. She also says [in the caption to Plate 1, Fig. B] that the notes were punched 'in previously marked positions'. But how these positions were fixed is not revealed.

Forster's practice shows that a great deal of sophisticated planning was undertaken to ensure that the finished print set forth the music in a seemly and economical fashion.

Egerton 2380 contains (fols 20,22,24) the tough brown wrapping paper in which the manuscripts of the 'Seven Last Words', the Sinfonias 1(X.82), 2(XI.87), 3(XIV.85), 4 (XIII.84), 5(XII.83) and 6(XV.86)[8], and three piano Trios (Hob. XV 9,2,10) were sent from Vienna to London.

It is tempting to suggest that as soon as the separate packets arrived Forster spread out the wrapping and started forthwith to estimate how he was going to publish their contents. Certainly each of the wrappers bears calculations relating to the music which travelled in them. The instruments specified are listed separately, work by work, and against each of them is placed a figure indicating the number of plates allocated to the part. Whoever made the estimate had a very clear idea as to how a 'standard' symphony—flute(s), oboes, bassoon(s), horns and strings—should be published. It should be encompassed on twenty-four plates. He took account of any extra instruments, such as the 'clarinetto' (clarino or trumpet), usually playing '*a due*', and the drum, to increase the target to twenty-seven plates, but he paid little regard to variations in length of the works he was preparing to compress into one mould.

These target estimates were taken forward to the next stage: the marking of the manuscript parts for engraving. At first sight it seemed reasonable to try to foretell the likely extent of a movement, when engraved, by simple calculation. Given that the size of a note punch (together with its necessary increment of space) and the length of the stave systems were known, the engraver would be able to calculate the number of notes that he could place on every line. If he knew, by counting, the total number of characters in the notation (notes, rests, accidentals, grace notes and the like) he could judge how many staves a movement would fill, and, allowing a given number of staves for a plate, how many plates were required to accommodate all the lines comfortably.[9]

The characters in movements selected at random from a number of the parts were counted, and a variety of calculations—adopting different values measured from the printed sheet for the unit width of note and space—were made. Approximations to the totals written in the manuscript were achieved in gross as it were, but no principle emerged which allowed the line-end marks to be predicted.

This result should have been foreseen. Notes have relative values: even when writing quickly a composer will tend to give more space in his line to those which are to sound longer. Notes are grouped into bars, and more extensive congeries, and it is important for the reader's understanding that these should not be broken. A well engraved plate should be planned with these considerations in mind. In Sinfonia 1(X.82), for example, there are 590 engraved lines in all the parts but there are no broken bars at line ends, and seldom do lines containing the same number of characters follow in succession.

Informed judgement rather than arithmetic is required to achieve these, characteristic, results. The parts suggest that a planner, perhaps a foreman engraver or some other craftsman of wide experience, chose a section with a variety of notation typical of the movement in question, and, knowing the size of his punches, judged how much copy would fit into an engraved line. Using this information as a gauge he worked through the movement cutting the music into lengths—not mechanically, but responding to the fall of bars within the line, and taking advantage of the opportunities that rests of many bars, or a long succession of accidentals, gave him to increase or reduce normal character spacing to preserve the integrity of bars or other structural features of the music. He marked the end of successive lines 1,2,3,4, etc until he reached the end of the movement and then he wrote down his decision about the number of plates to be used. This number also took account of the space required for titles, indications of speed, directions for transposing instruments and the like.[10]   Evidence of this procedure is abundant throughout the manuscripts, but alternative methods were sometimes used. In some sections of the *Seven last words* for example, the music is so homogeneous that the estimator was able to base his calculations on the number of bars that could be accommodated in a line; and in the Quartets Op 50 intended page numbers (2-3, 14-15 for example) were used to enumerate the plates required.

Taking the estimator's suggestions—however they were formulated—as a guide, the engraver scaled his plate for stave lines, placing his systems closer or more distant according to the range of the music—few or many ledger lines—and then used his point to indicate the notation on the metal. He then started to work through the processes described by Madame de Lusse.[11]   A comparison of the estimated extent of the Sinfonias listed on the wrapping in Egerton 2380 (fol 22) with the out-turn in printed sheets shows that the correspondence is tolerable, good even, except in the case of the violin parts. This is less true of the *Seven last words.*[12] It is difficult to say to what extent these disparities arose from judgement based upon a trusting eye and experience rather than calculation, and how much from the conventions of publishing.

The basic unit of production was a complete engraved plate and nature does not abhor a vacuum with more intensity than eighteenth century English music publishers—though not their Parisian and Viennese colleagues—abhorred unfilled plates. The number of stave systems on each plate throughout a work or part did not have to be uniform, but however many there were they had to be disposed to fill, or give the impression of filling, the metal. (The blank last stave on page 2 of the second violin part of the Quartet No 1 of Op 50 is a staring exception.) This concern had predictable results: the engraver 'made' lines by striking the notes closer together, or he drove his copy out by working to a looser standard. Although the Egerton music appears generally well spaced in the printed sheet, gross crowding in lines and between stave systems does mar the effectiveness of some parts. For example, in order to work the viola part of Quartet No 4 of Op 50 on to three plates, bars have been divided at the end of four successive lines and the player has not even been given the benefit of a direct to help his eye over the break. Many other cases could be cited. 'Loose' or 'open' punching, in its way as ungrateful to the eye as crowding, occurs less frequently.

The occurrence of blemishes of this kind should not be interpreted as evidence of an overriding determination by the publisher to compress his material into little room at all costs. The interplay of economic commercial practice and seemly presentation can be readily demonstrated from the manuscript and printed versions of Sinfonia 3(XIV.85). The manuscript of each of the instrumental parts (with the exception of the bassoon) has been marked by the estimator to indicate the number of plates required and, putting aside the violin parts, these estimates correspond with the preliminary calculations in Egerton 2380. Again with the exception of the violin parts, the number of plates engraved tallies with the estimate; one of the plates of the bass part had the largest number of staves (eighteen) and one of the plates of the flute part had the smallest number (thirteen). Still excluding the violin parts, plates with sixteen staves are the most frequent and the layout of the music on them is clear. The eighteen stave bass part is somewhat congested but is readable.

The first violin part is laid out as follows to make 6 plates.

Page	54	55	56	57	58	59
Staves engraved	15	15	12	12	11	11
Content	Adagio Vivace	Vivace (concluded)	Romance	Romance (concluded) 4 staves Minuet & Trio 8 staves	Finale	Finale

The music could equally well have been distributed as follows: leave pages 54 and 55 as originally planned; increase the number of staves on page 56 to sixteen to accommodate the whole of the Romance; increase the number of staves on page 57 to sixteen and allocate eight to the Minuet and Trio. Open the Finale on line 9 of page 57, and complete the movement in fourteen staves on page 58, leaving page 59 blank. This rearrangement would have saved a plate; but it would have entailed some congestion between the staves and, consequently, some reduction in legibility. It would certainly have been impossible to save two plates and so achieve the four desired in the original estimate.

The temptation to use five plates was resisted in part, perhaps, because the slight congestion that would have resulted was thought to be unacceptable, in part for technical reasons. It is noticeable that the estimates in Egerton 2380 generally aim at achieving an even number of plates through almost all the instrumental parts. This preference may well have been due to the method in which the plates were printed. Unbound, unsewn copies of orchestral parts in the form in which they were originally issued and which are now in Cambridge University Library (the Marion Scott Collection) show that Forster usually printed his music in folio: two page numbers were arranged to follow in correct succession when the sheets were inserted one within the other (quired) to complete the part. To print with two plates to view, rather than one, at every impression saved a great deal of time at the press. The technique was also used to produce two-page parts. For instance in the Cambridge copy of Overture IV (Hob. I 76) the bassoon and flute parts, each of which occupies the recto and verso of a leaf, are conjugate; the sheet on which they are printed has been folded but not separated. Other examples are to be found elsewhere among the overtures and symphonies in the Marion Scott Collection.

Analysis of the layout of the second violin music of Sinfonia 3(XIV.85) produced the same results as those derived from the examination of the first violin part and no good purpose would be served to repeat the detail here. The manuscript of this second violin part does, however, offer a neat example of an estimator choosing in a characteristic way between alternatives. Plate 2 reproduces fol 347 of Egerton 2379 and shows the end of the Romance, the complete

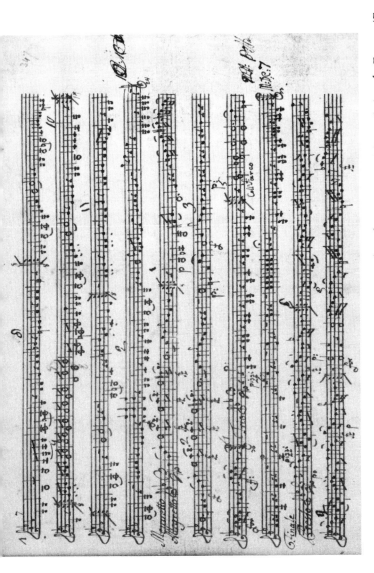

Plate 2. A reproduction of a page from the second violin part of Sinfonia 3 (XIV.85) *La Reine de France* (Egerton 2379, fol. 347). In addition to the points raised in the narrative, the letters 'E' (for error), and the pencil correction of a note in the second group of repeated semiquavers in line 2, bar 5, should be noted as evidence of some editorial supervision.

Menuetto and Trio and the opening bars of the Finale/Presto. The line ends are confidently marked, but the distribution of the music between plates is not straightforward, perhaps because the part is defective. The caret at the top left hand corner of the page indicates that something–the manuscript equivalent of one and a half engraved lines, it transpires–is missing.

The opposite folio (346v) is clearly marked to give two plates, each of thirteen staves, to the opening Adagio and associated Vivace. The first four lines of the Romance which are at the bottom of the folio are marked to give six engraved staves plus two bars of the otherwise absent seventh line. Allowing more than a whole line for the missing copy (fol 347) the estimator counted on to thirteen where he made a mark '1 pl(ate) 13 st(aves)'. It seems from an altered calculation that he planned to devote a plate of only eight staves to the Menuetto and Trio, but he abandoned this idea. Instead he continued with his figures into the Finale: a figure 8 appears above the repeat sign at the eighth full bar, and a figure 2 on the last line is clearly an altered 9. At this point he found himself in difficulty with the disposition of the rest of the movement and decided to review all the material again. He combined the whole of the Romance (incorporating the music provided to complete line 7) with the Menuetto and Trio to make two plates each of ten staves–the corrected allocation is shown on fol 347 as '2pl. 10 st.' written over '1pl. 8st.'–and then worked the last movement, Finale/Presto, to make two plates each of ten staves, though it appears from his figures (on fol 347v) that his first intention was to make two plates of eleven staves.

This conveniently explicit example demonstrates in simple terms the process of adjustment between what is required by the music and what is regarded as commercially desirable. The principle can be traced wherever estimate and music have survived together.

Egerton 2380 offers important evidence of other aspects of the relationship between publisher and engraver. Three of the Sinfonias (4,5,6) for which estimates are shown on fol 22 are also annotated to indicate the names of the engravers to whom Forster intended to entrust some of the parts. In Sinfonia 4(XIII.84) 'Scheren' (Scherer) is mentioned against bass and horns, and his name is joined with a brace across bassoon, flute and oboes with a note '16 plates', but the number of plates estimated for these parts is in fact only thirteen. The bassoon and horn parts of Sinfonia 4 are marked with a cross (X) as are the viola and bass parts of Sinfonia 6(XV.86). The plates allocated to the parts so marked do make sixteen.

There are other clues in Egerton 2379. On the blank verso of the last leaf of the bassoon part of Sinfonia 3(XIV.85) there is written 'Scherer to engrave'. 'No 6 Scherer' appears at fol 366v (on the blank verso of the last leaf of the first oboe part), at fol 375v (on the blank verso of the last leaf of the first bassoon part), and at fol 383v (within the viola part), all in Sinfonia 6(XV.86).

On fol 300 of Sinfonia 2(XI.87) 'Skillern' is written in the margin of the first page of the second violin part.

Can these rather vague pointers be used to arrive at some understanding of trade engraving practices in eighteenth century London? No contemporary account of the organization of a music engraver's shop in the eighteenth century seems to have survived, but if recent practice follows an earlier tradition then the master engraver would provide the punches for every character that was likely to be needed on a plate, and the employee would provide his own hand tools —the stave line scorer, the marking compass, burins, scraper and the like. If the shop were a large one the master would need to provide a number of different sets of punches, in diverse sizes and some more extensive than others, to meet the requirements of a wide range of music, and because it was not possible for two engravers to work with one set of punches at the same time. All the punches were cut and forged by hand and no two sets were identical. Thus a certain graphical difference might occur within a symphony or other extensive work. More substantial differences might appear if a manuscript were split and entrusted to two or more en-gravers—either in the same shop or in different shops—who worked on different parts simultaneously.

Is there any evidence to suggest that this might have happened?

The individual manuscripts in Egerton 2335 and 2379 certainly show that they have suffered very different usage as they have travelled their various ways. Many parts bear the normal patina that necessary handling and contact with metal and ink would produce. Some are much written over; some are badly stained, worn and cracked, with a strong fold across their long sides; others are clean and crisp and, except for line-end figures, unmarked. Some extensive parts have been given page numbers. Some parts carry signs that might well be 'danger signals' or warnings, used by particular engravers for their own guidance. Some parts have the word 'Done' written at the end of movements, presumably as an alert to prevent duplication by other engravers. In some parts the line and plate targets are indicated tidily, elegantly even, with a pen; in others the manuscript is obscured with a thick confusion of figures in crayon. In extreme cases the paper is abraded and pierced because directions have been scratched in with an engraver's needle.

It is unlikely that an engraver would treat the manuscript of one orchestral part gently and that of another roughly while it was on his bench. Indeed it is perhaps not too much to assume that differences in the attitudes and behaviour of individual engravers towards their copy reflect basic differences in their separate personalities. Can this be taken further? Are similar deep-seated individual differences, say in a characteristic use of tools, likely to be reproduced so consistently in the printed sheets that they can be identified as the unmistakable traits of a particular engraver?

Although verbal and musical texts are of their nature very different, it might be useful in seeking an answer to this question to adopt from the armoury of the bibliographer the distinction he makes between 'substantives'—the words—and 'accidentals'—the punctuation—in a work of literature. Just as one sixteenth century compositor might prefer to spell 'do', 'go' and 'heere' in this mode, and another, while setting the same substantive text with equal accuracy, might choose the alternatives 'doe', 'goe', and 'hire' and by their preferences leave distinctive trails of their handy-work through a play by Shakespeare, might not two engravers, both respecting the integrity of the notes and phrasing of the music—the 'essentials' —adopt consistent yet different preferences in such 'incidentals' as the presentation of, say, dynamics where convention admits acceptable alternatives? It was decided to test the validity of this assumption by seeking to establish the 'fingerprints', as it were, of particular engravers by means of a comparison of their treatment of 'incidentals'—the terms they used for the expression of dynamics, variations in speed, rests extending over a number of bars, the treatment of titles and the like. Such elements as the form of clefs, and the nature, size and design of other basic punches are also important, though in this connection less so for themselves than for the way in which they are used.

Egerton 2380 and the music in Egerton 2379 are both annotated to show that it was the intention to ask Scherer to engrave the bassoon part of Sinfonia 6(XV.86) and in view of this corroboration it was decided to examine the printed music of this part and record its salient graphical features. It was assumed that the punches would be in common use in Scherer's shop and that any particularities to be found in the engraving should be attributed to engraver 'S' (either Scherer himself or to a craftsman who worked with him). The printed images of the salient punches are set out in Plate 3. They have strong personality, and are quite unlike any others used in the Egerton music. What characteristics of the work of 'S' might encourage the observer to have confidence in his engraving if it were found elsewhere?

A comparison of the manuscript of the first bassoon part of Sinfonia 6 (Egerton 2379, fols 374-5) with the printed sheet reveals that he followed his copy closely: if f appears in the manuscript, it is engraved on the plate. Without exception the manuscript fz is so engraved: on the other hand, the manuscript *for* is invariably engraved as f. He tries to interpret from the manuscript what appear to be different usages for the dot and the stroke in staccato passages, and to stamp his plate accordingly. He reproduces turns and other graces, especially those peculiar to Haydn, with care and accuracy.[13] His work is not faultless, however. He occasionally omits decrescendo signs, or cuts them in the wrong direction, opening widely from *forte* to *piano* or pointing down from *piano* to *forte*. Sometimes he omits, or varies, an indication of speed set at the beginning of a movement. He works his plate dangerously close to the vertical edges and crowds some lines villainously in order to bring copy within his allotment of metal.

The personal traits of 'S'—the clues to his individual identity—are revealed in his attitude to the instrumentalist who is going to read the music. He introduces directs where required. When conventional abbreviations are used to express a repetitive pattern he always engraves at least a full bar in extended form before adopting a space-saving device,

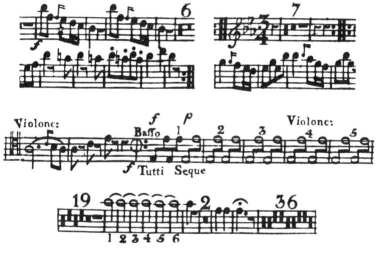

Plate 3. Characteristic traits of the style of engraver 'S': reproduced from the first bassoon part of Sinfonia 6 (XV.86) and from elsewhere through the Egerton music. (Reduction: 100:85.5).

and so on.[14]   A thoughtful man; a dedicated man, perhaps? In graphical terms the stamp of his individuality appears particularly in his treatment of grace notes. A typical example has a circular head about 1 mm in diameter, punched with the same tool that he uses for his therefore too prominent staccato dots, and attached to a stem as long as he can find space for. The tails are extraordinary: hand cut, or even scratched, they look in their irregular way rather like stiff tendrils in a breeze. Their form never varies. They are as idiosyncratic as a signature. All the Egerton music was examined, either in the original printed editions or in photocopies, against the repertory of the punches and with the traits of 'S' in mind. It was found that he had been heavily engaged in five of the six Sinfonias.[15]

The combination of distinctive personal traits into a consistent method of engraving may be said to constitute a style. The second violin part of Sinfonia 2(XI.87) marked 'Skillern' was also examined. The tools had peculiarities that would enable them to be identified in any context. The representation of 'incidentals' was characteristic too: the *fz* of the manuscript was consistently engraved *sf*: *po* became *p*, *for* became *f*. He was guilty of more omissions that 'S'. His attitude to the copy was 'formal': there were no supernumerary touches to aid the performer here. A cursory search associated this engraver with upper string parts. Close analysis could, no doubt, establish the elements of a distinctive, self-contained style for 'Skillern', as well as for other engravers whose fingerprints are discernible too in the Egerton music.

The examples just described show that complete instrumental parts of a work were distributed among engravers: material is not wanting to show that single parts were split too. For example the flute part of Sinfonia 2(XI.87) opens on printed page 21 in one style and concludes on the next page in the style of the 'S' engraver. A more extreme diversity is provided by the second violin part of Overture 5 (Hob. I 77), printed pages 16-19 (Egerton 2335, fols 11-13v), where the overall depth of staves, the intervals between stave systems, and the size and style of the note heads and of the letters used to indicate dynamics throughout pages 16, 18 and 19 are all fundamentally different from the corresponding elements on page 17.[16]

It has been shown that different engravers made, and adhered to, their own conventions for representing the incidentals of the music; to punch *fz* or *sf* for the ubiquitous *fz* in the manuscripts, *f* instead of *for, p* instead of *pia* or *po, f^mo* for *ff*, and the like. Was it personal style or preference, part of his conception of what was required, that led one engraver, but not necessarily another, to introduce on to his plate aids to the performer that did not appear in the manuscript copy? To strike 1, 2, 3 and more over a long succession of say, held minims, or of quavers tied across bar lines? Or to introduce directs where staves ended in bars unavoidably broken? Did this elaboration of an orchestral part spring wholly from the engraver's initiative? Or was he working under some form of direction?

Certainly instructions do crop up in the manuscripts. 'To be done longways' appears on the title page of the Piano Trio in G (Hob. XV 5, Egerton 2379, fol 85) and corrections and adjustments to the notation appear elsewhere in the same work. In the Piano Trio in C (Hob. XV 3, in fact by Pleyel, Egerton 2379, fols 69-83) there are several passages in the keyboard part marked to be transposed from the soprano clef in which they were written. Somebody must have given the engraver instructions to cue oboe solos into the violin parts of Symphonies 80 and 81 (Hob. I 80-81) and Overture VIII, from *Armida* (Hob. Ia 14); and bassoon solos from the same works into the bass parts. Perhaps it was Forster's sales manager who had the message 'NB This Overture may be play'd as a quartetto' stamped at the foot of the first page of the first violin part of all three works. Presumably somebody in the administration wrote to Haydn asking him to supply the copy missing from the second violin part of Sinfonia 3(XIV.85) at page 56. But who modified the horn parts of Sonata IV of the *Seven last words*? The printed versions differ from the manuscript originals.

If these shreds of evidence suggest that somebody had a general oversight of the publishing of the works, it is inevitable to ask why care was not taken to ensure more accurate presentation of the music itself as it passed through the engraver's hand. There are very few wrong notes, but the reproduction of much else is unsatisfactory, as the following representative examples show. How did 'Violino Pirmo' survive at the heading of the first violin part of Sinfonia 2(XI.87) not only in its first appearance as 'A Favorite Overture in all its Parts' (c1785) but also in 'A Grand Overture in Parts' issued about five years later? Who allowed copies to be issued though they were deficient in such imperatives as *'atacca subito il Terremoto'*, *'atacca subito'* (this not once but many times). Who did not seem to care that the first violin player was left without information as to the speed of the first movement of Quartet No 1 of Op 50, though Haydn had marked it 'Allegro'; or that a horn player was left pitched in C when the manuscript signalled a change to F. Who allowed SINFONIA to be contracted into an effervescent SIFONIA? The catalogue of missing elements could be extended at length through a range that includes fermatas, slurs, pauses, indications of dynamics, warnings—as *'solo'*, *'tutti'*, *'con sordino'*, *'segue trio'*—and the clear marking of first and second time bars.

No doubt some of the shortcomings arose during the preliminary marking up of the metal. If anything were omitted at this preparatory stage it would not be missed later because the engraver worked to his marked plate, not to the manuscript. Other shortcomings, and some of the errors, may with justice be attributed to the engraving copy itself. Among the Haydn manuscripts that have survived are the autograph scores of Symphonies 86 and 87. If these are compared with the authorized copies of the instrumental parts (Egerton 2379)[17] it becomes clear that there are hundreds of discrepancies between the two major sources of the text.[18] The criteria that the copyists used to interpret the autograph and the nature of the changes which they made could, perhaps, be generalized by a Haydn specialist. It must suffice here merely to indicate how in one small, but important particular the copy distorted communication between composer and performer.

   The autograph shows that in conformity with the practice of the day Haydn used both the dot (·) and the stroke (ʹ) to indicate staccato.   These signs were not alternatives: the staccato stroke implied a greater degree of articulation than the dot, and the use of one or the other was designed to produce a quite different sound in performance. Generally, Haydn's strokes and dots are well differentiated in the autograph, but the copyist often fails to transcribe them. The copies of Symphonies 86 and 87 that were sent to Forster were prepared on paper roughly 17 cm tall and 22 cm broad, with ten staves running parallel to the long edge on every page. The music is clearly written, but tightly compressed in the line and sometimes crushed between stave systems. Under these conditions it is easy to miss notational signs altogether. Certainly it is not always possible to distinguish a staccato dot from a stroke, and in some places they both seem to degenerate into a short horizontal dash as if to suggest some third form of nuance. Faced with these alternatives one engraver makes the best effort he can to stamp a dot or stroke as he interprets the sign in the copy; another applies strokes throughout in a quite arbitrary manner, thus giving support to David Boyden's view that the traditional distinction between the dot and the stroke was eventually lost because the printers used them interchangeably.[19] Too often the chances and changes along the road from autograph to printed sheet conspired to produce music that is neither Haydn *pur* nor Haydn as copied, but Haydn hit or missed.

Sometimes calligraphic ambiguity and the limitations of an engraver's tools interact to create passages of quite extraordinary muddle. Madame de Lusse considered twenty-four tools and a burin sufficient armoury for the engraver and wrote off as old fashioned those craftsmen who relied upon whole batteries of what she considered to be obsolete punches. It seems that some, at least, of the London engravers who were at work in the 1780s were equally unregenerate. Instead of cutting slurs with burins they used punches. Naturally these could not be made so as to span every combination of notes that was likely to crop up, and as a result ambiguities rise when a slur is placed over a group of notes which the punch cannot bridge entirely. Confusion is worse confounded when identical note patterns in the manuscript are engraved in a different form, not only in different instrumental parts of the same work, but also in the course of the same movement in one part. For example, in one place a spread of notes is pointed with staccato dots: five lines further on the same notation appears with staccato strokes. In some extreme examples the second violin part is engraved after the first violin part and the manuscript is abandoned altogether. Perhaps lacking the supervision and help of a musically educated supervisor on the spot—and it may be well to remember that the engraving of the separate parts of an orchestral work might be going on in shops as far apart as the Haymarket and St Martin's Lane in London—the engraver in difficulties was left to his own devices.

Granted that a publisher did not think it necessary to employ an editor to prepare a manuscript for press and oversee its reproduction in printed form, granted that he did not, or so it seems, adopt a straightforward 'house style' to guide his engravers, it is natural to assume that, in accordance with normal printing practice, proofs taken from the engraved plate would be examined, and errors corrected, before the sheets were printed off.

There are only two explicit references to correction in the material associated with the Egerton music. The title page of the *Seven last words* says that the music was 'Corrected by Mr Salpetro' (Giovanni Salpietro), but it has not been possible to discover what in fact he did.[20] A note on the blank verso of the last leaf of the manuscript of the first oboe part of Sinfonia 4(XIII.84) (Egerton 2379, fol 325v) reads 'To correct oboe 1mo No 4 done'. Whoever wrote the word 'done' was very careless: the printed part shows at least three errors—the omission of a long slur and three *f*s. On the other hand, careful examination of the printed copies against a variety of pencil marks recurring through the manuscripts reveals that corrections have been made by the engraver: a note head added, a stem extended, 'bis' written over a bar requiring a missing duplicate. The absurdities and errors that do occur throughout the Egerton music seem to represent not all the mistakes made by the engraver, but only the ones that 'got away'.

Why was not the same care taken to correct every discrepancy between the manuscript and the engraving? Was no independent comparison made between a proof of the engraver's 'corrected' plates and the manuscript? Was the engraver wholly and solely responsible for the accuracy of the engraved image? Did he have to make corrections 'in his own time', without pay? The material offers no answer to these fundamentally important questions.[21]

There is no need to stress the distorting effect that engraving practices brought to bear upon Haydn's music. Used as he was to composing with an accomplished orchestra at hand to test the effect of timbre against timbre, register against register and the subtle gradation of dynamics, Haydn created music in which refinement and delicacy went hand in hand with abrupt, sometimes extreme, contrast. To this end he often used conventional notation in an idiosyncratic way. He cared greatly about the way in which his directions were reproduced in print and observed in performance. Therefore the replacement of *for* by *f* throughout a symphony, ignoring the fact that in the manuscript *f* and *for* both occur frequently in neighbouring bars, may have removed a distinction intended by Haydn, just as the engraving of the staccato signs in a uniformly mechanical way, with no attempt to interpret the indications in the engraving copy (granted they were not always clear), certainly did.

Yet where no manuscripts with a genuine predigree going back to Haydn have survived, then printed editions, with all their faults, have to be accepted as sources, for what they are worth. The relationship between manuscript, autograph or copy, and printed versions has always been pursued by editors and other musicologists. In recent years this study has been given wider perspectives by scholars who are attempting to reconstruct the methods of instrumental performance current in past ages. This is but one line, among many, that specialists who have knowledge of the tradition of music engraving and printing techniques, and access to the original sources—manuscript and printed—might feel stimulated to pursue.

Would a comparison of the Egerton manuscripts and the Forster editions of, say, the Paris symphonies (Hob. I 82-87) with those issued by Artaria, Imbault, Sieber and Hummel throw light upon the varying technical and commercial practices of these leading European music publishers? Some of the confusion in the Forster editions arises from the inadequacy of tools—punches for slurs are a case in point; do European engravers make freer and more general use of the burin as Madame de Lusse advocated? And are the results more satisfactory than those achieved by London practice? A great deal of French music published in the eighteenth century is attributed to named engravers; do the engraving styles of, say, le Sieur Hue or Madame Vendôme produce characteristics that may be used to identify unsigned work? And would such enquiries make it possible to detect the ultimate provenance of some of the many unauthorized editions of Haydn's music circulating throughout Europe during the last twenty years of the eighteenth century?

If this study of the relationship between the music in Egerton 2335 and 2379 and Forster's editions encourages the investigation of such problems; if it results in the search for, discovery and examination of manuscripts that have been through a printer's hands, or proofs or printed copies marked up for publication in another format; if a determined effort is made by only a few specialist librarians and musicologists to familiarize themselves with the techniques and technology of plate engraving; and if in the short term it leads the way to the identification of the style of individual engravers and an assessment of their reliability, then this offering will have achieved its major purpose.[22]

REFERENCES

1 The edition was advertised in the *Amsterdamsche Courant* on 13. iv.1765 (Hob. i, p.302).
2 R S M Hughes 'Haydn at Oxford: 1773-1791' *Music & letters* XX 1939, 243.
3 W Sandys and S A Forster *The history of the violin and other instruments played on with the bow from the remotest times to the present* London, 1864, 334.

4 Sandys & Forster *op cit*, 314.

5 'The dates of the years when Haydn's works came' taken from 'the flyleaf of one of the old account books for 1786' (Sandys and Forster, *op cit*, 310, 311): *Overture 1* (Hob. I 74), 22 August 1781; *Overture 2* (Hob. I 70), 20 June 1782; *Overture 4* (Hob. I 76), 14 February 1784; *Overture 5* (Hob. I 77), 24 February 1784; *Overture 6* (Hob. I 78), 6 May 1784; *Overture 7* (Hob. I 81), 22 November 1784; *Overture 8*, the overture to *Armida* (Hob. Ia 14), 26 November 1784; *Overture 9* (Hob. I 80), 6 December 1784.

   'On 3 December 1787 there is an entry of "Paid postage of Six Overtures from Haydn £2.5.0". It is supposed these are the Sinfonias nos. 10 to 15' (Hob. I 82-87).

   Trios Op 38 (Hob IV 6-11), 6 July 1784.

   Sonatas Op 40 (Piano Trios, Hob. XV 3-5), 3 January 1785.

   Sonatas Op 42 (Piano Trios, Hob. XV 9,2,10), 26 December 1785.

   The manuscript of 'the Crucifixion published with the title of "Passione"' (the orchestral version of the *Seven last words*, Hob. XX/1) arrived on 16 July 1787. The *Quartets* 'Op 44' (Op 50, Hob. III 44-49) arrived on 5 October 1787.

   The dates in the account book do not always conincide with those on the wrapper in Egerton 2380.

6 Sandys & Forster, *op cit*, 312.

7 The detail is as follows: Artaria (1782), 1,240 staves on 98 plates of 296 x 218 mm; Hummel (1782, as Op 19), 845 staves on 59 plates of 284 x 201 mm; Guera (1782/3), 997 staves on 66 plates of 295 x 215 mm; Forster (originally Kerpen, 1783?), 1,077 staves on 74 plates of 280 x 203 mm.

8 The standard reference to any Sinfonia in this chapter starts with the original number (Haydn's?) written on the manuscript, followed (in brackets) by the number assigned to it by Forster in his series and the Hoboken number. Thus Sinfonia 1(X.82) refers to 'A Grand Overture in parts. Performed at the professional and other public concerts. No. X' (Hob. I 82). And so on.

9 Encouragement for this view of eighteenth century practice was offered by the flute (fols 266-267v), bassoon (fols 275-276v) and viola (fols 283-284v) parts of Sinfonia 1(X.82) in Egerton 2379 where figures accumulating to large numbers written throughout the individual movements suggested a comprehensive character count. A check by the writer produced numbers consistently below those in the manuscript, though predictions based upon the principles outlined in the text above and using the writer's figures did yield estimates for the numbers of engraved stave lines that were close enough to the printed copy to be encouraging.

The material was eventually shown to the most experienced music engraver in London and his view was that the count was a cast-off to establish money due for work done. He cited the practice, now discontinued but current in England during the working life of engravers still active, whereby every job was counted in the finest detail and priced character by character on a scale of farthings. A further count of the bassoon part by the writer—taking into account all the notes in the *divisi* sections which would not affect linear space when engraved but which would affect remuneration—came to 2,717, within three characters of the totals written in the manuscript, 2,720.

10 Sometimes the lines were marked off plate by plate. The appropriate breaks were clearly marked in the copy by a standard symbol.

11 It is likely that the London engravers used a punch rather than a graver to make the bar lines. In some of the parts, too, there is more that a suggestion that the notes were punched with a tool on which a note head and a stem were combined.

12 The normal instrumentation of the Sinfonias is violin 1, violin 2, viola, cello-bass, flute(s), oboe(s), horns, bassoon(s). Exceptionally clarini (trumpets) and drum are added. In the detail which follows no mention of an instrument means that the estimate proved to be accurate. In other cases a figure associated with an instrument shows by how many plates the printed part exceeded the estimate.

    Sinfonia 1(X.82). Total plates: estimated 27, actual 40 (this included 2 plates for clarini, alternative to horns, for which no provision was made in the estimate). Violin 1 (+2), violin 2 (+2), viola (+1), bass (+1), oboes (+2), horns (+2), bassoons (+1). *Sinfonia 2*(XI.87) 24 plates. The estimates were accurate throughout. *Sinfonia 3*(XIV.85). Total plates: estimated 24, actual 28, violin 1 (+2), violin 2 (+2), horns (+2), bassoons (+2).

13 Haydn naturally laid great store by accurate representation of these features, particularly his half mordent. See a letter dated from Estoras on December 10 1785, where he complains at length—with useful examples—about the inadequacy of Artaria's engravers. See H C R Landon *The collected correspondence and London notebooks of Joseph Haydn* London, 1959, 51.

14 This proceeding is in the spirit of Haydn's own practice. (See H C R Landon *The symphonies of Joseph Haydn* London, 1955, for detail.) A reading of the whole of Chapter IV 'Textual Problems: the Use of Sources' would provide background information about the origin of many of the problems the engraver had to face.

15 The hand of 'Engraver S' has been identified in the following parts through the Sinfonias: *Sinfonia 1*(X.82) Viola, bass, flute, clarino (1&2), tympano, bassoons. *Sinfonia 2*(XI.87) viola, bass, flute, horn

(1&2), oboe (1&2), bassoons. *Sinfonia 3*(XIV.85) viola, bass, flute, horn (1&2), bassoons. *Sinfonia 4*(XIII.84) flute, oboe (1&2), horn (1&2), bassoons (these are the only parts that have survived). *Sinfonia 5*(XII.83) Only the first violin part has survived. It shows none of the characteristics associated with 'Engraver S'. *Sinfonia 6* (XV.86) viola, bass, flute, oboe (1&2), horn (1&2), clarino (1&2), tympano, bassoon (1&2).

16 It is difficult to account for this rather bizarre intrusion. The manuscript part of violin 2 has been paginated 1 to 6 in a large contemporary 'workshop' hand to indicate the order of the music— probably in the interests of safety because the recto of the first leaf contains the last seven lines of the Finale.

The first movement (Vivace) opens on the verso (1v) of the first leaf and is numbered 1. 'Overture V. 14-15-16-17' also appears there, written in a second contemporary hand. Overture V is clearly Forster's publication number ('Sinfonia/di me giuseppe Haydn/in b fa' in the composer's hand is all that appears on the title page): '14-15-16-17' indicates the planned ordering of the printed pages of the second violin part through Forster's series of Overtures or Symphonies. In fact the sequence of the pages appears as '16-17-18-19'.

Perhaps as a result of some dreadful confusion the copy which now appears on page 17 was overlooked and had to be engraved in a compressed style so that the material could find its proper place between two existing plates. Or do the two conflicting sets of page numbers hint at some larger miscalculation; or to an accident?

17 Complete except for the second violin part of Forster's Sinfonia 5 (XII.83) (Egerton 2379, fols 306-320).

18 It cannot be assumed that the Egerton parts were copied from the Paris autographs (Bibliothèque Nationale, Rés. Vm^7. 541. 3 and 2). If they were related in this way it is remarkable how many details of phrasing and dynamics that are perfectly clear and unambiguous in the autograph have been omitted from, or misplaced in, the copies, particularly as they bear corrections in Haydn's hand. It is within the province of the specialist to interpret the musical significance of these dissimilarities, but the consequences of some of them are unmistakable on the printed sheet.

19 D D Boyden *The history of violin playing from its origins to 1761* Oxford, 1965, 410.

20 It might be possible to assess Salpietro's methods by comparing two editions of Wanhal's Op III: the one published by Hummel in about 1776 and 'Mr. Salpietro's' version published by Bland in about 1782 (*Deux quatuors a deux violins, alto et basso. Selected from his Op: III^d. Corrected 1782 by Mr. Salpietro*).

21 Presumably the engraver corrected his own work; if so the bassoon part of Sinfonia 3(XIV.85) presents a conundrum. The part extends over two pages, numbered 30 and 31, and the plates show all the characteristics of the 'S' engraver. Some foreign elements are to be seen, however, in the last line of page 30 and the first line of page 31 which span the end of the Romance. In these lines grace notes appear with tails sharply punched descending at a steep angle, whereas all the others in the part are cut by hand and horizontal in the style of the 'S' engraver. The bass clef at the beginning of the two lines is different in style from all others: so is a figure 2 over the rest bar on page 31. Although the black notes appear to be standard throughout the part, two minims on page 31 have not been punched but drawn in with an engraving point.

The place where the turn over should have come is marked in the manuscript. This has been ignored, and four extra bars have been squeezed in to make a very crowded last line on page 30 and a correspondingly 'loose' first line on page 31, though had the mark in the manuscript been observed both lines would have been conventionally spaced. The imprint line on page 30 is not in the style of the 'S' engraver. All in all enough to raise speculation about copy left unfinished by one engraver and completed by another.

22 For active help in the preparation of this chapter the writer is grateful to D W Williams and his colleagues in the Music Department of Cambridge University Library; to Margaret Cranmer, Librarian of the Rowe Music Library, King's College, Cambridge; and to Richard Andrewes, Librarian of the Pendlebury Library, University of Cambridge all of whom made the original Forster, and other early editions of Haydn's work available for investigation under ideal conditions.

He is indebted no less to L W Duck, Music Librarian, the Central Library, Manchester and to V J Kite of the Avon County Library (Bath Reference Library) who willingly supplied photocopies of unique Haydn material in their collections.

Preliminary study of the Egerton manuscripts was undertaken with copies provided by the reprographic service of the British Library; Cambridge University Library Photographic Department (G D Bye) undertook like service for the printed material in the Marion Scott Collection, and the Bibliothèque Nationale (Paris) kindly provided microfilm of the autograph scores of three of Haydn's symphonies.

Pamela Willetts, Deputy Keeper, Department of Manuscripts, the British Library, David McKitterick (Rare Books Room, Cambridge University Library) and G L Hinder all provided essential assistance at critical stages of the work.

THE ORIGINS OF MOZART'S 'HUNT' QUARTET, K 458

ALAN TYSON

Mozart spent something like two and a half years in writing and at times rewriting the six string quartets that he dedicated to Haydn in September 1785. The long and laborious effort (as he describes it) is reflected in the number of different papers that he used in the six autographs, which have been in the British Museum (and subsequently the British Library) since 1907.

More than that: the variety of papers within the autographs is sometimes our best clue to the times at which the various parts of the autographs were written down. This is true even though for four of the quartets Mozart himself supplies a date. At the beginning of the G major quartet K 387 he writes 'li 31 di decembre 1782 in vieña', and the last three quartets were entered by him in the little catalogue of his works that runs from February 1784 up to his death: the 'Hunt', K 458, with the date of November 1784, and the A major, K 464 and the C major K 465, with the dates of January 10 and 14 1785. But what do those dates represent? Perhaps only the dates at which those four works were for the first time ready to be copied and rehearsed—an event that did not necessarily preclude further alteration or improvement almost up to the moment of their publication in the autumn of 1785. So even in the case of these four quartets it is still worth while attempting to determine rather more closely the period over which each was composed. And for the two remaining quartets, the second in D minor, K 421/ 417b and the third in E flat, K 428/421b, we should be grateful for whatever clues to their dates we can obtain, since we have nothing more to go on than a story told by

Constanze Mozart to Friedrich Rochlitz some time after her husband's death. According to this anecdote, the D minor was being written during her first confinement—ie in June 1783.[1]

In the present essay I shall try to present evidence that bears on the period during which the 'Hunt' Quartet was being composed.

The quartet has come down to us on three different paper-types, recognizable by their watermarks and by differences in the vertical span of the staves, which number twelve on each page. We can distinguish them as Types I, II, and III. From the table below it will be seen that Type I was used for the first two leaves of the first movement, and that the whole of the rest of the quartet is on paper of Type II, with the exception of the minuet and trio, on a single leaf of Type III:

Movement	Foliation	Paper-type	Quadrant	
I	23	I	1B	
	24	I	4B	
	25	II	3A	
	26	II	2A	= a sheet
II	−27	III	1A	
III	28	II	4A	
	29	II	1A	
IV	30	II	2B	
	31	II	3B	= a sheet
	32	II	1B	
	33	II	4B	

Types II and III are familiar to students of Mozart from many of his other scores from this period. It is not even necessary to go outside the six 'Haydn' quartets, for we encounter Type II again in the fifth quartet, K 464, and Type III is represented in all the first three quartets as well as here in the minuet and trio of the fourth. But for a long time Type I was a puzzle, at any rate to those few scholars who have made a study of the paper-types used by Mozart in his Vienna days. The problem was that it was impossible to match it elsewhere. The bifolium that is formed by the first two leaves of the 'Hunt' Quartet is the lower half of a sheet, the watermarks being (fol 1) the lower part of three moons and (fol 2) the letters 'GF'. On the analogy of similar water-marks (such as that of Type II here), one might expect that the watermarks in the unrepresented upper half of the sheet would consist of the remaining part of the three moons, and (over the 'GF') a device such as a crown. But among the Mozart autographs of the Vienna period no leaves could be found either to match fols 1 and 2 of the 'Hunt' or to complement them. One was forced to the conclusion that the paper-type found there was a unique specimen—a disappointment, since *unica* cannot contribute anything to the question of dating.

It was therefore with considerable surprise and interest that while working in Berlin in the summer of 1978 I came across four scores by Mozart which not only included leaves of Paper-type I but provided them in sufficient quantity for the precise form of the watermark in both the 'twin' forms to be determined. (These watermarks are reproduced on the following pages.) The most bewildering aspect was that three of the four scores come from more than a decade before the 'Hunt' Quartet. The scores are:

1. K 51/46a, *La finta semplice* (opera buffa): four un-numbered leaves before fol 219, with a new version of no. 23, Ninetta's aria 'Sono in amore, voglio marito'. Staatsbibliothek Preussischer Kulturbesitz, Berlin.
2. K 139/47a, Mass in C minor: fols 17-46. Staatsbibliothek Preussischer Kulturbesitz, Berlin.
3. K 108/74d, *Regina Coeli*: all 20 leaves. Deutsche Staatsbibliothek, Berlin.
4. K 427/417a, Mass in C minor: fols 7-10. Deutsche Staatsbibliothek, Berlin.

The last two of these autographs were dated by Mozart. The *Regina Coeli* is inscribed 'nel mese di Maggio 1771', and the Kyrie of the unfinished C minor Mass is dated '1783'. The first two autographs are not dated, but perhaps we shall not go far wrong if we ascribe the revised version of the aria in *La finta semplice* (written in Vienna between April and July 1768) either to 1768 or to 1769; and it seems that the early C minor Mass falls within the same period as well.[2]

We appear, then, to have three examples of Paper-type I in scores dating from between 1768 and 1771, and (with the 'Hunt') two examples in scores from around 1783 or 1784. It is natural to suspect that the watermarks are not after all identical, and that we have more than one paper-type before us. Yet tracings of the watermarks in the 'early' and 'late' examples match perfectly, and the vertical span of the twelve staves is exactly the same in all five scores. And there is a further small feature that is, I believe, sufficient to confirm that we are dealing with a single batch of paper. In each of the five scores one can observe the same peculiarity in the inking of the stave-ruling: the second line of the first stave, and the first and fifth lines of the second stave, are darker than the others. (This feature can be seen in the 1969 facsimile of K 458.) I think it is safe, therefore, to assume that the paper is the same, and that Mozart acquired it in or

2A

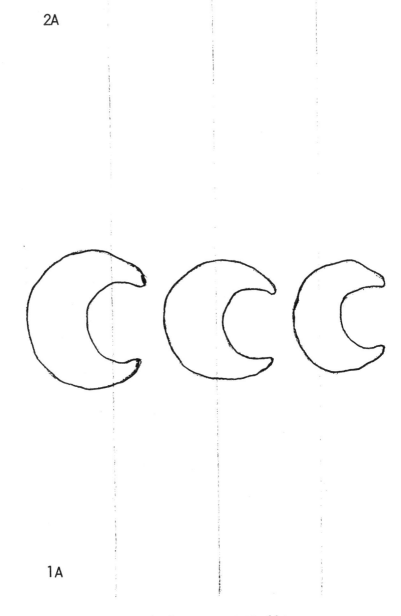

1A

Watermark of Paper-type I: Mould A.

3A

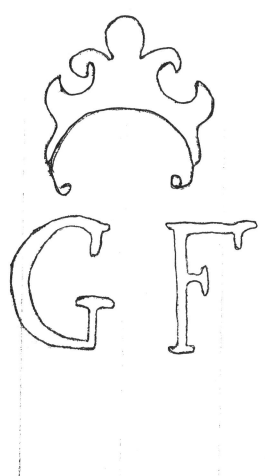

4A

2B

1B

Watermark of Paper-type I: Mould B.

3B

4B

around the year 1768, almost certainly in Vienna. What still has to be explained is his subsequent use of it in 1771 and in 1783 or 1784.

'Almost certainly in Vienna': that is an assumption that goes some way ahead of the evidence so far presented, and it needs to be justified. The paper we are considering is of the standard-sized oblong format ('Querformat'), and the evenness of the stave-ruling shows that all the staves were ruled simultaneously by a machine. Since paper of this size and shape, originating for the most part from Italian paper-mills, was used by Mozart not only on his Italian journeys but also in Salzburg, as well as throughout the last ten years of his life in Vienna, its physical appearance cannot be used to decide where it was purchased. But the fact that it was machine-ruled with twelve staves weighs heavily against its having been acquired in Salzburg. For music paper seems in the normal way to have been ruled not at the place of manufacture, the paper-mill, but at the retail outlet; and the evidence is stronger and stronger that Mozart could not get paper machine-ruled with twelve staves in Salzburg.

There were instead three possibilities open to him. He could rule a dozen staves singly with a *Lineal* (a kind of five-nibbed pen); or he could purchase 12-stave paper elsewhere and bring it to Salzburg; or he could content himself with 10-stave paper. This last was much the commonest solution. For most of his needs in Salzburg 10-stave paper was quite adequate, and he became adept at accommodating himself to it; in fact it was usually only choral works with an orchestra that included trumpets and drums as well as strings and woodwind which called for some ingenuity. It is however striking that from the moment of his arrival in Vienna in April 1781 his choice fell upon paper with twelve staves. This remained his preference until his death ten years later;

he very rarely returned to 10-stave paper, and even when very large forces were involved, he pointedly eschewed 16-stave paper, the kind adopted by Beethoven for most purposes from the time at which he settled in Vienna in November 1792.

This is not the place to review all the instances of Mozart using machine-ruled 12-stave paper in Salzburg and to demonstrate that the paper was acquired elsewhere.   But a few examples can be given.   The autograph of K 125, the earlier of Mozart's two *Litaniae de venerabili altaris sacramento*, is dated 'nel Mese di Marzo 1772', and although it is on 12-stave paper there is no reason to doubt that it was written in Salzburg.   But the source of the paper is easily explained, for it is found also in the choruses of his serenata *Ascanio in Alba*, K 111, composed in Milan some six months earlier. Several other examples that apparently show machine-ruled 12-stave paper being bought and used by Mozart in Salzburg prove on examination to be not what they seem.   Some are post-1781 fragments wrongly ascribed to the Salzburg years: for example K 196a (Anh. 16), K 323 (Anh. 15), K 323a (Anh. 20), and K 258a (Anh. 13).   Others prove on examination not to have twelve staves, eg K 166g (Anh. 19) where in any case the staves have been ruled singly with a *Lineal*. And the 1776 concerto for three pianos K 242 is on 12-stave paper, but only ten of the twelve are machine-ruled, since the first and the twelfth staves are drawn with a *Lineal*. Would Mozart have gone to this trouble if he had been able at that time to have twelve staves ruled by machine?

In the light of the foregoing we can assume, I think, that Mozart acquired his stock of Paper-type I in Vienna in the course of the year 1768 (he arrived there on January 10 and left at the end of December).   We need not be surprised that he preserved a sufficient quantity of it to enable him to write out K 74d (108), the *Regina Coeli* of 1771, on it; that, after all, was a choral work with an orchestra that included oboes, horns, trumpets, and timpani. But what of the two works of his Vienna years that include this paper? I have come to the paradoxical conclusion that the parts of those scores that are on Paper-type I were in fact written in Salzburg.

The C minor Mass K 427/417a was undertaken in fulfilment of a vow. From Mozart's letter of January 4 1783 we learn that he had 'promised in his heart' before he was married that if he were to bring Constanze to Salzburg as his bride, he would perform a new mass of his composition there. He claimed at that time that the score of half such a mass had been finished. Yet when the work was finally performed in Salzburg on October 26 1783, with Constanze taking the soprano part, only four movements had been completed: the Kyrie, Gloria, Sanctus, and Benedictus. (No doubt the remaining numbers were supplied from other masses.) The score that has come down to us today, in the Deutsche Staatsbibliothek, Berlin, is not as complete as it once was. Some of the portions that Mozart finished, though they were known to Ludwig von Köchel, are no longer extant. But the score contains a substantial portion of the unfinished Credo, down to the words 'Et homo factus est'.

Most of the surviving parts of the score are on 12-stave paper—as one would expect of a Mozart score written in Vienna after his arrival there in April 1781. But there are also nine leaves of 10-stave paper, today bound in at the end of the score. These contain extra wind parts for the Gloria and the Sanctus (of the Sanctus, indeed, they are all that survives in autograph). We know from other works that such wind parts were very frequently written out by Mozart after the rest of a score. When we bear in mind that Mozart and his wife arrived in Salzburg on July 29 1783, and that the mass, still uncompleted, was not performed there till October

26, the very day before the couple left Salzburg for their journey back, it seems almost certain that the supplementary wind parts were written in the course of Mozart's stay in Salzburg (no doubt near the end), and that that is the reason why they are not on Viennese 12-stave but on Salzburg 10-stave paper.

There are some interesting parallels here with another work composed around this time partly in Salzburg and partly in Vienna; it too remained a fragment. This was the 'dramma giocoso' *L'oca del Cairo*, K 422. Although the history of that undertaking remains in part conjectural, it was during Mozart's stay in Salzburg that the Abbé Varesco furnished him with a draft libretto of the first act. Mozart evidently set to work at once, and on December 6 1783, only a few days after his return to Vienna, he was reporting in a letter to his father that the first act had been finished apart from three arias. Subsequent letters indicate Mozart's increasing dissatisfaction with the libretto and with his inability to extract necessary changes in it from the Abbé; by February 1784 he had suspended work on it. The portions of the score that have come down to us (Staatsbibliothek Preussischer Kulturbesitz, Berlin) are, as in the case of the C minor Mass, partly on 10-stave and partly on 12-stave paper; and it is precisely the earliest numbers, which we might suppose him to have tackled first, that are on 10-stave paper identical with that used for the extra wind parts in the mass.[3]

All this provides a useful confirmation of my claim that Mozart could not purchase 12-stave paper in Salzburg. Yet there were some situations in which it must have seemed almost essential for him to procure some. I suggest that the completion of the C minor Mass's four performed movements was one of these.

The fact that almost all of the surviving portions of the main score are on 12-stave paper of types that Mozart was using in Vienna in 1782 and 1783 lends support to his claim in January 1783 that 'the score of half a mass' had been completed; some of it at least must have been well in hand. The four leaves of Type I come near the beginning; they are fols 7–10.   On 7 recto is the conclusion of the Kyrie fugue. 7 verso is blank apart from a deleted bar containing music on the dominant of D minor. 'No. 2', the start of the Gloria, begins on fol 8 recto, and continues up to 10 recto (10 verso is blank).   And here Type I ends.   The continuation of the Gloria ('No. 3', Laudamus te) is on a different paper, found in Vienna works of the second half of 1782. Although other explanations are possible, it strikes me as highly probable that the music on Type I represents a last-minute rewriting of the end of the Kyrie and the beginning of the Gloria. This rewriting will have required Mozart to find 12-stave paper in Salzburg.

Since such paper could not be purchased, it looks as though Mozart had recourse to the collection of his old scores which was kept by Leopold. (He would have been looking at them anyway if he was searching out old movements with which to fill out his uncompleted Mass.) And no doubt it was there that he found a small amount of 12-stave paper left over from 1768.   Luckily, not much of Type I was needed. Four leaves (two bifolia) were sufficient to fill the gap in the mass.   A further bifolium was put to another use: on it he wrote a substantial part of the quartet movement in B flat which is now the first movement of the 'Hunt' Quartet.

This has been a somewhat circuitous journey, but its conclusion is clear enough: Mozart began writing the 'Hunt' Quartet in Salzburg in the late summer or autumn of 1783. Or perhaps we should say: it was there and then that he began to write a first movement which satisfied him—for we do not know how many false starts he made and rejected.

How much of the first movement he wrote at that time is less certain.   Examination of the ink suggests that he broke off at bar 106, after the first 16 bars of the development. (This is the third bar on the fourth side.)   And it is quite likely that, with the exception of the minuet and trio, he completed no more of the quartet for a whole year after that. This time the evidence comes not from the ink but from the paper.   The rest of the first movement, the slow movement and finale are all on paper of a single type—Type II—that he also used for approximately the first half (opening allegro, minuet and trio, and three sides of the variation movement) of the fifth quartet, K 464 in A major—a work not entered in Mozart's *Verzeichnüss* till January 1785.   Since the 'Hunt' Quartet, as we have seen, is dated 'November 1784' in the *Verzeichnüss*, it is a plausible suggestion that not only most of the 'Hunt' but also about half of K 464 was finished around that time.

That still leaves the minuet and trio of K 458 unaccounted for.   Its paper-type—Type III—is found in the latter parts of the two preceding quartets, K 421/417b and K 428/421b, as well as in a single leaf inserted into the first quartet, K 387 (this is fol 10, with a revised version of bars 125-142 of the last movement).   It would certainly be convenient if Mozart's use of this paper-type (with 12-stave pages and a total stave-span of 182.5-183 mm)[4] could be confined to the time preceding his journey to Salzburg at the end of July 1783. But that is not possible: Mozart uses it again in K 426, the fugue for two pianos in C minor dated December 29 1783, a month after his return from Salzburg to Vienna.[5]   I know of no instance of this paper-type dated after the end of 1783 —although a left-over single leaf might be used by Mozart after the rest of a paper supply had been exhuasted.   With some hesitation and qualification, then, we may ascribe the composition of the minuet and trio of the 'Hunt', like the start of its first movement, to the year 1783. A fragment of the opening of the minuet, showing the first nine and a half bars in an earlier version, and preserved in the Musée Adam-Mickiewicz of the Bibliothèque Polonaise in Paris, is on the same paper.

Two other fragments for string quartet, both in B flat, were tentatively assigned to the year 1784 by Einstein in the third edition of Köchel. These are K 458a (Anhang 75), nine bars of an Allegretto in 3/4 metre (with only the first violin and violoncello entered), and K 458b (Anhang 71), ten bars obviously of a fast tempo in 2/4 metre. Both fragments are in the Mozarteum, Salzburg, and have been published in the NMA (VIII/20/1, Bd. 3, p. 138, edited by Ludwig Finscher).

Paper-studies, however, indicate that the link with the 'Hunt' Quartet is unacceptable, since both fragments are on paper of a type that does not appear in the surviving autographs of Mozart before the end of 1789.[6] It is the principal paper-type of the second (at present the only accessible) act of *Cosi fan tutte*, K 588. And, more to the point, it is found in the autographs of both the second and the third 'Prussian' quartets, K 589 in B flat and K 590 in F, works entered in Mozart's *Verzeichnüss* in May and June 1790 respectively.[7] Given this information, we can hardly doubt that the two fragments K 458a and K 458b represent attempts to compose a minuet and a finale for the late B flat quartet K 589.

But there is a third fragment for string quartet in the Mozarteum which is on a paper-type appropriate to the 'Hunt', but which by an irony of scholarship was assigned by Einstein to K 589 and therefore given the provisional date of 'May 1790'. This is K 589a (Anhang 68), a substantial draft for what must surely have been intended as a finale. It is in B flat, in 3/4 metre, and has the character of a polonaise, fully scored for eight bars and with the first violin only for a further 57. It has been published in the NMA (VIII/20/1, Bd. 3, pp. 148-9).

The paper is of Type III, like the minuet and trio of the 'Hunt'. And since there is (so far as I can see) nothing to connect the fragment with K 589 except its key of B flat, it is much more plausible to link it with Mozart's earlier quartet in B flat from the Vienna years. I conclude that K 589a is an attempt, later abandoned by Mozart, to write a finale for the 'Hunt' in 1783.

We have seen that the first of the six 'Haydn' quartets bears the date of the last day of 1782. Moreover, as early as April 26 1783 Mozart was offering a set of six quartets to the Paris publisher Sieber. But the dedicatory letter at the beginning of the first edition is dated 'il p.^{mo} Settembre 1785'. Can he have foreseen that it would be almost two and a half years after the Sieber letter before they would be ready for the public?

One is certainly left with the impression that the whole project cost Mozart much more effort than he had foreseen: the quartets seem truly to have been, as he says in the dedicatory letter, 'il frutto di una lunga, e laboriosa fatica'. In that respect the present enquiry throws light on two points. Firstly, the traditional division of Mozart's work on the quartets into two short bursts of activity, the first from December 1782 to around July 1783 (quartets 1-3), and the second from November 1784 to January 1785 (quartets 4-6), is blurred once we accept that some of the 'Hunt'—the fourth quartet—was written and still more of it was attempted in the year 1783. And secondly, the claim that each quartet was conceived as a whole by Mozart in his head, and then at

once written down—a notion for which there is little evidence
in the sources and which is increasingly coming under challenge—must stand abashed before a demonstration that
several movements were begun and then given up, and that
over a year separates the earliest from the latest portions of
the completed 'Hunt' Quartet.

REFERENCES

1 *Allgemeine musikalische Zeitung*, i, cols. 854-5 (September 1799).
2 Intrigues prevented a Vienna performance of *La finta semplice* in
   1768, but it was performed in Salzburg in 1769. See O E Deutsch
   Mozart: Die Dokumente seines Lebens Kassel, 1961, 82-3; R Anger-
   müller 'Ein neuentdecktes Salzburger Libretto (1769) zu Mozarts
   "La Finta semplice" ' *Die Musikforschung* xxxi 1978, 318-22. In
   his edition of the masses, Walter Senn fixes the composition of the
   C minor Mass K 139/47a between the autumn of 1768 and the
   middle of 1769: see NMA I/i/i (1968), p. xi.
3 For a fuller discussion of the internal chronology of *L'oca del Cairo*,
   see my essay 'The Date of Mozart's Piano Sonata in B Flat, KV
   333/315c: the "Linz" Sonata?', in: *Musik—Edition—Interpretation,
   Gedenkschrift für Günter Henle* ed. M Bente, Munich, 1980.
4 The number of staves and their total vertical span are important
   qualifications here. For in Salzburg in 1783 Mozart used paper
   with the same watermark but with ten staves, not twelve, their total
   span being 183 mm. Later in Vienna he used 12-stave paper with a
   total span of 188.5-189 mm in 1785, and again in 1791. The
   1791 paper can be recognised by the vertical lines at the beginnings
   and ends of the staves.
5 I am assuming here that K 426 is correctly dated by Mozart. In fact
   the autograph (Pierpont Morgan Library, New York) shows that the
   year was originally written down as '1782'.
6 The watermark is found a little earlier, in March 1789, in the copyists'
   score (with additions by Mozart) of Handel's *Messiah*, K 572.
7 See A Tyson 'New light on Mozart's "Prussian" Quartets' *Musical
   times* cxvi 1975, 126-30.

SOME ASPECTS OF MUSIC PUBLISHING IN NINETEENTH-CENTURY BERLIN

RUDOLF ELVERS

Berlin assumed a prominent role in the history of music printing and the music trade much later than other music publishing centres in Germany. It was only in 1616 that Georg Runge began to print and Martin Guth to publish music in Berlin, most of it sacred, including books of psalms and hymns for the evangelical church. In his Rostock dissertation of 1932 (*Der Berliner Musikdruck von seinen Anfängen bis zur Mitte des 18. Jahrhunderts*) Hans Ulrich Lenz was able to cite no more than 150 titles between 1616 and 1740, including hymn books with music as well as more considerable musical publications; one example is Johann Crüger's *Praxis pietatis melica*, of which thirty-four editions appeared in less than 100 years.

Modern music publishing is usually thought of as dating from the second half of the eighteenth century. Many publishing houses were founded in Germany at that time, and a number of them still flourish today. Immanuel Breitkopf of Leipzig, who is sometimes described in histories of music as the reviver of the art of Petrucci, must still be accounted the most important figure of the period. He carried his enthusiasm for modernizing musical typography with movable pieces to the point of trying to produce maps on the same principle. However, the aesthetic value of his new type apart, his invention achieved greater success in the literature of music printing than it represented in practice. Breitkopf's real importance for music publishing lay in the field of advertising. He brought out catalogues systematically, beginning in 1762 with his six-part *Catalogo delle sinfonie* in which only manuscripts were offered. A sprinkling of printed editions then gradually made their appearance in the sixteen supplements issued up to 1787.

In Berlin Johann Carl Friedrich Rellstab, the father of Ludwig Rellstab, followed the example of his Leipzig colleague. After taking over Georg Ludwig Winter's stocks of music in 1784 he began publishing music himself, and issued a series of fourteen catalogues. Although Rellstab built on similar foundations to Breitkopf, both men having acquired from their fathers printing shops with histories that can be traced back to the sixteenth century, he was much less well placed as a Prussian than his Leipzig rival. For Frederick the Great had, in 1773, granted the privilege for music publishing to the Amsterdam publisher Johann Julius Hummel. Consequently Hummel, who had promptly opened a branch in Berlin in 1774, was able to engrave virtually anything which he thought might turn out profitably. He had the better composers, and in addition worked quicker because he engraved his editions, whereas Rellstab used type; moreover for some years he had two engraving shops, one in Amsterdam and one in Berlin.

Both firms survived into the next century, but succumbed to the economic difficulties brought about by Napoleon's conquest of Prussia. Rellstab offered his firm for sale in 1806, though in the event it was not wound up till 1808. He had brought out a total of not more than 400 titles, among them the first vocal scores of operas by Gluck. Hummel produced very little after 1806. The business was closed officially in 1822, having published some 2000 works.

How matters stood with the music trade when the French troops entered Berlin can be discovered easily from the contemporary 'Baedeker' of the town. On page 405 of his *Lexicon von Berlin und der umliegenden Gegend* (1806) Johann Christian Gaedicke lists the following businesses: '(1) Rellstab, Jägerstrasse No.18. (2) Werkmeister, Jägerstrasse

No. 33. (3) Concha, Stechbahn No.4. (4) J. C. Windaus, unter den Linden No.13. (5) Schauspieler Böheim, Behrensstrasse No.29. (6) J.J. Hummel, an der Gertrauten- und Spreegassen-Brücke No.51; und (7) mehrere Buchhändler.'

These can be divided into three groups:

1. Music publishers with a retail department and their own production line: Rellstab, Hummel, Werckmeister.

2. Private individuals who dealt from their own houses, primarily in their own works: the actor Böheim.

3. Retail businesses which dealt principally in books but included some music as well: Windhaus and the 'several bookshops'.

In a new edition of his book, which came out in 1828 under the title *Der Berliner Nachweiser zu allen hiesigen Sehens- und Merkwürdigkeiten*, Gaedicke says summarily on page 203: 'We have ten music businesses, and the majority not only have their own thriving publishing concern and sell all the latest music, but offer old musical works as well, especially Trautwein, Breitestrasse No.8'. By 'music businesses' Gaedicke evidently means publishers with or without a retail department or shop, for exactly ten firms can be counted in Berlin in 1828. They are (in addition to Trautwein) Cosmar & Krause, A M Schlesinger, Gustav Bethge, Julie Concha, Gröbenschütz & Seiler, Friedrich Laue, Ferdinand Samuel Lischke, Heinrich Wagenführ and the Magazin für Kunst, Geographie und Musik. Besides these publishing houses there were also a considerable number of bookshops which not only sold music but occasionally published it themselves, such as Sander, Rücker, Nauck, Starcke, Logier, Mylius, Boike and Duncker & Humblot.

The number of music publishers rose to seventeen by 1850. While firms such as Concha, Lischke, Laue and Gröbenschütz went out of business or passed into other hands, the following new ones were founded: Bote & Bock, Challier & Co,

Damköhler, Esslinger, Guttentag, Horn, Leo, Paez, Stern &
Co.

It was typical of many firms founded before 1838, the
year when Bote & Bock opened, that they rose from quite
small beginnings and failed to survive for long. Rudolf
Werckmeister is an example. He started a music lending
library in Oranienburg in 1802, moved to Berlin in 1804,
gave up his publishing business in 1809 but kept his lending
library till 1813. Werckmeister was, with Hummel, one of
the first reprinters of works by Beethoven in Berlin and, as
it chanced, brought out the first separate work of E T A
Hoffmann (the 'Trois canzonettes', in May 1808).

All these small firms like Concha and Lischke went in for
reprinting. As a result, their editions were often not included
in Hofmeister's music bibliographies (published from 1829
onwards)—so strictly was their code observed even then—
which makes life difficult for the music bibliographer. Such
editions consist in general of only four, six or at most eight
pages. Besides Berlin popular music everything saleable was
extracted from the more successful operas in the Berlin
repertory—as Rellstab had done earlier. Only with the gradual
improvement in copyright law, dating roughly from the
foundation of the Leipzig 'Börsenverein der deutschen Buchhändler' in 1825 and the 'Verein der deutschen Musikalien-
händler' in 1829, did attitudes change. As an outward sign
of this the words 'Eingetragen in das Vereins-Archiv' ('entered
in the Association's records'—ie the records of the Association
of German Music Dealers in Leipzig) began to appear on
titlepages.

The most important personality among Berlin publishers
of the first quarter of the century was undoubtedly Adolph
Martin (really Abraham Moses) Schlesinger, who came from
Sülz in Silesia. He started before 1795 with a book distribution agency, ran a French lending library for a long time

and also sold music and maps. In 1810 he opened a shop, and the following year began to bring out his own publications. It is no surprise to find that his Op 1 was an 'Auswahl von Ouvertüren, Gesängen, Märschen und Tänzen aus den neuesten Opern, welche auf dem Königl. Nationaltheater in Berlin aufgeführt werden', in this case excerpts from Spontini's *La Vestale* arranged for piano by Carl Wilhelm Henning. A selection from Reichardt's *Der Taucher* followed, then one from Bernhard Anselm Weber's *Deodata* and a string quartet arrangement of Fioravanti's *Die Dorfsängerinnen* (*Le cantatrici villane*). However, after the wars in which Prussia regained her independence he achieved what would today be called his 'big breakthrough' by becoming Carl Maria von Weber's publisher. The sizes of the various printings of one of his most popular publications of this time are known. The first issue of the first book of Weber's *Leyer und Schwerdt*, which appeared in January 1815, consisted of 300 copies, 100 more were printed in February, 50 in March, 50 on October 6 and finally a further 50 in January 1816. The second book then came out in a first printing of 550 copies.

In 1819 a connection with Beethoven was established through Schlesinger's son Moritz. The opening by Moritz of an independent business in Paris in 1821 made possible not only joint publication, but the acquisition of German rights for French operas—the so-called 'grosse Rechte'. It still remains the dream of every music publisher to possess as many such rights as possible for popular operas. Thus Schlesinger became the first importer of French operas to Berlin—a type of import destined to remain a Berlin speciality (a later example is Adolph Fürstner, founded in 1868). At the same time he held the publication rights for all marches in use by the Prussian army, and in addition brought out three very influential periodicals: *Berliner allgemeine musikal.*

Zeitung (1824-30), edited by A B Marx, ten years of *Der Freimüthige* (1825-35), which had previously been published by Dr Kuhn, and *Das Berliner Conversationsblatt* (1827-38), for which Friedrich Förster and Willibald Alexis were responsible.

Schlesinger's third son Heinrich took over the firm in 1838, and ran it at first on behalf of his mother, with whom he had jointly inherited a million Thaler, and later alone. He published Liszt and Cornelius and bought Chopin's posthumous works, though he turned down Wagner's *Holländer*. Although Heinrich was a difficult man and something of a recluse —the Mendelssohns thought him ghastly—he put the firm into far better order. For example he had all his publications produced by the Leipzig printing firm of C G Röder from the time of its establishment in 1848. Schlesinger's vast store of plates perished only during the bombardment of Leipzig in the second world war. When Heinrich, who had no heirs, sold his business to Robert Lienau in 1864, he could look back on over 6000 titles of every description—a veritable department-store of music.

In 1838, the year of A M Schlesinger's death, Bote & Bock was founded through the purchase of the small business of Fröhlich & Co. It began quite modestly with small works by minor Berlin composers, published, more by chance than design, the Op 1 (three songs to poems by Mickiewicz) of Stanisław Moniuszko, who was at that time a pupil of Rungenhagen's, and very quickly conquered the dance market with the music of Josef Gung'l (whose output eventually totalled more than 400 works). The firm broke into opera with Otto Nicolai's *Lustige Weiber von Windsor* in 1849, and crowned its endeavours in this sphere by acquiring the German rights of all Offenbach's stage works in 1858. By that year it had published about 5000 works.

Trautwein & Co, founded in 1820, presented a very

different picture. While Traugott Trautwein, who had been trained at Breitkopf & Härtel's, provided the practical expertise, the '& Co' concealed the ruling spirit of the house, a member of an old Berlin family named Ferdinand Mendheim, whose motto was 'classic and correct'. This partnership was responsible for the first German complete edition of Haydn's string quartets, described as a de luxe edition, with a chronological thematic index and a historical preface, and for the appearance in Berlin of the first editions of Bach's St John Passion (1829) and many of his cantatas, with 'correct performance material'. Trautwein also published the first collected edition of Gluck's songs and odes, the motets of Rungenhagen (who provided him with a link with the famous 'Sing-Akademie'), the first 'complete edition' to appear in Berlin (that of Karl Christian Friedrich Fasch, 1839) and finally—drawing on the collection of the Royal Library, which collaborated in the project—the *Auswahl vorzüglicher Musikwerke in gebundener Schreibart von Meistern alter und neuer Zeit, zur Beförderung des höheren Studiums der Musik, unter Aufsicht der musicalischen Section der Kgl. Akademie der Künste in Berlin.* The connection with musical scholarship lasted till after 1860, by which time about 1500 titles had appeared. Martin Bahn then acquired the business. It was he who launched Robert Eitner's *Monatshefte für Musikgeschichte* (1869) and the Publications of the 'Gesellschaft für Musikforschung' (1873).

A glance at the firm of Heinrich Wagenführ will serve as a final example. It was founded in 1828 and taken over by Challier in 1868. Wagenführ published cheap music. His catalogue of 1838—the only one that seems to be extant— lists 290 titles, the product of ten years, of which 80 per cent cost between 2½ and 15 silver Groschen. They were mostly dances, from the *Fakeltanz zur höchsten Vermählung der Prinzessin Louise von Preussen mit dem Prinzen Friedrich der*

Niederlande and *Der russische Schumna-Galopp* to the *Besänftigungswalzer als Antwort auf den Berliner Desperations- oder sanften Heinrichswalzer*. The two most expensive items were Carl Loewe's three String Quartets Op 24 and the same composer's oratorio for four male voices *Die Apostel von Philippi* Op 48 (at 3 Rthlr 15 Sgr).

If Berlin held four publishers within its walls in 1806, ten in 1828 and seventeen by the mid-century, the number soon grew considerably. Twenty-three are known in 1870, at least thirty-three in 1880 and more than seventy by the end of the century. The swift increase is easily explained: Berlin had become the capital city, the centre of the German empire. But there was another factor, an invention by a Berliner which permitted a vast reduction in the cost of the production of music.

Julius Friedländer devised a mechanical press for printing music, though he employed it at first for a Leipzig firm. Having founded, in partnership with a Herr Stern, the firm of Stern & Co before 1840, he opened a business under his own name in 1845, took over sole direction of Stern & Co in 1852, amalgamating it with his own firm, went into partnership with Heinrich Jacoby and Gustav Heintze in 1860 and in the same year took over C F Peters in Leipzig. For this last enterprise he borrowed 29,000 Taler from the Leipzig bank of Vatter & Co, which remained the owner of Peters until the debt was paid off. Friedländer's contribution to the firm was his invention of the mechanical press which, as the Peters general catalogue (Leipzig and Berlin, 1861) proclaimed, enabled music to be printed from the highest quality plates on sized paper at a cost reduction of 800 per cent. Friedländer did not leave Peters till 1880, having directed the firm at times from Berlin.

Friedländer is an example of a figure in the publishing world to whom history has paid little attention, but whose

emergence had important consequences. The radical reduction in the production cost of large print-runs led to the
establishment of the *Edition Peters* and other cheap popular
editions and 'Volksausgaben'. Previously the price of music
had remained remarkably constant. In 1801 Hummel's
vocal score of Mozart's *Die Zauberflöte* cost 8 Taler, 5
Groschen. Twenty years later Schlesinger was charging 6
Taler, 12 Groschen for the first edition of the vocal score of
Weber's *Der Freischütz*. About 1840 Bote & Bock asked
almost the same price for their *Freischütz* vocal score as
Schlesinger (6 Taler, 15 Groschen), and 7 Taler for Adolphe
Adam's *Le postillon de Longjumeau*. Even the relatively
late introduction of lithography in Berlin, probably through
Schlesinger, had no effect on prices, although more pulls
could be taken from a stone than a plate. Yet shortly before
1870 the cost of the Peters vocal score of *Der Freischütz*
was only 20 Groschen–or 2 Marks after 1872–on sized
paper!

Cheap music printing brought a change in the quantity of
music published. The output of a firm can readily be assessed
by its plate numbers. It will be remembered that J J Hummel,
an international North-European publisher, brought out some
2000 titles (not counting reissues) in almost fifty years,
Rellstab only 400 in twenty years and Werckmeister about
250 in only four years. On the other hand Schlesinger
reached about 9000 titles between 1810 and 1900, Bote &
Bock 15,000 between 1838 and 1900, and Fürstner 4000
between 1868 and 1900 (omitting reissues in each case).

The yearly output of new editions and reissues may be
illustrated by two samples based on Hofmeister's *Jahresver-
zeichnis* for the relevant years (see facing page).

Comparing the output for the year 1852, in which thirteen
publishers produced 326 titles, with the figures for 1880,
when thirty-two publishers brought out about 1000 editions,

it becomes evident that a certain amount of fragmentation has taken place: a greater number of small and medium-sized firms were scarcely producing more in percentage terms than was the case in 1852. This tendency becomes progressively more marked up to 1900. It should be mentioned that the 1880 figures for Bote & Bock, Schlesinger and Carl Simon are all relatively high because all three simultaneously produced series of Chopin's works, copyright in which had run out in that year!

	1880		1852
Bote & Bock	186	. . . .	48
Schlesinger	136	. . . .	185
Carl Simon	135		
Hermann Erler	90		
A Fürstner	55		
Challier & Co.	42	. . . .	22
Bahn (Trautwein-			
Guttentag)	36	. . . .	36
Kühling	26	Damköhler . . .	10
Philipp	23		
Raabe & Plothow	23		
Paez	20	. . . .	9
Sulzbach	20	Stern & Co. . .	5
Simrock	20	Horn	3
Hermann Schroeder	17	Leo	3
Güttner	10	Geelhaar.	2
and seventeen firms with		and three firms with	
fewer than ten titles each.		only one title each.	

To arrive at a complete picture it would be necessary to consider the size of printings. For understandable reasons —which, however, become much less understandable when one thinks of modern book production—these figures, like dates of publication, have mostly been and remained the closely guarded secrets of the publishers. Care should also be taken not to judge the health of a firm by the number of new publications in a year: Simrock produced in general very few titles in his later Berlin years, but he was the publisher of Brahms and Dvořák. The same goes for Fürstner who, besides acting as agent for French publishers (including Heugel), took great trouble to obtain operatic rights and so eventually became the chief publisher of the operas of Richard Strauss. That development belonged to the twentieth century, by which time Leipzig, despite the competition presented by the capital Berlin, had become the world centre of music publishing, even though Berlin could boast more publishers. Prussia was conquered by Saxony through the marketing system: the book distribution and commission agencies. Business was now even quicker off the mark in Leipzig than in Berlin.

THE EARLY NOVELLO OCTAVO EDITIONS

MIRIAM MILLER

There exists a belief that the Novello octavo editions of vocal scores of the standard choral repertory and the *Musical times* owe their common size and format to one another. This is something of an over-simplification, as an examination of the history of these publications will show and will, in its turn, throw many interesting sidelights on printing, publishing and education in mid-nineteenth-century England.

The *Musical times* was initially the creation of Joseph Mainzer, a German music educationist who came to England in 1841. He was an advocate of the singing-class method of musical instruction as opposed to individual tuition, and published a treatise, *Singing for the million*, in 1842 to demonstrate his method. Mainzer was a priest, and saw the instruction of the masses in singing as 'a powerful auxiliary in the religious and moral education of the people'.[1] Mainzer's methods were adopted widely and with enthusiasm. It may be that Nettel's comment[2] that one result of the Industrial Revolution in England was to transform the children of a generation of folk-singers into a generation of choral singers is yet another over-simplification, but there is no doubt that the factory-workers of the major industrial towns were the children of agricultural labourers, scarcely literate and poor. Many of the singing-classes set up under Mainzer's influence were closely connected with factories in which the singers worked. It was one thing, however, to set up singing-classes, but quite another to maintain the initial enthusiasm and to satisfy a growing national appetite for vocal music at a price which singing-class members could afford. Accordingly, Mainzer inaugurated *Mainzer's musical times and singing circular* in 1842, a journal which appeared on the first day of each month. It was octavo sized and included a short piece of choral music in unaccompanied chorus score format, as well as one or two brief articles on class singing and some notes and news on group singing activities throughout the country. The price was 1d. For two years the choral items in each issue bore the imprint 'London: at the office of Mainzer's Musical Times, 340 Strand...', but in January 1844 this was altered to 'London: published by B. Cowderoy, 340, Strand...'. Cowderoy's role as publisher had always been acknowledged in the colophon statement of each issue together with that of William Stevens, 37 Bell Yard, Temple Bar, as the printer, but in May of the same year the journal was taken over by J Alfred Novello, together with the agency for Mainzer's own publications, which were numerous.

Novello absorbed the journal into an already well established family business at the London Sacred Music Warehouse, 69 Dean Street, Soho, and declared his intention of improving both the quality and the coverage of what he called *The musical times and singing-class circular*[3], but retaining the price, size and format of Mainzer's original. His reason, as given, was to allow the new series to be conveniently bound with the old numbers, but it is doubtful whether he could have improved the presentation of what had clearly become an immensely popular publication. What he did improve, immediately, was the quality of the music and of its printing. Novello had pointed out in his preface to the first issue of the new journal that as the 'proprietor of many important copyright works' he intended to make extracts from them available at a much cheaper price, and this he did with marked effect. The appearance of the music pages also improved dramatically from what had been rather a rough, cobbled impression to one of neatness and clarity in which can already be seen the beginnings of the distinctive and familiar octavo edition style. The printer appears in the colophon statement from 1844 until 1846 as Thomas Richards, 100 St Martin's Lane; from 1846 until 1847 as Thomas Harvey, 24 Cornwall Road, Lambeth, with J Alfred Novello as publisher; but from the beginning of 1847, Novello appears as both printer and publisher, 'at his Printing Office, Dean's Yard, Dean Street. . .'. We cannot be certain that either Richards or Harvey printed the music pages. Even with their names appearing in the colophons, it is highly possible that they were responsible for the letterpress printing only. The case of J Alfred Novello, however, was quite different.

A short history of cheap music. . . in. . . the house of Novello, Ewer & Co[4] describes how Novello set up his own printing house. Disputes within the printing trade over rates of pay and the adoption of new methods of printing obliged him to use non-union workmen and become a printer 'outside the trade'. The steady development of the Novello business made this an untenable situation and dissatisfaction with existing techniques led him to re-examine methods of producing the cheap music to which the *Short history* is dedicated. The result of this examination may be read in *Some account of the methods of musick printing*[5], a short pamphlet published in 1847 with the intention of advertising the fact that the house of Novello was now willing to undertake printing commissions. Samples of several music founts are illustrated and, in an accompanying discussion, Novello makes clear his preference for stereotyping as the method most suited to his purpose. Engraving he rejects as being too costly and declares that pewter plates wear out too quickly, after 'from 1300 to 2000 impressions according to the goodness of the workmanship'. In the *Short history* lithography is also rejected as being 'not then perfectly understood', an interesting comment in view of the fact that it had been adopted by Breitkopf & Härtel in 1805[6] and was to be adopted on a large scale for music-printing in England by Augener & Co in 1853.[7] It seems probable that Novello was influenced by the experience of William Clowes & Son, a long-established general printing house, at Stamford Street, Blackfriars[8], because in adopting stereotyping for music Novello was not an innovator. The Clowes firm is mentioned in the *Short history* as being responsible for notable improvements in music typography, but their problems with their workmen were so severe as to make them consider destroying their music founts (p 33). Novello's decision to establish his own printing works, staffed with non-union workmen, appears to have relieved him of that particular anxiety. In the *Musical times* of April 1 1848 there appears the advertisement:

> 'Apprentice wanted to the Letter-press Printing Business in all its branches, including the composition of music types. A Premium will be required. Apply to Mr.J. Alfred Novello, London Sacred Music Warehouse, 69, Dean Street, Soho & 24, Poultry.'

Similar advertisements appear throughout the years with regard to vacancies in the printing house and other areas of the Novello business. The demand for a premium may seem surprising today, but was common practice at that time.

Stereotyping, the method of printing adopted by Novello for his infant printing-house, involves the making of a plaster mould of a forme of type, then filling the mould with molten metal. When the metal has cooled, the plaster is stripped away leaving a metal stereotype 'plate', an exact duplicate of the original forme. The great advantage of this method is that it allows several 'plates' to be made from one forme of type, thus speeding up the printing operation and saving the original type from damage. It also has the advantage of minimizing the breaks in stave lines etc, which is such a common feature of music printed from type—indeed, in the Novello imprints, those become clear only under magnification.

Above all, the method produced music cheaply, and this was a most important consideration for Novello if he was to keep down the cost of the *Musical times* and print music its readers could afford. The *Short history*, however, declares that even at this relatively early stage in the history of the firm, Novello was dissatisfied with the music type available to him, and determined to improve it. We know from his *Methods of music printing* that he had two of the founts offered there as samples specially cut. They are a Pearl-Nonpareil (No 3) and a Gregorian fount, but although a Gem fount is also offered in this leaflet, Novello decided to have a completely new fount cut in this style for use with the octavo choruses and editions. The *Short history* tells us that the fount took over six years to perfect, and that the punches were cut by 'Mr.Palmer of the Soho Type Foundry'. This was presumably Henry William Palmer, 'A stereotype and letter founder' whose address was 6A West Street in the Seven Dials district of Soho in 1852.[9] The type was finally adopted in 1853-54, by which time the Novello octavo editions were an integral part of British musical life.

The octavo editions began in 1846, when the *Musical times* announced 'the cheapest musical publication ever offered to the public'. This was Vincent Novello's vocal score reduction of Handel's *Messiah*, to be sold in twelve monthly numbers, beginning in August 1846 and costing 6d per number. The result would be a complete octavo-sized vocal score of the work, costing six shillings, a price within the grasp of most choir singers. The edition was immediately popular (even the *Athenaeum* approved) and was followed by similar presentations of Haydn's *Creation* and Handel's *Judas Maccabeus*. As a further development, J Alfred Novello published the choruses from these vocal score editions at about half the price of the complete work, 'for the poorer Choral Societies, who want a large number of the Choruses'. He adds, in the same announcement, 'The Quarto Pianoforte Edition will be convenient to the Pianist, from only requiring half the usual number of leaves to be turned over'—an immensely practical statement, but also indicative of the fact that the house of Novello was producing large quantities of other editions besides the octavos. A folio edition was also available for those who wanted it, as well as orchestral material.

The relative cheapness of the octavo editions must have been a very strong selling point, but the high quality of the production was another. Even before the introduction of the improved Gem fount, the printing is clear and crisp, and there is no doubt that accurate registration and careful underlay of text make for easy reading. Phrasing and other dynamic markings are kept to a minimum so that even an inexperienced chorister can hold his or her part without confusion. The octavo size makes the music comfortable for choristers to carry and hold, whether sitting or standing, and when singing from copies of this size they may easily see their conductor. These comments may well seem self-evident to musicians who have come to accept the upright octavo as the only size for a vocal score, but in the mid-nineteenth century it was still something of an innovation. Vincent Novello, when he published his collection of masses by Mozart and Haydn around 1825, adopted an oblong octavo format. One interesting detail is the determined adoption of the treble clef for all the upper voices. This was still a matter of some contention as late as 1850, when J Alfred Novello alluded to it in his preface to volume III of the *Musical times*.

Mention of Vincent Novello, the founder of the business and father of J Alfred, obliges one to examine his role in the creation of the octavo editions, and a very important one it proves to have been. All the available evidence demonstrates that while his son devoted his energies to the business side of the enterprise, it was Vincent who retained artistic control. The vocal score reductions were all Vincent's work, as were those published with the *Musical times*. Also it would appear that it was the elder Novello who selected the repertory. He was himself a deeply religious man, and, like Mainzer, may have looked upon music as an improving influence in an age where there was much to improve. Certainly the early octavo editions offered what we have now come to accept as the standard oratorio repertory, major choral works by Beethoven, Handel, Haydn, Mozart and Mendelssohn, and if there is rather a preponderance of Handel, this is only natural in view of his perennial popularity in Britain.

But no matter how good the quality of the music, how clear the printing, convenient the size or cheap the price, the Novello octavo editions would never have achieved their success had not a ready market existed for them, and it is here that the true inter-relationship between the octavo editions and the *Musical times* may be found. When J Alfred Novello took over Mainzer's journal in 1844, he must have realized what a valuable advertising medium it could be for an enterprising publisher. The subscribers to the journal could only be teachers and others actively involved with a choir or singing-class, and therefore hungry for music their choristers could sing. Music of this nature was not readily available in the 1840s, at least not in the smaller provincial towns, and this was a void which Novello's was unusually well qualified to fill. Further, the journal allowed the firm to keep in touch with its customers. Ever since Mainzer's day, a column of reports on musical activities among subscribers had been a regular feature. Under Novello's influence this became much enlarged into 'A Brief Chronicle of the Last Month', and later a section of answers to questions sent by correspondents further extended his insight into the nation's musical life. Thus he was able to anticipate demand, advertise his wares and sell his existing stock while, at the same time, running a highly successful periodical. A present-day music publisher would ask for little more. It was a natural progression that a singing-class which developed into a choral society would tire of singing and performing a number of short pieces and wish to tackle a major work, hence the publication of Handel's *Messiah* in 1846. The repertory offered was acceptable to such a public, these works being very well suited to the talents of a large amateur chorus, and sufficiently 'uplifting' to satisfy a nineteenth-century audience. The 'Brief Chronicles' each month yield fascinating information on how widespread choral singing had become, and not only in the larger provincial cities. Reports appear from Sale, Dewsbury, Kilmarnock, Ormskirk, Shoreham-by-Sea, Birkenhead, Dunfermline and hundreds of other small towns, demonstrating the extent of the *Musical times* subscription list and Novello's market.

It was a market which Novello studied and served for a number of years, although not without problems. The success of his firm's octavo editions encouraged other publishers to copy the series and thus affect his sales, but it is clear that he was a good deal more perturbed by evidence that private, individual copies were being made of his copyrights, as the following note, printed in the *Musical times* for July 1849 shows:

'To Choral Societies. J. Alfred Novello would respectfully call the attention of all who may require the use of separate Vocal Parts of Oratorios, Masses, Motetts, Anthems, etc. to the large Catalogue of that class of Music which he prints, and to the great reduction which he has made in the price of it since the Ist of January last. All separate Vocal Parts are now published for THREE HALF-PENCE PER PAGE, which will be found less costly than the blank music paper necessary to copy out the same quantity of music. Good printed copies can thus be obtained not only for less than the blank paper, but saving all the trouble or cost of copying, and ensuring a correctness which is unattainable in manuscript copies.'

The point is shrewdly argued, but in the end Novello was obliged to prosecute to protect his copyrights (*Short history*, p 59). His claim on the reduction of prices in 1849 is correct, and indicative of his policy of keeping the price of copies as low as possible. The steady increase in sales was an important factor in the operation of this policy, and by 1854 Novello was able to offer four of his major productions, bound in scarlet cloth, with gilt lettering, as follows:

```
HAYDN'S CREATION . . . . . . . . . . . . . .3s
HANDEL'S MESSIAH  . . . . . . . . . . . . . .4s
    "        JUDAS MACCABAEUS. . . .4s
    "        SAMSON . . . . . . . . . . . . . . .4s
```

When one considers that the original cost of the *Messiah* edition in twelve separate monthly parts was six shillings, one is impressed by the achievement. Novello's experiment of eight years earlier had become accepted as a standard series and was to continue to influence the musical life of the nation for many years to come.

REFERENCES

1 *Mainzer's musical times and singing circular* New series i 1843, 6.
2 R Nettel *Music in the Five Towns, 1840-1914* London, 1944, 1.
3 *Musical times and singing-class circular* i 1844, 1.
4 *A short history of cheap music as exemplified in the records of the house of Novello, Ewer & Co* London, 1887. Published anonymously, but in fact by Joseph Bennett.
5 J A Novello *Some account of the methods of musick printing with specimens of the various sizes of musical types* London, 1847.

6 See the article on the firm in *Grove's Dictionary* 5th ed London, 1954.

7 C Humphries and W C Smith *Music publishing in the British Isles* London, 1954, 35.

8 *ibid*, 108.

9 *Watkins's commercial and general London directory* London, 1853.

MEYERBEER'S ITALIAN OPERAS

WINTON DEAN

Historians of opera have sometimes interpreted Meyerbeer's career—two operas produced in Germany (1812-13), six in Italy (1817-24) and six in France (1831-65, the last posthumous)—as an epitome of opportunism or a paradigm of the wandering Jew. This is wisdom after the event. He *was* a Jew and an opportunist, and he wandered, but then so did many other composers of his and previous generations. Until Weber and Spohr began to establish a national school about 1816, German opera scarcely existed above the Singspiel level. True, this had produced three isolated masterpieces in *Die Entführung aus dem Serail, Die Zauberflöte* and *Fidelio*, but they did not amount to a tradition, and there was nothing else of consequence. Most of the operas written for Germany, which, like Italy, was a divided country with many court theatres, were Italian, even when composed by Germans. Gluck, the leading opera composer of his age, never set a libretto in his own language.

The only flourishing alternative to the Italian school was the French, whose strong local tradition in the treatment of the sung text gave it a sturdy independence. But Paris was the capital of a united and prosperous nation with a rich culture, especially in the theatre, and from the time of Lully and even earlier it had attracted foreign musicians. Moreover French opera seemed to require an infusion of foreign blood —especially Italian blood—before it could thrive. An astonishing proportion of its leading composers—Lully, Gluck, Piccinni, Sacchini, Salieri, Cherubini, Spontini, Rossini and Meyerbeer himself—were either Italians or had learned their craft in Italy. Many lesser figures, including J C Bach,

Paisiello, Reichardt, Paer and Winter, travelled the same path. Several of them—Italians as well as Germans—set librettos in all three current languages, thereby confirming opera's status as an international art. It was through no fault of his own that Mozart did not add a French opera to his Italian and German tally.

Only the strictures of Weber, Wagner and other German nationalists have branded Meyerbeer's career as retrograde. One of the most gifted composers of the next generation, Otto Nicolai, wrote a series of Italian operas before his single German masterpiece. But Meyerbeer's sensational success in Paris has tended to eclipse his Italian period, which was its necessary pre-requisite and only comparatively less of a triumph. It is worth examining his Italian operas to determine how much of the essential Meyerbeer (if we can assume that such a thing exists) antedated his arrival in Paris, at Rossini's invitation, in 1825.

These operas are generally dismissed as mere imitations of Rossini (his junior by six months). It is true that on reaching Venice in 1815 Meyerbeer fell at once under the spell of *Tancredi*, and that Rossini is an overwhelming influence on his Italian operas (and a palpable one on his French operas as well). That was inevitable. Rossini-fever was a germ that within a few years could be caught anywhere in Europe, and it was highly infectious. Very few composers escaped it, even the most nationally or locally orientated, such as Schubert, Weber and Marschner. What is interesting about Meyerbeer's Italian operas is the presence of characteristic traits that he is commonly supposed to have acquired in Paris.

One of the six, *Semiramide riconosciuta* (1819), is a setting of Metastasio, whose librettos were still tempting composers even in Germany (Poissl produced operas based on *L'Olimpiade* in 1815 and *Nitteti* in 1817). In the others

Meyerbeer collaborated with two of the most prolific and successful librettists of the day. Gaetano Rossi, the author of *Romilda e Costanza* (1817), *Emma di Resburgo* (1819) and *Il crociato in Egitto* (1824), worked for Mayr, Rossini (*Il cambiale di matrimonio, La scala di seta, Tancredi, Semiramide*), Mercadante (*Il giuramento, Il bravo*), Donizetti (*Maria Padilla, Linda di Chamounix*) and Nicolai (*Il proscritto*, originally intended for Verdi). Felice Romani, who supplied the texts for *Margherita d'Anjou* (1820) and *L'esule di Granata* (1822), was the most distinguished Italian librettist between Da Ponte and Boito and scarcely needs an introduction. Several of these scores are inaccessible, but the two most successful give a vivid and no doubt representative picture. *Margherita d'Anjou* was performed all over Europe for twenty years. *Il crociato in Egitto* lasted longer and travelled further, reaching places as remote as Havana, Mexico City, Corfu, Constantinople and St Petersburg by 1841. It received a concert performance in London, said to be the first for more than a century, in January 1972.

It is hard to know how much say Meyerbeer had in the choice or treatment of his subjects at this period, but both librettos, especially *Il crociato in Egitto*, have an ominous flavour of Scribe. Rossi was always addicted to strained situations and melodramatic extravagance, with the characters dancing attendance on the plot instead of controlling it. Romani was capable of better things, as we know from his collaboration with Bellini in *Norma* and *La sonnambula*. But his libretto for *Margherita d'Anjou*, based like so many others of the period on a French *mélodrame* by Pixérécourt, does not show him at his best. Admittedly it is an *opera semiseria*, a deliberate mixing of the genres, in which the heroic postures of the old *opera seria* were modified by two strains from *opéra-comique*, the *comédie larmoyante* that was part of Rousseau's legacy and the realism of the first

Revolutionary decade. (*La sonnambula* is a specimen of the type at its best.) *Opera semiseria* admitted comic characters on an equal basis with their social superiors, though the comedy tended to become more and more sentimental. Some examples, including Mayr's treatment of stories set by Cherubini in *Elisa* and Beethoven in *Fidelio*, bore the title *farsa sentimentale*. It was one of the growing points of the Romantic movement in opera.

The plot of *Margherita* is nothing if not romantic.[1] The action takes place near Hexham during the Wars of the Roses (which had inspired Mayr's *opera seria* of seven years earlier, *La rosa rossa e la rosa bianca*, likewise by Romani out of Pixérécourt) and concerns a successful campaign by Henry VI's widowed Queen against the Yorkists; the links with history are negligible. It is full of stratagems and spoils, battles, disguises, conspiracies and tergiversations of every kind, such as might be thought not unsuited to that turbulent period. Much of it, as in many of the Revolution *opéras-comiques*, takes place in darkness. The motley collection of characters includes the Grand Seneschal of Normandy (tenor), who is supposed to be in love with the Queen but has no love scene with her (there is no love music in the opera); his wife Isaura, who follows him across the Channel disguised as a knight and obtains employment as his page, without being recognized, in order to watch his steps (she is then required to carry his love messages to the Queen); Norcester (*sic*), a Yorkist baron disguised as a Highland chieftain, who goes over to the beaten side when his own has avenged his wrongs, presumably to prevent the opera ending an act too soon; a cowardly Gascon surgeon named Morin (originally Michele), a substantial *buffo* part designed as foil to the high-born characters and a vehicle for comic relief; and the villainous Richard of Gloucester, who does not appear till the middle of Act III. He then gets everyone else in his power, only for the tables to be turned in a most incongruously happy ending. We encounter many of the favourite ingredients of early Romantic opera—prayers, hymns, storms, an aria in polacca rhythm for the surgeon, a mute child (the young Prince Edward) threatened with death on the stage, and 'characteristic' choruses. Each act begins with one of these: French soldiers playing cards, drinking and wenching to a bouncy tune that may have been Meyerbeer's idea of a Northumberland jig in Act I, English soldiers vowing death to the French in Act II, Highlanders addressing a hymn to the sunrise in Act III.

The music is as mixed in style as the libretto. As one might expect, the Rossini of the early comedies dominates the serious as well as the lighter scenes. The score is full of clattering march rhythms, brilliant coloratura (especially for the Queen) and—a Rossini trait that Meyerbeer never outgrew —loud thumps in pianissimo passages, generally off the beat and often in the most unsuitable contexts, such as the prayer quartet in the first finale. Even the amiable hymn to the sunrise for no obvious reason sports a fortissimo penultimate chord. Yet there is a positive if fitful attempt to evoke an appropriate dramatic atmosphere and to develop the action in musical terms. A number of set pieces lead into one another without a break; Romani's design may have been a help here, as it was to Mayr in *Le due duchesse*. Meyerbeer makes rather crude efforts to differentiate the characters in duets, of which there are three in Act I: for the Queen and the disguised Norcester, both praying hard for different things (and Norcester cursing in the cabaletta); for Morin and Isaura, she professing such devotion to her husband that she must always be with him, however badly he behaves, Morin dismissing these sentiments as obsolete (she ought to take a lover); and for Isaura in her knightly disguise and her unsuspecting husband. It is during this piece that he enlists her in his household.

More successful is the evocation of night, mystery and shady business afoot in two trios in Acts II and III and the early part of the second finale. In the Act II trio, after a battle, Isaura is lost and frightened, the Seneschal defeated and ignorant of the Queen's fate, Morin thankful to the darkness for aiding his escape. Each has a long solo with its own music, but bringing in a common main theme at different points to the same words (about night); then they meet and recognize one another. Several times they think they hear Gloucester's soldiers, but decide it is the wind or the river or the echo of their own voices. The music has a light touch and an individual flavour, and culminates in a return of the main theme in augmentation. The coda leads into a substantial finale, which begins with a band of Highlanders searching for the Queen and proposing to throw her in the river. Solo voices answer one another in the darkness over a creeping orchestral ostinato, first in G minor, later, as the full cast assembles, in G major. After an Andante sostenuto quintet of perplexity in A flat—the favourite key for a slow concertato in finales of this period, especially those of Mayr and Rossini—another rhythmic ostinato takes over when Norcester horrifies the defeated Lancastrians by revealing his identity, but promptly joins them and persuades his Highlanders to do the same. The resourceful treatment of ostinato is Rossinian, and so is much of the structure of the finale, but it lacks Rossini's formal balance, both between fast and slow sections and in tonality. The principal components are in G minor and major (fast), A flat major (slow), A major with excursions to D minor and F major (fast, with one short Andante) and D major (fast). The ensemble in which all thank Norcester is very Mozartian in theme and harmony, but this will never do to end an act, so the Queen introduces a poor Rossinian tune with triplets and gallops away with the coda.

The Act III trio for three basses (Norcester, Morin and Gloucester), though of clear *buffo* descent, has considerable character. Gloucester, who has not previously sung in the opera, tries to induce the other two to betray themselves by revealing their loyalties. Morin admits that he does not hate the Queen, but evades the trap by saying he cannot hate anyone: he only wishes the war would go away and make life tolerable for ordinary folk like himself. Gloucester then orders Norcester to produce his wife, knowing that the woman masquerading as such is in fact the Queen. Morin covers Norcester's embarrassment by saying he is a notoriously jealous husband. The situation is temporarily saved, but Gloucester's suspicions are confirmed. Meyerbeer gets a good deal of vitality and dramatic irony into the music, which is *Staccato sotto voce marcato* almost throughout, and is saved from pretentiousness by the presence of the down-to-earth Gascon. Episodes of this kind—the ironical male-voice trio 'Sous votre bannière' in Act III of *Le Prophète* is another —are among the most successful in Meyerbeer's operas. The more ambitious scenes of *Margherita d'Anjou* are apt to be precarious in style and hollow in sentiment.

There is nothing remotely comic about *Il crociato in Egitto* —in intention, at least. It is a very grand *opera seria* set in the period of the Crusades, with rival nationalities and religions, Christian and Islamic, at each other's throats throughout, and the usual emotional cross-currents and complications. Armando, a knight of Rhodes left for dead on the battlefield, has enlisted in the service of the Sultan Aladino under another name, conquered his new master's enemies, and had a son by his daughter Palmide. The Egyptians are prepared to regularize the union, but Armando confesses his deception to Palmide: he has betrayed everyone, including his uncle Adriano di Monfort, the Grand Master of his Order, and Felicia, his childhood companion and destined bride. When Adriano arrives with an embassy to solemize a peace treaty, he is horrified to discover Armando in Saracen costume.. He demands and breaks in two the sword he has dishonoured (the opera must have been expensive in cutlery, for the entire Christian chorus does this in Act II), and the family quarrel develops into a renewal of hostilities. Armando says Palmide will die of grief if he deserts her; Adriano says Armando's behaviour will kill his mother; Armando returns penitent to the Christian fold. Felicia arrives disguised as a knight (not an unusual situation for a mezzo at this period) in search of Armando's tomb. The two women meet in the palace garden and find a common link in a melody that turns out to be Armando's favourite song (shades of Grétry's *Richard Coeur de Lion*); Felicia recognizes his happiness with Palmide and the child, and offers to give him up, the scene culminating in a soulful trio on the melody aforesaid.

The first finale begins with a peace conference and ends with a declaration of war. In between Aladino proclaims Armando his son-in-law and heir and releases all Christian prisoners; Armando rejects Palmide and the throne; Adriano tries to stab him; Felicia, claiming to be his brother, insists on dying first; everyone says farewell to sweet dreams of love and honour (in a canonic round, predictably in A flat); each side unfurls its banners and draws up in line of battle, the infidels summoning the faithful with the aid of a 'bronzo tremendo'.

At the start of Act II all the Christians are in prison. The first two numbers are big arias for the two women, both devoted to Armando. Aladino threatens to kill his grandson, but cannot hold out against Palmide's pleas and the kneeling child, and goes to the other extreme, not only sparing the boy but releasing Armando, Adriano and all the other Christians as well. Meanwhile the vizier Osmino is hatching a plot with the Emirs to overthrow Aladino. Palmide announces her conversion to Christianity and is hailed by Felicia as a sister and embraced by Adriano; they pray in a quartet with Armando. This goads Aladino to fury, and he despatches all the Christians back inside (quintet and chorus).

The prison scene begins with another prayer and a Hymn of Death led by Adriano, after which the Christians break their swords (it is not clear why they still have them). Armando says farewell to Palmide and his son. At this point Osmino and the Emirs take control. In a double male chorus they whisper to the knights, *sotto voce staccato, con mistero*, that all will be well; the knights reply *sotto voce e staccatissimo, con sorpresa*—as well they might. The two parties march out conspiring, and in very short order everything is sorted out to produce the statutory happy end—but not before Armando has saved Aladino from Osmino, Adriano has ordered his knights to defend the betrayed Sultan, Armando has declared himself once more Aladino's prisoner, and Osmino (whose revolt saved everyone's bacon) has been unceremoniously put to the sword. (Meyerbeer made many changes for revivals, and some versions may not agree with the above synopsis.)

Much of this reads like pure Scribe—the capitalization of religion as a stage gambit, massive confrontations brought about by the flimsiest motivation, prominent use of the chorus (all male, but often divided into four parts and two nations), and the absurdly quixotic behaviour of the central characters. Armando, a Crusader Pinkerton, cuts a contemptible figure throughout; Aladino with his alternate imprisonment and release of the Christians is a singularly inept Sultan. The two long-suffering heroines, wronged by the same man, and the mute child threatened with violence on stage are conventional Romantic tear-jerkers. Meyerbeer makes no serious attempt at characterization; he plays each scene for all it is worth and passes on to the next. Everything is pushed to extremes—in dramatic posture, vocal compass and sheer volume of sound. This is the Rossini of *Semiramide* yoked to a high-pressure German engine. The vocal writing is of extreme virtuosity, especially that of Armando (one of the last great parts written for a castrato—Velluti, who sang it in London in 1825) and Adriano, a freak tenor whose C major *Allegro marziale* entrance aria, with a compass of two octaves and a fifth (G to d″) and the orchestra competing against a stage band, verges on unintended parody. The ornaments and cadenzas, unlike Rossini's and Donizetti's at their best, are applied rather than organic and therefore never expressive. Like Le Sueur in France Meyerbeer plasters the voice parts with hortatory instructions designed to supply what he may have failed to convey in the music: *con impeto doloroso* and similar phrases in the first chorus, *soffocato* and *con trasportata della disperazione* in the Act I love duet, *con amara ironia* in the first scene for Armando and Adriano. He abuses the *vibrato* effect said to have been introduced by Rubini, asking for it repeatedly, and sometimes for *molto vibrato* (even in chorus parts) and *vibratissimo*. Armando at one point has *sospiro vibrato* over a fermata.

In style the music combines the attributes of Janus and a weathercock. It faces several directions, often in the same piece: back beyond Rossini to Mozart, sideways (or northwards) to Weber, forward to the pulsating energy of early Verdi. The prominence given to the castrato is incongruous, yet symptomatic. Even national influences do not derive from the same period; archaic Mozartian formulae jostle harmonic frissons derived from *Der Freischütz*. Meyerbeer possessed Puccini's knack of picking up the latest tricks, as well as his tendency to aim too low. The immensely spectacular first finale begins with echoes of Mozart, including 'Il mio tesoro'. The round (headed *Canone*) lacks the melodic inspiration of its Rossinian models, but is partly redeemed by an attractive instrumental texture with prominent flutes. The big double chorus with its brass fanfares and two stage bands, equipped with a powerful Turkish battery, reflects Spontini's *Fernand Cortez*, perhaps by way of *Semiramide*. Again Meyerbeer abjures the symmetry of Rossini's finales (the key scheme is E flat—G major and minor—A flat—C—F minor and major), but he does his best to work action into the music.

Despite extravagances the orchestration is one of the opera's stronger features. The free use of solo instruments, especially the woodwind, had been anticipated by Mayr and Rossini, not to mention Mozart; but Meyerbeer's handling is often fresh and varied, for example in the clarinet solos of Palmide's cavatina and her duet with Armando in Act I and the rich accompaniment of Felicia's rondo at the beginning of Act II.

Even the early German operas contain interesting experiments in orchestral sonority, perhaps inspired by Vogler; this was a sphere in which Meyerbeer was always a pioneer, as Berlioz recognized by many citations in his *Traité de l'instrumentation*. Harmonically too the score of *Il crociato* is enterprising for its day; here we are reminded of Weber rather than Rossini. The modulations are well prepared and often strikingly dramatic. The weaknesses are melodic and rhythmic (the ease with which the elements can be separated is itself significant). The tunes, with a few exceptions (the beautiful trio for Armando and the two women in the garden is the most conspicuous—though at the end Meyerbeer all but throws away his advantage in a vacuous multiple cadenza), tend to be short-breathed, derivative and commonplace, the rhythms in the quicker movements to fall into a galumphing banality suggestive of a circus elephant. The occasional attempts to galvanize them—for example the heavy emphasis on the third quaver of each beat in 12/8 time in the Act I chorus of Egyptian priests and Christian knights—merely draw attention to the limitation.

Disappointment arises not from the badness of some of the score but from the startling inconsistency of nearly all of it. There is no fixative to fuse the elements together, no warning of the tumbles from the potentially sublime to the patently ridiculous. Many happy ideas are either ill executed or let down by some disastrous consequent. The opening *Pantomima ed introduzione*, in which Christian slaves labour at the fortifications under the lashes of their overseers and lament the loss of wives, children and country, is an interesting and dramatic idea, well calculated to launch the opera, but after the Weberish chromaticism of the orchestral introduction it lapses into triviality; the conception is stronger than the invention. The Act II quintet in which the Christians are sent back to prison ends with a section (Allegro moderato 2/4 E major) almost worthy of Verdi both in its melody, introduced by each voice in turn, and its contrapuntally and harmonically arresting development, but dissolves into trashy coloratura in the coda.

Meyerbeer seems to have invented that special brand of conspiracy music, evolved from the *buffo* ensemble but treated with a straight face, that Sullivan parodied so hilariously in *The Pirates of Penzance*. There are two sterling specimens in *Il crociato*, the four-part chorus of Egyptian conspirators near the beginning of Act II and the double chorus of Emirs and knights towards the end. The former begins impressively with drums alone and much harmonic suspense, including a splendid plunge from E flat to G flat followed by a gradual and well-managed return, but the entire effect is destroyed when the voices enter with an absurdly jaunty tune. Here, and in the double chorus with its comic flourishes between the vocal phrases, a posse of policemen seems to emerge from the wings.

The finest music in the opera occurs in the prison scene. The long orchestral introduction and Adriano's arioso conjure up the grim atmosphere most impressively; the sudden chord of A flat after C major at the mention of death is a thrilling moment. The F minor Hymn of Death, with harp accompaniment and longer than usual phrases, sustains the tension, and the F major section at the end, again faintly Verdian, would be a not unworthy companion to the famous prayers in *Mosé* and *Nabucco* but for the otiose scales and cadenzas.

There are enough flashes of imagination to suggest that a potential operatic genius was lost in Meyerbeer. But tantalizing lapses of taste were characteristic of his whole career. He was to achieve—had already achieved in fair measure—an easily recognizable manner, but never a coherent style. In a few later scenes—the blessing of the daggers and the love duet in Act IV of *Les Huguenots*, the coronation scene in *Le Prophète*, the finales of Acts II, IV and V and the opening of Act III of *L'Africaine*—he was to surpass anything in *Il crociato*. But he never rid himself of its faults. He never outgrew the short square melodic phrases (Wagner had a similar weakness to overcome), the Rossinian thumps, the tendency to spoil an eloquent vocal movement with extraneous flummery, the debasement of religion and politics to the level of stage carpentry (so unlike their treatment by Verdi or Musorgsky), above all the subordination of character to intrigue and dramatic emotion to hollow rhetoric.

The explanation lies in his character. He was constitutionally a timid man, afraid of failure, afraid of his public (whom he attempted to bribe, both by giving them what he knew they liked and, in his Paris days, more literally by lavish payments to the claque and other influential persons), afraid of trusting his own real gifts, afraid to let go of the past and advance into the unknown. Rossini too had a touch of this; it is the most likely explanation of his early retirement from the theatre. Meyerbeer's insecurity was more basic. It made him afraid to be sincere. He mortgaged his future fame to enjoy the plaudits of contemporaries. By no means a negligible composer, he remained a hopelessly flawed one —and the central flaw has exposed itself to posterity in the most damning form, as a want of artistic integrity.

His arrival in Paris in 1825, to supervise a production of *Il crociato*, did not elicit anything new. One of the most enjoyable features of his French operas, the gift for ballet music and attractive diversions, is adumbrated in the Chorus of Disembarcation in Act I of *Il crociato*, as the ship carrying the Christian embassy is wafted by gentle breezes down the Nile. Besides the task of mastering French declamation, Paris merely gave him a larger theatre of operations—literally and figuratively, for it was still the Mecca of opera composers. And it introduced him to a librettist, Scribe, whose stock-broker attitude to theatrical enterprise coincided all too precisely with his own. Scribe's vast cenotaphs were to chill the bones of Donizetti and Verdi; they must have appeared to Meyerbeer the perfect habitation for his muse.

REFERENCE

1 There are several versions of the opera, as of so many others at this period (including *Il crociato in Egitto*), all produced within a few years and published without date. The one described here appears to be a Paris arrangement made in 1826, expanded from two to three acts with extra music borrowed from *Emma di Resburgo*. Romani should not be held responsible for every extravagance, though the essentials of the plot and the characters remain; the music all dates from Meyerbeer's Italian years.

CHELARD'S 'PALLADIUM DES ARTISTES':
a project for a music periodical

RICHARD MACNUTT

On October 1 1829 the French composer Hippolyte Chélard
drafted a letter[1] to an un-named correspondent who was
evidently canvassing views on the founding of a new music
periodical. This must have been intended either as a rival or
complement to the *Revue musicale*, which had been launched
by Fétis in February 1827. Chélard, honoured to have been
consulted, hastens to add his remarks to all the 'excellent
advice that will already have been given'. Eleven foolscap
pages and some 3,500 words later the addressee—if the letter
was ever sent—may well have regretted having made the
approach; but he certainly had in fullest detail a recipe for a
somewhat novel form of periodical, and we ourselves can
glimpse through its pages the frustrations experienced by a
talented but unappreciated composer—'a true artist', Berlioz[2]
later called him—who was trying to make his way in the
establishment-ridden musical life of Paris.

Chélard was forty when he wrote this letter. Born in Paris
in 1789, the son of a clarinettist at the Opéra, his musical
education had followed the normal pattern. In 1800 he took
his first lessons in solfège from the sixteen-year-old Fétis and
in 1803 was admitted to Rodolphe Kreutzer's violin class at
the Paris Conservatoire, where he subsequently also studied
composition with Gossec. In 1811 he won the Prix de Rome
and went to Italy, studying with Baini and Zingarelli, and
also with Paisiello who persuaded the Teatro dei Fiorentini
in Naples to mount his comic opera *La casa da vendere* in
1815. The production was a success and Chélard must have
been full of optimism when he returned to Paris, especially
when the Théâtre Favart agreed to stage the opera. But it

failed, even with Manuel García and Cinti-Damoreau in the cast, and Chélard was obliged to spend the following ten years leading a humdrum existence as a teacher and orchestral violinist.

A composer in early nineteenth-century Paris could best achieve wide popularity by writing agreeable salon music or producing successful stage works. Chélard evidently saw himself as an opera composer, and one can easily appreciate his sense of frustration at finding his work totally neglected after such a propitious start to his career. Eventually his opera *Macbeth*, to a libretto by Rouget de Lisle and Auguste Hix, was accepted by the Opéra and produced there in June 1827 with a cast that included Cinti-Damoreau, Adolphe Nourrit and Dérivis, but once again his hopes were cruelly dashed: the piece was withdrawn after only five performances and was never revived in Paris.

Fétis himself wrote a long review of the première in the *Revue musicale*[3] and Chélard can hardly have complained that it was unsympathetic or unfair. After referring to severe weaknesses in the construction of the libretto, Fétis turns to the composer, lamenting the French system which allows a promising musician to 'languish in the obscurity of an orchestra' for ten years without finding any opportunity to work in the theatre, to have his music performed or to give any proof of his abilities. Now, with no experience or chance to learn from his mistakes in the course of composing smaller pieces, Chélard has to 'make his début with an immense work in our leading opera house. . . . If he has surmounted only some of the obstacles, we must take into account the good things he has done and postpone final judgment until he has an opportunity to profit from the observations that he will have made on his first work.' Fétis goes on to criticize adversely several specific and general aspects of both the opera and the performance, but concludes by praising Chélard's dramatic sense and orchestration and by stressing his genuine talent.

After the failure of *Macbeth* Chélard's disenchantment with musical life in Paris led him to look for opportunities abroad, and from August 1828, when a revised version of *Macbeth* was produced in Munich, Germany was gradually to become the centre of his operations. He did, however, make one last attempt to establish a foothold in his native city. At the time of writing his long letter about the proposed periodical, in October 1829, he must have been making the final preparations for the staging of *La table et le logement* at the Opéra-Comique, where it was to be given two months later, on December 24.

Against this background it is no surprise to find Chélard at the beginning of his letter pointing out that, having himself encountered 'every kind of vicissitude and obstacle', he considers that he has a fairly accurate idea of what is required from the new periodical. 'A specialised periodical and several *impeccably* edited newspaper columns devoted to the same topic already exist. . . . For a new undertaking of this kind to have any hope of success, it must have a purpose of undeniable importance and be original and striking in appearance; without this it will be merely the vehicle for a pointless attempt at competition. . .'

Chélard's main complaint about existing writing on music is that it takes no account of the opinions of practising artists —the

> 'composers and performers who submit their work or their talent to the judgment of the public. If in fact we examine articles devoted to music we find that they are in general written by persons in society—writers endowed with wit and taste, no doubt, but for the most part lacking real knowledge of an art which is for them no

more than a diversion but upon which their influence is nonetheless great. A few enlightened enthusiasts and several very competent artists, struck by this unsatisfactory state of affairs, have tried to lessen its effects and have brought to publications the salutary assistance of their zeal and knowledge. But owing to their disproportionally small number, their writings appear, among so many competing interests, to be merely the expression of their personal views or, at most, those of a small section of public opinion. Thus most practising artists are excluded from those important discussions of which they are the prime subject and which concern their closest interests.'

He points out that, although it is the business of writers to interpret public reaction and to criticize musical works, the fact that composers have no means of defending themselves is unjust and

'gives rise to a number of abuses which corrupt criticism and hinder or misdirect the progress of the art. . . . The main basis of this unfortunate state of affairs lies, in my view, in the shortage of money and time which this class of persons, impecunious and almost fully occupied in work essential to their subsistence, cannot remedy. Furthermore, fully absorbed as they are in specialized studies of very long duration, they have little time for science or literature and, intimidated by the idea of writing in public, they sentence themselves to silence or give vent in private to sometimes unjust, often exaggerated, and always useless complaints that are motivated by despondency or personal dissatisfaction rather than by general considerations of an elevated nature.'

Chélard considers that the time has arrived when rivalries between differing genres, conflicts of principle, the wider dissemination of music and 'a certain restlessness which seems to portend one of those epochal crises called *revolution*' are demanding a condition in which all types of talent can compete on an equal footing. This 'could become the subject of an enterprise which is both noble and fruitful; no more worthy assignment can ever have been proposed to a financial sponsor! I will go further: the principle the results of which I am about to enlarge upon and which I am confining for the present to music will, I doubt not, extend to the other arts and one day restore to periodical-writing the purity, philanthropy and catholicity without which it is merely an offensive weapon placed in the hands of the few to the detriment of the many.'

Having outlined what he regards as the basic purpose of the new periodical, Chélard proceeds to draft a sixteen-point plan for its realization, following it with an elucidation of his points, a summary of the merits of the scheme and a supplementary list of twenty-three compulsory regulations for the contributors and publisher of the *Palladium des artistes*—the name he has chosen for the journal. It is not necessary to give here all the details of the synopsis, for many of the points are repeated between the two numbered lists and several are concerned with very minor administrative matters. The essential features are described below.

First, Chélard concerns himself with the contributors, who must be practising artists (including academics and writers) and may be of any nationality. All articles must be signed, so that petty intrigue, denigration and exaggeration may be replaced by frankness, emulation and moderation; and no contributor will be paid, so that articles may be above any suspicion of venality. Any artist may announce, describe, review, criticize or defend his own work or his own talent—though never those of others.

> 'By forbidding criticism of the work of others I shut the
> door on those passionate conflicts which bring artists
> into disrepute and oblige a lone figure to fight against
> innumerable attackers. . . . It is true that criticism will
> be deprived of its lively but ill-intentioned scrutiny of
> the faults of works which their authors will probably
> treat with rather suspect and sometimes tedious moder-
> ation; but it will be amply recompensed for this by the
> feast of new fare that I will offer it. It will be active in
> just retaliation against judgments expressed, reviews,
> the actions of authorities, and the measures and systems
> of administrations; it will laugh at pretentious and
> powerful ignorance, will unmask intrigues, and will
> fight prejudice, error and caprice; and finally, as a free
> and enlightened opposition, it will in its turn bring the
> public before the judgment of artists and connoisseurs.
> Praise be to God, sir: I have no fear that criticism,
> provided with a feast of this kind, will faint with hunger
> in this journal.

'Discussions of all kinds concerning history, science,
administration, doctrine and general subjects are permitted,
bringing attack and defence together either in the same
number or in subsequent numbers. . . .' By this method
Chélard hopes both to educate the public and, by drawing
together artists whose isolation narrows their point of view,
to establish certain fundamental principles.

The publisher may not interfere in editorial matters, but
he will have the right to suppress material in whole or in part
when the laws of the press are contravened or personal
remarks made. Thus Chélard intends to release writing
'from influences desirous of imposing constraints upon it'.

Evidently Chélard felt in some way uncomfortable about the impracticability of his scheme, for he provides, rather surprisingly, for an appendix to each number which will not be subject to the general rules and regulations. It will contain, apart from commercial advertisements, reports and criticism by writers other than the interested parties. These are to be chosen by the publisher, but Chélard insists further that all articles be signed and defence allowed in the following number—a procedure he would like to see adopted by all journals. The remainder of Chélard's points relate to the organization of the journal. He refers briefly to the financial sponsor, who alone will be entitled to any profits; to the jury, composed of French and foreign artists, who will have the task of settling any disputes that may arise; to the amount of space to be allocated to various features; and to the institution of two annual general meetings ('philharmoniques').

Drawing towards the close of his letter, Chélard promises that the *Palladium des artistes* 'will occupy an area different from that of other journals and will complement their methods, without containing anything liable to displease them; on the contrary, I see only too well that, uncharitable as they are, it will sometimes cause them amusement. It is, however, up to artists to be careful to remain within the confines of truth, justice, modesty and good taste, on pain of public ridicule and censure.'

He encourages the publisher by providing a list of some thirty probable contributors—including Cherubini, Rossini, Spontini, Spohr, Hummel, Meyerbeer, Le Sueur, Boieldieu and Auber among the composers, and Choron, Fétis, Baini, Rinck and Rochlitz among the scholars. 'Appeal to these leading personalities and they will respond with generous haste!', he confidently exclaims.

There are of course bound to be undesirable features, he admits:

'tiresome nonentities, petty vanities and gossip will throw their vexatious weight into the balance! But is this not the fate of all institutions?. . . Fear of abuse must not prevent one from taking action. . . . Rest assured, sir: an enterprise of this kind dedicated to the interest and the instruction of all will have a success with the public equal to the influence that it will exert on the progress of the art and on the future and the character of artists.'

It is a zealous appeal, growing in enthusiasm as the letter advances. But if the letter was read at all the appeal evidently fell upon deaf ears, and by the time that the next new French music periodical appeared in 1833 (Heugel's *Le Ménestrel*, which was not of course conceived along Chélard's lines), Chélard himself had abandoned Paris. His new opera, *La table et le logement*, failed at the Opéra-Comique in December 1829. It was again given a long review in the *Revue musicale*[4] but this time the tone was utterly discouraging. 'If it can scarcely be imagined that the director of a theatre should ever have received [a libretto] of such silliness, still less can it be that a musician, a man of experience and good sense, should have considered setting it to music.' Every feature of the work is thereupon attacked, though the writer (anonymous, ironically, but certainly Fétis himself) regrets deeply that he is obliged to be so severe on an artist whose talent and person he much respects.

This fresh disappointment, together with the failure (coincident with the July Revolution of 1830) of the small music-publishing business that he had started in the early 1820s, finally forced Chélard to turn towards Germany, where he had already been encouraged by the success of his *Macbeth* in 1828. From this point his career at last began to flourish. *Macbeth* was given occasional revivals, including a production in London in 1832. Another opera, *Mitternacht* (written for but not produced in Paris), was given at Munich in 1831. *La table et le logement* was revised and produced as *Der Student* in Germany and, with Malibran, as *The students of Jena* at Drury Lane in 1833; and *Der Hermannsschlacht*, his most important work, was given successfully in various German theatres from 1835 onwards. In 1840 he was appointed Kapellmeister at Weimar, holding the post for twelve years. Thereafter he spent two years in Paris before returning in 1854 to Weimar, where he remained until his death in 1861.

REFERENCES

1 The autograph, unsigned, is in the possession of the writer of this contribution.
2 In his *Mémoires* Chapter 51, Letter 3.
3 i 1827, 520-6.
4 vi 1830, 543-9.

MUSICAL PERIODICALS IN 'BOURGEOIS RUSSIA'

GERALD ABRAHAM

The date 1861 is a milestone in the cultural as well as the political history of Russia. As Lenin wrote, the emancipation of the serfs marked 'the beginning of the new bourgeois Russia'. And the intellectual climate of the new Russia affected attitudes to music like everything else; the musical *intelligentsiya*—it is a Russian word—were more serious than the amateur singers and pianists of earlier generations. The Russian Musical Society was already two years old and in 1862 two schools of music were opened in St Petersburg—the official Conservatoire and the Balakirev-Lomakin Free School of Music. The Moscow Conservatoire was founded in 1866. Up to then Russian 'musical periodicals' had consisted mainly of 'almanacs', collections of piano music and songs which met the demand for salon music of various grades of difficulty and sometimes offered music of more substance. The most important and longest lived, for it survived in one form or another until the very eve of the revolution, was the *Nuvellist*, a publication with an interesting, and at some periods not undistinguished, history.

It was founded in 1840 with a French title, *Nouvelliste*, by a Petersburg publisher, K F Golts (presumably Holz) but was taken over in 1842 by Matvey (Moritz) Bernard who soon russified the title and introduced much more Russian music, including songs and piano pieces by Glinka, indeed a good proportion of worthwhile music, both Russian and foreign (unprotected by copyright), as well as ephemera. He commissioned Liszt to write for the *Nuvellist* his well-known transcription of Alyab'ev's song 'The Nightingale' and the practice of commissioning from distinguished composers was continued after his death by his brother, who commissioned Chaykovsky's *Seasons*, op37a, for piano. When the *Nuvellist* had passed from the Bernard family a later owner, Baron Wrangel (Vrangel'), at once invited Balakirev to make his delightful and too little known four-hand arrangements of thirty Russian folk-songs. During part of its existence, however, the *Nuvellist* did not consist solely of music. In 1844 Bernard provided a 'literary supplement' containing

> news of Russian, Italian, and German operas and concerts given in St. Petersburg and Moscow, news of happenings in the field of music, critical notices of new operas and ballets given in the chief cities of Europe; biographies of eminent musicians; announcements of new musical compositions published in Russia and abroad, descriptions of newly invented instruments, correspondence, etc.

The level was not very high. Most of the contents—anecdotes, obituaries and so on—were lifted from Western magazines and newspapers; they ranged from Schumann's *Musikalische Haus-und Lebensregeln* to accounts of happenings not only in the capitals but in Russian provincial cities. Bernard contributed his 'recollections of an old musician' to nos. 7, 10 and 12 in 1847. All this did not amount to very much, yet in the forties and the first half of the fifties the literary supplements to the *Nuvellist* were, unless we reckon the half-foreign *Muzïkalny svet* [1847-78], 'the only specifically musical journal in Russia'.[1] However the supplements came to an end in 1875, though in 1878 an attempt was made to replace them with a 'musico-theatrical gazette' or 'review' conducted by the composer Mikhail Ivanov, which reported the musical life of St Petersburg and specialized in celebratory and obituary articles. For instance, in 1881 it characteristically 'borrowed' from the *Moskovskiya vedomosti* Chaykovsky's article on 'The last days in the life of N G Rubinstein'.

In 1856 a more serious periodical was launched by the publisher Stellovsky—the *Muzïkal'ny i teatral'ny vestnik* which changed its name two years later to *Teatral'ny i muzïkal'ny vestnik* and collapsed in 1860. (The original title was confusingly revived in the 1880s.) The most important contributor was Serov, not yet known as a composer, who provided not only such substantial criticism as his study of Dargomïzhsky's *Rusalka*, which ran through ten numbers of its first year[2], but also a series of 'Letters from abroad' telling of his visit to Liszt at Weimar and his meetings with Berlioz and Meyerbeer at Baden-Baden, and a 'Course of musical technique' 'not for professionals but for music-lovers. . . . not to teach them how to compose or perform, but how to listen to music with understanding. . . to give them the means of enjoying the art better and judging it with sense', all very useful for the 'new bourgeois Russia'.

In 1867 Serov with his wife started a 'critical gazette' of his own, *Muzïka i teatr*, proclaiming that criticism 'must above all be capable of demonstration based on historical data'. But only seventeen numbers appeared and Serov found a new platform—other than the general press—in another short-lived periodical *Muzïkal'ny sezon* (1869-71) to which he contributed three path-opening articles on 'Russian folk-song as a subject for scientific study'.

The *Sezon* was edited by the celebrated—or notorious—critic Aleksandr Sergeevich Famintsïn who was also enlisted in the less ephemeral *Muzïkal'ny listok* which succeeded it. The *Listok* was the brain-child of Vasily Vasil'evich Bessel', who had founded his famous publishing house in 1869. Bessel' was a remarkable man, a viola-player, one of the first graduates of the new Petersburg Conservatoire, and a very enterprising publisher, the first in Russia to bring out full orchestral scores. The image reflected in the letters and memoirs of composers whom he afterwards lost to his rivals does him much less than justice, particularly when one considers their expensive habit of making wholesale revisions of their already published scores and his compliance with their wishes. The *Listok* (the word means 'leaflet'), a 'weekly musical gazette', announced itself as 'published under the editorship of the free artist[3] V Bessel'' but he relied to some extent on a group of musicians including Hermann Laroche (Larosh), Famintsïn and a couple of Serov's protégés. They were not markedly friendly to the composers of the 'mighty handful' whose works were handled at the time by Bessel', but the publisher was a strong character and the editorial statement of intent prefixed to the first number of the *Listok* (September 3 1872) bears his personal stamp. After remarking that in Russia 'we have not a single specifically musical journal', he acknowledges that in launching a new one 'our task is admittedly not easy; the failure of all previous musical journals published among us up to now has not been forgotten', and then announces, among other parts of his programme, his aim to introduce 'among the waverings of musical judgments and the changes of public taste ideas of sound standards, carefully separating the good from the bad in all productions and with all composers'.

The first number was modest enough, sixteen pages in small format, of which five were given over to advertisements—four of the publications of the Leipzig firm of Forberg, one of works by Dargomïzhsky published by Bessel'. The only review, signed A∗∗∗, was also of a Bessel' publication, the *Six songs* Op 7 by Cui (Kyui), but was by no means a mere puff. The second number contained the first instalment of a long article by Laroche on 'The historical method of teaching the theory of music'. Later numbers of the first year included substantial reviews of more Bessel' publications.

Laroche wrote on Rubinstein's 'musical pictures' *Ivan the Terrible* and *Don Quixote*, 'V.V.' (Bessel' himself) on the first production of Rimsky-Korsakov's *Maid of Pskov* and the famous production of three scenes from *Boris Godunov*. They are fair enough and Famintsïn was allowed to handle the 'complete' *Boris* and its first performance very roughly in the issues of February 3 and 10 1874. By then Bessel''s little weekly was carrying substantial articles, reviews and concert criticisms, as well as musical news from home and abroad; it was a real milestone in the history of the Russian musical periodical. All the same, it lasted only until May 1877. Later Bessel' tried again with another weekly, *Muzïkal'noe obozrenie*. It was edited by Cui, ran from September 1885 to December 1888 and had a monthly musical supplement of piano pieces and songs by Rubinstein, Borodin, Rimsky-Korsakov, Chaykovsky and such younger men as Lyadov and Glazunov. They failed to save it. It seemed that no Russian musical periodical—and there were others during the 1880s—could establish a permanent footing.

The first to do so, if we except the *Ezhegodnik Imperator-skikh Teatrov* (Year-book of the Imperial Theatres), was the *Russkaya muzïkal'naya gazeta* published and edited by Nikolay Findeisen (Findeyzen) initially in 1894 as a monthly, from 1899 as a weekly. Both were products of the 1890s; the first *Ezhegodnik* appeared in 1892, two years before the *Gazeta*. Both were casualties of the revolution, although the *Gazeta* lingered on till 1918. Otherwise they had nothing in common. The *Gazeta* was a straightforward 'musical periodical'—a very good one—and very much a matter of private enterprise[4], the *Ezhegodnik* was an official publication, at first largely statistical and always concerned not only with the State opera-houses but with the other Imperial theatres in St Petersburg and Moscow. Each issue lists the previous year's productions with dates and other information, and

gives the names of the entire personnel of every theatre
—actors, vocal soloists, chorus members, dancers, conductors,
orchestral players, administrators, librarians, prompters,
backstage staff—with the date of his or her original engage-
ment. And this information is repeated year by year so that
one can, for instance, trace that Karl Karlovich Grimm,
percussion-player in the Petersburg opera orchestra in the
1890-91 season (the first recorded), had been engaged on
January 1 1855—and what happened to him later. Much
more interesting is the 'Review of the activities of the Imperial
stages in the season 1890-91' which gives scene by scene
accounts of the action of every new production—opera, ballet
or play—copiously illustrated by drawings and photographs
of the scenes, singers and actors in the original costumes.
The second year (1893: season 1891-92) had a named editor,
A E Molchanov, who took advantage of the fiftieth anniversary of the original production of *Ruslan and Lyudmila* to
print a 55-page study of the opera by Stasov, plus lists of all
the exponents of each part—and the box-office takings—at
every performance since 1842. (The half-centenaries of
Gogol''s *Marriage* and *Gambler* and the centenary of Fonvizin's
death were celebrated similarly but less generously.)

Thus from the first the *Ezhegodnik* included an important
musical element, and in its fourth year the non-statistical
material overflowed into three supplements, all including
substantial musical articles: Laroche on 'P I Chaykovsky as a
dramatic composer', Mikhail Ivanov on 'The first decade of
the regular Italian theatre in Petersburg in the XIXth century
(1843-1853)', 'My evenings: reminiscences of L I Shestakova'
(Glinka's sister), 'New materials for the biography of M I
Glinka' by Stasov and 'New materials for the biography of A N
Serov' by Findeisen. Such supplements not only continued to
be a constant feature of the *Ezhegodnik*; they proliferated.
In 1913, for instance, there were no fewer than seven.

Long before then there had been a revolution in the *Ezhegodnik*'s format. In 1900 Molchanov was replaced as editor by a brilliant and influential young man, Sergey Dyagilev, who had not long before launched his famous art periodical *Mir iskusstva*. The new editor at once introduced a larger format, new type, and better paper, but otherwise his first number (season 1898-99) was retrograde. Presumably taking over at short notice and having his hands full with *Mir iskusstva*, he printed merely the statistical part of the year-book with no editorial matter whatever. But he made amends the following year with a handsome—and handsomely illustrated—volume, including a section which should have appeared in the previous one and banishing the statistical part to the end. The first of the three supplements has articles on *Les Troyens à Carthage* by Kashkin, 'Glazunov as ballet-composer' by A Koptyaev and 'Concerning *Walküre*, Richard Wagner and Wagnerism' by Laroche. Unfortunately the expense of this production horrified the Court Minister. There was a row, Dyagilev resigned or was dismissed, and his successor, L A Gel'mersen, gradually imposed economies, although there was no return to the pre-Dyagilev format.

When Findeisen founded his *Russkaya muzïkal'naya gazeta* he was twenty-six, two years younger than Dyagilev when he took over the *Ezhegodnik*. He was a man of outstanding ability and industry—editor, publisher, biographer, historian—and besides the *Gazeta* he produced during 1903-11 six issues of an occasional publication, *Muzïkal'naya starina*, collections of 'articles and materials for the history of music in Russia'. The *Gazeta* was lively and well illustrated. Attracting plenty of advertisements, it quickly flourished and in its third year, 1896, the monthly issues expanded from forty pages to seventy-six and the next year to 112. The change to weekly publication in 1899 was fully justified and the annual volumes —monthly or weekly—ran to 700 or more pages. Findeisen and his contributors filled them with interesting and valuable material; a great deal of biographical information about Russian musicians, including their letters, was first published in the *Gazeta*; new works were discussed and analyzed. In 1896 Glazunov gave a fairly full account of his and Rimsky-Korsakov's completion of *Prince Igor*, much more reliable than the one he offered in later years. Old treatises were unearthed and discussed at length; in 1897 Vasily Metallov contributed an eighteen-page account of Diletsky's now famous but then unknown *Musikiyskaya grammatika* which he had found in the library of the Synodal College. Foreign composers were not neglected; translations of Wagner's *Kunstwerk der Zukunft* and *Über das Dirigieren* were serialized in 1897 and 1899. Folk-music, ethnomusicology, instruments, church music, harmonic theory, acoustics—the recently published *Populäre Darstellung der Akustik* of Ludwig (not Hugo) Riemann was translated and serialized through fourteen numbers during 1897-98—it is difficult to think of any aspect of music not well represented in the *Gazeta*. As for musical life, concert and opera notices and news from abroad abound. Jubilees, deaths and centenaries were marked by special numbers or a special double number might be 'Dedicated to Contemporary Polish Composers', with facsimiles of autographs by Szymanowski, Różycki, Młynarski and Opieński (September 2-9 1912). And Findeisen and his team had their fun, making merry over the 'literary achievements' of the composer-critic Mikhail Ivanov who was to be accused by a later writer of having 'systematically hounded all the most significant composers, beginning with the Handful and ending with Skryabin'[5]. One of his 'achievements' had been owing to a last-minute change of programme, to pronounce on a Haydn quartet under the impression that it was a quintet by Mozart; he appears to have been addicted to criticism of concerts that had not taken place and artists who had not performed.

In 1896 Findeisen lamented the demise of the Moscow *Artist* which, though not a musical periodical, had always treated music seriously, and greeted with scorn a new German-language publication, the Petersburg *Russlands Musik-Zeitung*. (It collapsed almost immediately.) 'Leaving out of consideration the splendid *Ezhegodnik Imperatorskikh Teatrov*, incomparably rich in appearance and content, the *Russkaya muzïkal'naya gazeta* is now', he claimed, 'the only organ exclusively devoted to music in Russia'. It remained so, with only insignificant and ephemeral rivals, until December 1910, when its uniqueness, though not its supremacy, was challenged by a plucky little weekly, *Muzïka*, brought out in Moscow by another editor-publisher, Vladimir Derzhanovsky. *Muzïka* consisted of only twenty-eight or thirty-two small pages, including advertisements, but Derzhanovsky managed to pack a great many worthwhile things into his limited space. The first few numbers contain a serialized article on 'Contemporary tendencies' (Strauss, Debussy, Skryabin) by Leonid Sabaneev, letters from Rimsky-Korsakov and other composers (including Rimsky-Korsakov's correspondence with Stasov about the history of *Sadko*), a thematic analysis of Skryabin's Fourth Sonata with the relevant text from the 'Poème de l'extase', French original and Russian translation, 'texts for music' by Bal'mont, Bryusov, Bely, Gippius and others. To take only one instance of the *trouvailles* for the student of Russian music in *Muzïka*, the October 5 1913 number has an unpublished passage from *Tsar' Saltan*. The accent was very much on the contemporary and *Muzïka* stood in roughly the same relationship to the *Russkaya muzïkal'naya gazeta* as *The Chesterian* to *The Musical times*. But *Muzïka* was a war casualty of 1916 whereas the *Gazeta* survived the October revolution for several months.

They had recently been joined by a third 'journal of musical art' which eclipsed both of them in format and typography, indeed compared favourably with the *Ezhegodnik*. This was the Petrograd *Muzïkal'ny sovremennik*, edited by Andrey Rimsky-Korsakov, the composer's son, who was co-publisher with Pëtr Suvchinsky. Eight numbers a year were contemplated and duly appeared from September 1915 to April 1917[6], with a satellite two to four times a month. These were quite substantial and equally well produced *Khroniki* of—mostly Petrograd—concert and opera notices, reviews and occasional pages devoted to, for instance, 'Musical vandalisms' (including Albert Coates's performance of *Tsar' Saltan* minus the whole of Act IV, sc 1) or 'Flowers of publishers' eloquence'. During its short life the *Sovremennik* printed source material of the highest importance, notably the Balakirev—Rimsky-Korsakov correspondence which was serialized from the first number and just concluded in the last. It was available nowhere else until its publication in Vol V of Rimsky-Korsakov's 'Literary productions and correspondence' in 1963. Rimsky-Korsakov's correspondence with Lyadov was also first published in the *Sovremennik*. Two double numbers, no 4-5, 1916, devoted to Skryabin (including Yuly Engel's 90-page 'Biographical sketch'), and no 5-6, 1917, to Musorgsky, and the Taneev number, no 8, 1916, are fundamental items in bibliographies of those composers. Vyacheslav Paskhalov's serialized study of 'Chopin and Polish folk-music' probably remains the most authoritative monograph on the subject; it was reprinted in book form in 1949.

Muzïkal'naya sovremennik survived the February revolution but not the October one. After a five-year interval Andrey Rimsky-Korsakov tried to revive it in a *Muzïkal'naya letopis'* published by the Petrograd publishing co-operative 'Mïsl'' in 1922. A second number, which appeared in 1923, actually concluded P N Stolpyansky's lengthy study of 'Music and music-making in old Petersburg' begun in the *Sovremennik*. But the third (1926) was the last. The *Letopis'* never achieved periodical publication and, although its contents were worthy of the *Sovremennik*, its format—which changed with each number—was vastly inferior. It was the only direct link, a slim one, between the pre-revolution and post-revolution periodicals. The revolution drew a firm line at the end of a chapter.

As things began to settle down in 1921 various musical groups with antagonistic aims were formed and periodicals began to proliferate, only to die fairly quickly.[7] Another *Muzïka* was started in Moscow in 1922, proudly claiming to celebrate the fifth anniversary of the October revolution with 'the appearance of the *first* number of the *first* musical journal in the RSFSR' (Russian Socialist Federal Soviet Republic), but it vanished after the fourth number. Even more brief was the life of *K novïm beregam* (Toward new shores). Although sponsored by 'Muzsektor', the music section of the State Publishing House, in 1923, edited by Viktor Belyaev and Vladimir Derzhanovsky of the original *Muzïka*, and well produced, only three numbers appeared. The contributors—'Igor' Glebov' (Boris Asaf'ev) and Leonid Sabaneev among the most prominent—were all champions of genuine contemporary music. But *Muzïkal'naya nov'*, the organ of their foes, the Association of Proletarian Musicians, also published by 'Muzsektor', hardly fared better; its double number 6-7 in 1924 was the last. The Association for Contemporary Music, founded in 1924, had better luck with their little organ *Sovremennaya muzïka*, edited mainly by Belyaev, Derzhanovsky, and Sabaneev. Small in format, not very well produced, and irregular in appearance—six numbers in 1924, four in 1925, four (two of them 'double') in 1926, and so on—it staggered along until 1928 and its thirty-two numbers contain substantial material, particularly analyses of new Russian works with pages of musical examples. But it was not narrowly Russian: the first number carried articles on Hindemith's *Quartet no 1* and *Sonatas* Op 11 as well as a five-page report on the historic Salzburg Festival of Contemporary Music 'from our Vienna correspondent' Paul Pisk.

Like its contemporaries the more eclectic and better produced *Muzïka i revolyutsiya* (1926-29), *Muzïkal'noe obrazovanie* (Musical education) (1925-30) and an annual series of article-collections *De Musica* (1923, 1925-28), it succumbed to the hostility of the 'proletarians' and for several years, indeed until the Union of Soviet Composers launched *Sovetskaya muzïka* in 1933, the intelligent Russian musician or music-lover had to be content with the *soupe maigre* of purely 'proletarian' periodicals. 'Bourgeois Russia' had gone for good.

REFERENCES

1 B Vol'man *Russkie notnïe izdaniya XIX-nachala XX veka* Leningrad 1970, 92.
2 Stellovsky bought the publication rights of the opera only later, in March 1857.
3 'Free artists' were one of the hierarchic categories between the 'nobility' and the serfs; Rubinstein was a 'free artist', Chaykovsky was 'noble'.
4 Findeisen, like Bessel', was his own publisher. But whereas Bessel' was a music-publisher who produced periodicals as a subsidiary activity, the 'Tipografiya N Findeyzena', as it was originally called, existed primarily to print the *Gazeta*, although it did embark on other musical publications, eg translations of Berlioz's *Mémoires* and Gounod's *Mémoires d'un artiste*, and Stasov's *Liszt, Schumann and Berlioz in Russia*.
5 *Khronika zhurnala 'Muzïkal'ny sovremennik'* no 21 1916, 19.
6 The numbering on the wrappers is confusing since the volumes were not numbered; thus no 8, 1916, is followed by no 1, 1916.

7 An extended survey of 'Musical periodicals for 15 years (1917-1932)' by A Steinberg (Shteynberg) appeared in *Sovetskaya muzïka* i, no 2 1933, 132-48, and a chronological list with bibliographical details, *ibid* no 6, 147-58.

ALFRED CORTOT AS COLLECTOR OF MUSIC

ALBI ROSENTHAL

In his recent biography of Alfred Cortot (1877-1962), Bernard Gavoty devotes barely three pages to the famous collection amassed by the great pianist in the course of his life[1], confining himself to a brief list of some authors represented in the music theory section of the library[2], a cursory enumeration of the more notable autograph manuscripts (though omitting, for example, the Liszt Piano Sonata, Cortot's last major acquisition), and a few anecdotes (not all correct). Yet, when the full extent and details of this music collection become known, Cortot's significance as a collector will be seen to rival his stature as one of the great interpreters and teachers of his epoch. Within the confines of a short paper any attempt at listing even the more important books, editions, autograph manuscripts and letters and other musical treasures would be futile. It may, on the other hand be worthwhile to outline the aims and achievements of Cortot as collector and to relate them both to his personality and to trends in music collecting in the first half of the twentieth century.

Alfred Cortot is best known throughout the world for his interpretations of romantic music, for the poetry, the lyricism, the delicacy and the ineffable artistry of his interpretations. His study editions of Chopin, Schumann and others, however, reveal his painstaking, indeed pedantic attention to detail, and his strict, methodical approach to every aspect of music. This lesser known side of his personality is also reflected in the exemplary organization and cataloguing of his vast collection (including his working editions, books and scores). Indeed, he once said that, had he not been pressed by his parents to become a musician ('for which I had neither preference nor aptitude'), he would have loved to become an apothecary or a librarian.

As a boy, Alfred Cortot was an avid reader[3]. However, the first episode to give evidence of his collecting instincts and vocation occurred after his first piano recital in Berlin, when he was in his early twenties. Against the advice of his teacher Louis Diémer he read what the critics wrote in the newspapers on the following day and decided to express personally his gratitude to the most enthusiastic among them, Herr Max Springer, who was also director of the Musik-abteilung of the Preussische Staatsbibliothek at the time. He was warmly received at the Library and, on being en-couraged to name any manuscript he would most like to see, he asked for that of the Ninth Symphony. It was placed before him and he spent an hour or two studying every page. While turning over a particular leaf, he noted that a tiny piece of a blank corner was hanging loosely by a bare thread, almost falling off. He turned the leaf back and forth, found himself unobserved, quickly plucked the minute paper triangle, a fraction of an inch long, from its tenuous moorings with a deft movement of his right hand, and hid it in his note-book. When asked, later in life, which piece in his collection he treasured most, Cortot used to open a little gold pendant hanging from his watch chain: 'le voilà–un morceau de la Neuvième Simphonie!'. It accompanied him throughout his life.

While this anecdote may not serve as an example to be re-commended for starting a collection, it throws light on Cortot's personality. The choice of the Ninth Symphony would be that of a young musician deeply involved in Beethoven's piano works at the time[4] and also of a conductor who had received his apprenticeship as repetiteur at Bayreuth and who had just conducted the first performance of *Götterdämmerung* in France. The rapt enthusiasm, the revelation at handling the score written by the composer himself, and the desire, born at that moment, to possess a tangible, if in this case microscopic witness of the process of artistic creation are in direct relation to the mainsprings of Cortot's qualities as an artist.

It was Henry Prunières (1886-1942), the distinguished French music historian, who not only awakened in Cortot the latent passion for systematic collecting by introducing him to his own remarkable private library, but also provided him with a comprehensive framework of classification in which every book, manuscript or other document would find its organic place within the collection as soon as it was acquired.[5] The catalogue of Cortot's library was divided into the following categories:

Théorie musicale (TM)
Esthétique musicale (EM) (including a special section on the 'Querelle des Bouffons' controversy)
Histoire de musique (HM)
Méthodes (MET)
Histoire des instruments (HI)
Bibliographie musicale (BIB)
Dictionnaires de musique (DIC)
Catalogues (CAT) Subsections: Auteurs, (Catals. thématiques), Bibliothèques, Expositions, Editeurs, Libraires, Ventes.
Périodiques musicaux (PM)
Biographie musicale (BM)
Mémoires & correspondances (MC)
Ouvrages relatifs à la musique (ORM)
Notation musicale (NOT)

Musique instrumentale antérieure à 1800 (MIA)
Musique vocale religieuse (MVR)
Liturgie (LIT)
Musique vocale profane (MVP)
Folklore (FOL)
Musique dramatique (MD)
Danse—chorégraphie (D)

Interprétation (INT)
Facsimilés (FACS)
Iconographie (ICON)

MSS autographes
Lettres autographes

Musique instrumentale postérieure à 1800
Premières éditions de Mozart, Beethoven, Schubert,
    Liszt, Chopin, &c.
Partitions d'orchestre
Matériel d'orchestre
Partitions de poche
Éditions de travail

Cortot wrote a 'fiche', of the usual 6 x 4 inch size, for every item in his library, from the plainest working edition to the choicest rarity. On it he entered the full bibliographical particulars, as well as the source, date and price of purchase, the classification symbol and shelfmark. The two latter were also entered in each book or edition, next to his bookplate, and each item was marked with a small green stamp with his monogram. Every piece could thus be located at once by anyone, particularly by his devoted chauffeur and factotum Pierre Malézieux, on any of the shelves on the four floors of his splendid villa at 5, rue de Jaman in Lausanne. The entire vast 'fichier' is preserved and remains after the removal and dispersal of the collection[6] as a monumental record of a lifetime of intensive collecting.

The classification system of a private collection embracing every aspect of music does not differ greatly from that of a major public library. Both are influenced and shaped by systems applied to musicology as a whole, as defined, for instance, by Friedrich Chrysander, Hugo Riemann, or more fully by Guido Adler (cf *Vierteljahrsschrift für Musikwissenschaft*, i, 1885, and his *Methode der Musikgeschichte*, 1919). The guidelines followed by the great music collectors of the first half of the twentieth century like Paul Hirsch, Werner Wolffheim, Henry Prunières and Alfred Cortot reflect the ideas, principles and systems formulated by the above-named scholars. The collections differ from those amassed in the eighteenth and nineteenth centuries inasmuch as they reveal their creators' awareness of the developments and aims of music scholarship, including music bibliography. Whereas a Burney, Hawkins or other eighteenth-century collector[7] tried to gather musical documents of earlier centuries rather like an explorer bringing home specimens of hitherto unknown and partly still mysterious species from newly found territories, the twentieth-century collectors were able to build on the massive foundation of nineteenth and early twentieth-century musical scholarship. Werner Wolffheim and Paul Hirsch may be regarded as being in the mainstream of German and Austrian 'Musikwissenschaft', Prunières and, through his influence, Cortot leaning more toward systems of French 'musicologie', combining them with French bibliophile taste and aspirations. Cortot, the only professional musician among these collectors—most music collectors are musicians manqués and most musicians choose their collecting hobbies from other fields—added further dimensions by supplementing his library with valuable collections of musicians' portraits, coins and medals, as well as postage stamps with musical associations. For Cortot, collecting was a quest for a documentary 'Gesamtkunstwerk', in which every aspect of music had its legitimate place.

In his teaching, Cortot asked his pupils to submit papers embodying their thoughts and literary or poetic associations with the sonata or other piece they had prepared for him. Historical aspects, literary and philosophical parallels, and other not strictly musical considerations were regarded by him as necessary adjuncts to musical analysis and performance. Both the music of the great masters of the past and that of the contemporaries he pioneered was always seen by him in the context of tradition, of which his library was a visible expression.

Cortot, author of numerous articles and several books, never wrote about his library and collections. Collecting was not an object of theorizing or self-glorification for him, but a passionate pursuit and a vital background to his art as interpreter. He led the nomadic existence typical of internationally celebrated musicians, giving upwards of seven thousand public concerts in numerous countries, including North and South America and Japan. Wherever he stopped he visited the local book and antique shops, and particularly in the smaller European provincial centres, where his tours took him regularly, 'les antiquaires' greeted him with items of musical interest they had kept aside for him. In the larger centres like Paris, London, Brussels, Amsterdam, Berlin, Munich, Florence, Vienna and many others, all the major firms, particularly those dealing exclusively or partly in music books and manuscripts treated him as a most-favoured client, and he often underlined his indebtedness to them. Thus the firms of Reeves, Maggs and Quaritch in England, Leo Liepmannssohn (later Otto Haas, London) and Martin Breslauer in Berlin, Jacques and Ludwig Rosenthal in Munich, the Olschkis in Florence and Rome, Hiersemann in Leipzig, Hinterberger in Vienna and the Paris firms of Legouix, Georges Heilbrun, Arthur Rau and many others figure prominently as suppliers in the card index. He was represented at the auctions of Leo Liepmannssohn, Henrici, Stargardt, Karl & Faber, Hoepli, Sotheby, Christie and others by local dealers.

Like every true collector, Cortot had a fund of stories of lucky finds and purchases. On opening the door of a little antique shop in Pisa, the chime of the bell, dangling from a string, appeared to him to have an unusual sound. On closer inspection it turned out to be one of the rarest and finest portrait medallions of Paganini, cast in solid bronze in the 1830s. He was allowed to acquire it in exchange for a new bell. One of the coincidences bordering on the miraculous which he used to talk about again and again, concerned the original manuscript of Fauré's 7th Nocturne. The manuscript, lacking the first two pages, which had been in the possession of one of the composer's English pupils who had died near Oxford, was offered to him by the present writer and sent to Lausanne at Cortot's request. Barely three weeks later an unknown French gentleman resident in Nice sent Cortot as a gesture of admiration and gratitude for a transaction involving the purchase of a youthful portrait of Liszt, the gift of 'un feuillet autographe de Fauré' which turned out to be the missing portion of the Nocturne manuscript. More than forty years earlier Cortot had given the first performance of the piece in Fauré's presence; the two portions of the manuscript were reunited in his house after being separated for several decades.

Alfred Cortot was the last of the great music collectors whose libraries aimed, within certain limits, at universality in their representation of music and musical history, and who could achieve their aim to a remarkable degree, thanks to the conjunction of availability of the material and the means to acquire it. The drying up of sources has often been lamented, but unforeseen events such as sales by institutions (and in the more distant past the secularisation of the monasteries in Central Europe) provided new opportunities for acquisitions. It is, however, safe to say that a collection like that of Alfred Cortot can and will never be brought together again, not only because his generation had opportunities denied to subsequent ones, but because the ideal of a private library of such comprehensiveness is rooted in a nineteenth century faith in such an achievement which could not survive in the second half of our century. The collection was also intimately bound up with a life-style and a seigneurial grandeur more akin to the 'fin-de-siècle' than to the last decades of the twentieth century. Thus the collection is becoming in itself an object of history and the expression of an epoch in which familiarity with original sources could fertilize the interpretative art of a great musician like Alfred Cortot.

REFERENCES

1 B Gavoty *Alfred Cortot* Paris, 1977, 285-288.
2 Partly catalogued in F Goldbeck and A Fehr *Bibliothèque Alfred Cortot, Première partie, Théorie de la musique* Paris, 1936.
3 A copy of a book entitled *Les naufrages aëriens* by Albert Laporte, Paris, 1886, with many graphic illustrations of ballooning disasters is in the writer's possession. It is signed 'Alfred Cortot 1er Janvier 1887'; he was 9 years old at the time.
4 Cortot played a great deal of Beethoven in his early years. He included op 106 in his first London recital.
5 See the preface by Henry Prunières to the printed catalogue, *op cit*.
6 cf A H King and O W Neighbour 'Printed music from the collection of Alfred Cortot' *The British Museum quarterly* xxxi 1966, 8-16, pl. ii-v; also F Traficante 'The Alfred Cortot Collection at the University of Kentucky Libraries' *University of Kentucky Library Notes* i no 3, 1-19. Major sections of the Library were acquired by

the Newberry Library, Chicago and the Music Library of the University of California at Berkeley. The autograph manuscripts were acquired by Mr Robert O Lehman in the spring of 1962, many of them being now on deposit in the Pierpont Morgan Library, New York. Many of the autograph letters were purchased by the Comtesse de Chambure.

7 cf A H King, *Some British collectors of music c.1600-1960* Cambridge, 1963.

THE PAST, PRESENT AND FUTURE OF THE MUSIC LIBRARY THEMATIC CATALOGUE

BARRY S BROOK

When, almost exactly a quarter of a century ago, Alec King published his illuminating article, 'The past, present and future of the thematic catalogue'[1], he concentrated on the individual composer. And while he also discussed publishers' catalogues and multiple-composer (eg genre) catalogues, he gave only passing mention to library thematic catalogues since at the time there were only a handful of printed ones in existence. He concluded his essay with the outline of a 'scheme for all the necessary sections' of a thematic catalogue of an individual composer's works, adding that 'much discussion between compilers and users would be necessary before agreement could be reached on a definitive but reasonably consistent scheme. . . [The scheme] outlined. . . may at least provide, apparently for the first time, a beginning for the discussion.'

I have previously contributed to such a discussion as regards composers' catalogues.[2] At this time, in homage to —and in the footsteps of—a fine scholar and friend of many years, I should like to confront the past, present and future of the rapidly growing field of the music library thematic catalogue and to present three schemes 'for all the necessary sections' thereof as 'a beginning for discussion'. I will pay special attention to three recent catalogues dealing with manuscripts c 1600-1800 (a period under inadequate bibliographic control), to the relationship of library cataloguing practices to the International Repertory of Musical Sources (RISM) Series A/I and A/II, and to cataloguing methods and their potentials involving the computer.

The past[3]

Awareness of the vital significance to music research of complete thematic catalogues of library holdings has developed all too gradually. Up to the present time surprisingly few catalogues of this type have been published, even for repositories rich in early sources. Of these few, it is often only the manuscripts that are catalogued with incipits; sometimes only anonyma are thus treated. One may speculate on the reasons for this. First, publishers have almost invariably preferred catalogues without incipits to avoid the additional expense (until very recently the production of non-thematic library catalogues outnumbered thematic ones by perhaps fifty to one). Secondly, compilers of library inventories have usually been so closely involved with their libraries that, with the music itself readily at hand, inclusion of incipits seemed unnecessary. Finally, scholars and doctoral students, bent on investigating specific genres or composers, have taken down incipits relevant to their own needs, but have not, as a rule, catalogued the contents of an entire collection.

Scholarly thematic cataloguing of library holdings has lagged many decades behind that of individual composers' works. The initial model for the new scientific approach to the composer catalogue was Ludwig Ritter von Köchel's *Chronologisch-thematisches Verzeichnis* of Mozart's works, published in 1862. It was not until the 1890s that a comparable library thematic catalogue appeared: Otto Kade's *Die Musikalien-Sammlung des Grossherzoglich Mecklenburg-Schweriner Fürstenhauses* (1893). Including its supplement (1899), it contains many thousands of multi-stave incipits in 1,050 information-packed pages. Only about half-a-dozen other library catalogues were published with incipits before 1900; these were only partially thematic.[4]

Virtually all other eighteenth and nineteenth-century library catalogues containing themes are in manuscript, in

the form of summary lists intended for record-keeping purposes such as notating accessions or indicating shelf locations.
Such catalogues, which often contain dated entries, are of
immense historical and sociological significance, especially
if the collection itself has been dispersed.[5] Possibly the
earliest surviving manuscript catalogue of this type is that of
the music collection of the Prussian general Friedrich Otto
von Wittenhorst-Sonsfeld (1678-1755). (The extant portion
of his collection is now located in the Bibliotheca Fürsten-
berginana in Herdringen.) The catalogue contains thematic
incipits of 365 works acquired between 1728 and 1760 and
written by almost 100 composers ranging from Abel to Biber
to Marcello to Telemann to Werner. Similar manuscript
catalogues from the eighteenth century exist for library
holdings in Rheda, Uppsala, Karlsruhe, Munich (Maria Anna
of Bavaria), Herzogenburg, Brno, Sigmaringen, Lambach,
Rajhrad, Regensburg, Prague, Basel, etc; and for private
collections such as those of Dunwalt, the Count d'Ogny,
the Sharp family, etc.[6]

A further stage in the cataloguing of an individual composer's works, stressing comprehensiveness of source control
and reference to related literature, was exemplified (albeit
inconsistently) by Alfred Einstein's third edition of Köchel,
published in 1937. With few exceptions[7], this model was not
adopted for library holdings until the 1960s, and then rather
slowly, as a number of 'modern' thematic library catalogues
began to appear.[8]

In retrospect, the achievement of Otto Kade (1819-1900) in
bringing out the Schwerin catalogue in 1893-1899 is astonishing. It was not equalled in bibliographic thoroughness and
breadth of reference until the 1970s, when the *Kataloge bayerischer Musiksammlungen* began to appear. Kade's catalogue
provides full diplomatic transcriptions of each title, brief
biographies of little-known composers, reproductions of

signatures, incipits for both prints and manuscripts in as many staves as can be useful, including all voices of anonyma and polyphonic works; it reproduces integrally many introductions, dedications, and archival documents. To this day, no complete thematic catalogue of a major library as large as Schwerin has been published.

Another aspect of the history of music library thematic cataloguing must be mentioned. In a number of libraries containing early sources, one may find catalogue cards that contain incipits, in addition to the usual bibliographic information. This cataloguing practice is—as is the card itself—largely a twentieth-century phenomenon, and has almost invariably and most unfortunately been sporadically employed. At times it seems as if the cataloguer, not knowing how to deal with a knotty identification problem, felt obliged to add the incipit as the only means of minimizing ambiguity.

I use the phrase 'almost invariably' because at least one man early in our century was fully aware of how valuable incipits on library cards could be for bibliographic control. He was Vladimir Helfert (1886-1945), an outstanding scholar and Professor of Musicology in Brno, whose career was cut short by his imprisonment in a Nazi concentration camp. In 1919 he founded the Musical Archives of what is now the Music History Institute of the Moravian Museum in Brno. He made the inclusion of musical incipits a basic requisite for the cataloguing of manuscript music. For this reason, the card catalogue of the Institute's collection, which, after half a century, numbers almost 60,000 items, is a joy to use.

And when I suggested above that it was 'most unfortunate' that incipits were found only sporadically on catalogue cards, I had in mind the many potential uses to which files of complete incipit-provided entries can be put. The cards can be photographically reproduced, the copies sorted in a variety of ways, and a whole series of specialized thematic indexes created. These could be organized by genre, by key, or by date. They could be kept in special card files or, conceivably, when arranged in groups of ten cards (5 x 2) or twenty-one cards (7 x 3), photo-offset for publication in pamphlet or book form (similar to the G K Hall publication of the catalogue of the Music Division of the New York Public Library).

The present

In the 1970s the pace of music library thematic cataloguing has increased dramatically. A number of individual library catalogues have appeared and many more are in progress.[9] Several publishers and professional societies have actively begun to bring out thematic catalogues and indexes singly and in series, for composers, genres, publishers, libraries and specific collections. Among these are Henle (Munich), Bärenreiter (Kassel), Detroit Information Coordinators, Schneider (Tutzing), Pendragon Press (New York), Supraphon (Prague), the Music Library Association (USA) and (in the planning stage) the Italian Musicological Society.

More important, several major regional and national catalogue series have been established. Among them are:

> *Tabulae musicae austriacae: Kataloge österreichischer Musiküberlieferung* which began in 1964, and by 1979 had produced nine volumes on various Austrian composers and library collections by such scholars as Karl Schnürl, Rudolf Flotzinger, Theophil Antonick, Elisabeth Maier and Karl Mitterschiffthaler.

> The Moravian Music Foundation's 10,000 musical documents, of which approximately the first 500 manuscripts (in the Peters Memorial Library in Winston Salem, North Carolina) have been inventoried in Marilyn Gombosi's *Catalogue of the Herbst Collection* (University of North Carolina Press, 1970).

Catalogus artis musicae in Bohemia et Moravia cultae
of which two volumes have appeared: Oldřich Pulkert's
Domus Lauretana Pragensis (1973) and Jaroslav Holeček's
*J. A. Seydl Decani Beronensis operum artis musicae
collectio* (1976).

*Katalog tematyczny rekopiśmiennych zabytków
dawnej musyki w Polsce* which began in 1969 with
Elżbieta Gluszcz-Zwolińska's Wawel catalogue of early
music manuscripts, to be followed by catalogues of
holdings at Sandomierz, Kowicz, and the areas surrounding Crakow.

Kataloge bayerischer Musiksammlungen (including
church, court, and public libraries), of which three
volumes have appeared since 1971. They have been
produced by a team under the direction of Robert
Münster. Six other volumes are awaiting publication,
with another twenty planned for the near future. The
third volume in this series (Schloss Harburg) will be
described below.

And, of greatest significance, RISM Series A/II has
finally been formally launched with the appearance of
two pilot catalogues, one (manuscripts in Schloss
Langenburg) prepared by the international editorial
office in Kassel, the other (pre-1800 manuscripts in the
libraries of Denmark, in microfiche) a product of the
Danish RISM team. Both will be discussed below.

RISM has been the catalyst of a far-reaching effort to
catalogue all extant early (western) music and music literature sources in libraries and private collections throughout
the world. RISM has concentrated thus far on western music
to 1800. It has unfortunately not always recognized the
long-range significance to bibliographic source control of
cataloguing with musical incipits. Its 'systematic' Series B

includes inventories (already out or in preparation) on Hebrew, Greek, and Arabic sources; volumes on specific genres, repertories and theoretical writings of the Medieval and Renaissance periods; and volumes on printed recueils and published literature 1500-1800. In some—but not in all—appropriate cases, these Series B volumes have included incipits. We are more directly concerned here with Series A, the 'new Eitner', which is divided into two sub-series, each organized alphabetically by composer; A/I, individual composer's printed works to 1800, which is not thematic; and series A/II, music manuscripts 1600-1800, which is. Publication of A/I is virtually complete except for the supplementary volumes; data are still being gathered for A/II and computer applications are still being tested.

The cataloguing done in various countries in fulfilment of national RISM Series A objectives has already resulted not only in several publications, singly and in series, but also in the establishment of extensive national incipit files. In Czechoslovakia, for example, in cataloguing centres in Prague, Brno, and Bratislava, several hundred thousand manuscripts and prints have already been catalogued, all with incipits. This is the most comprehensive and impressive project of its kind ever undertaken, with extremely detailed catalogue cards and upwards of a million items to be dealt with. In France, which had originally decided to do without incipits, the entire manuscript contents—to 1800!—of the Département de la Musique of the Bibliothèque Nationale is now being thematically inventoried. In Stockholm and in Munich, the catalogues of the holdings of all libraries thus far completed for the respective countries have been interfiled by incipits so that ready identification of anonyma and works with multiple ascriptions is possible.

We will now examine the organization of three thematic library catalogues that have recently appeared, all related to

RISM in one way or another. The first uses a computer to format and index the data, a photo-composition device driven by computer to create both incipits and text, and conventional offset printing thereafter. The second presents a great wealth of data in compact form simply by photographing the (typed) catalogue cards. The third catalogue also uses the computer to format, index and print the data (both coded incipits and text), but it is printed directly on to a microfiche master.

Catalogue I
The first catalogue to be examined is entitled 'Fürstlich Hohenlohe-Langenburg'sche Schlossbibliothek Katalog der Musikhandschriften'. It is a pilot project within the Series A/II of RISM. It was commissioned by RISM and published in *Fontes artis musicae* xxv/4 1978 from computer-generated photo-composed output. Its general approach was established by RISM's Advisory Research Commission made up of Kurt Dorfmüller (President), Israel Adler, Norbert Böker-Heil, Barry S Brook, Alexander Hyatt King, François Lesure and Pierluigi Petrobelli. Editing was in the hands of Helmut Rösing and Gertraut Haberkamp. Computer programming, automated indexing, and photo-composed output formatting were the responsibility of Norbert Böker-Heil. Ursula Böker-Heil did the encoding of the incipits.

The collection, containing 249 items, is almost entirely secular (arias, concertos, sonatas, symphonies, etc) and mainly from the later eighteenth and early nineteenth centuries. As Kurt Dorfmüller indicates in his preface, the entries are very detailed and such exhaustiveness (copyist, previous owners, first performance, etc) is too costly except for small catalogues. The external form of the catalogue also raises problems since 'too little account was taken of how the output should look'. Each entry is presented in a solid block of run-on type containing a wealth of data that is very difficult to differentiate despite the varieties of type-fonts used. On the other hand, the incipits, which were auto-matically photo-composed from the 'Plaine and easie code', are beautifully produced and eminently readable.

The preparation of this catalogue provided invaluable lessons. It was clear from a preliminary printing, distributed to a small group of specialists, that readers were not ready to accept coded incipits, and that the run-on format of the text was unacceptable. For that reason the catalogue, as finally printed in *Fontes*, contained incipits in conventional notation (created automatically by computer from the coded input). In addition, since it was not financially feasible at the time to reformat the block-printed catalogue data, a page of examples showing 'how we envisage the future form of the entries' (p 292) and a 'checklist RISM A/II' (p 293) showing the revised scheme was included in Dorfmüller's preface.

The scheme employs a space-saving numerical system for designating solo voices, choir voices, solo instruments and orchestral instruments. For example, 'VSol: 1000. choir 1111. orch: 11101.0200.200' indicates the following instru-mentation: (vocal solo) soprano, (choir) soprano, alto, tenor, bass; (orchestra) two violins, viola, bass, two oboes, two horns.

The scheme is made up of 30 discrete elements divided into six distinct areas:

RISM A/II Checklist

Filing Area	00	composer's name, standardized ◊ date of birth, date of death
	01	filing-title
	02	thematic index number ◊ opus-number ◊ key

Description Area	03	exact transcription of the title
	04	author of text ◊ arranger or co-composer ◊ performer ◊ dedicatee
	05	manuscript or autograph ◊ date of manuscript ◊ writer's name
	06	collation (score, parts, etc., number of volumes or fascicles, pagination)
	07	list of parts if mentioned in 06; statement of missing parts
	08	size; watermark
Area of contents and incipits	09	description of the sections (parts, movements, numbers) of the work, or description of the contents of a collective manuscript
	10	text incipit
	11	musical incipit
Index Area	12	solo vocal parts (S, A, T, B,) ◊ additional solo vocal parts
	13	choir parts (S,A,T,B) ◊ additional choir parts
	14	solo instruments
	15	string instruments (vl 1, 2, vla, vlc, b) ◊ wood wind instruments (fl, ob, cl, fag) ◊ brass wind instruments (cor, tr, trb) ◊ additional instruments
	16	keyboard instrument(s) or plucked instrument(s)
	17	non-standardized name of composer
	18	other title information
	19	genre(s) if given in the source
	20	roles
	21	former depository or owner; provenance

	22	control number of the collective manuscript to which the single work belongs, or control number of single work belonging to a collective manuscript, or control number(s) of other copies of the same work
Notes Area	23	former shelf-number
	24	dates or dating references
	25	references to other RISM series
	26	additional data taken from the source
	27	data taken from secondary literature ◊ miscellaneous
Location Area	28	RISM sigla: country ◊ library
	29	shelf-number
	99	control number

As appendices to the catalogue there are five invaluable and automatically printed-out indexes:

Text incipits

Filing titles (organized where appropriate by medium and key)

Genres (when and as named in the title)

Names (other than composers) eg arrangers, copyists, authors of the texts, dedicatees, etc

Incipit Index

The Incipit Index, named 'Melischer Index' by Böker-Heil, is an ingenious finding tool, organized by movement of melodic intervals, designed to identify anonyma and locate multiple attributions. It lists all incipits in 'Plaine and easie code', one line for each, followed by catalogue number and composer. Preceding each coded incipit are four numbers representing the first four intervals given in half steps like the system used by Nanie Bridgman (+ for upward, 0 for a repeated note, − for downward); the arrangement is from the largest ascending interval to the largest descending interval. Thus *Frère Jacques* would appear thus: +2 +2 −4 0; it would precede *God save the queen* which would be listed as follows: 0 +2 −3 +1. When duplication occurs at this admittedly limited four-interval level, the complete coded incipits that follow may be compared to ascertain if they are indeed identical (or identical except for being transposed).

Whatever difficulties the Langenburg catalogue may have undergone, the potential of automated thematic cataloguing, indexing and photo-composition of incipits for RISM A/II has been demonstrated, and most important, in its preface, an excellent scheme for the format of each entry has been presented.

Catalogue II

The first catalogue to be described is the third in the *Kataloge bayerischer Musiksammlungen* (KBM) series which is under the general editorship of Robert Münster, head of the music division of the Bayerische Staatsbibliothek, and which is being produced with support from the Deutsche Forschungsgemeinschaft and in close association with the West German RISM office.

The three volumes of the KBM that have been published thus far represent the same kind of giant step forward from Kade that Einstein made from Köchel. They should be regarded as a model for library catalogues dealing with seventeenth, eighteenth and nineteenth-century manuscript sources, setting a standard for thoroughness, accuracy, clarity of presentation, and wealth of documentation that would be difficult to surpass.

One reason for the accuracy of the entries in the KBM volumes is that the compilers have availed themselves of the rich reference potential of the Bayerische Staatsbibliothek's music division, and especially of the dependable multi-indexed incipit files of the adjacent West German RISM office. This steadily-growing incipit bank includes 60,000 titles in its composer file alone (a single title may represent a manuscript with as many as twelve works by a single composer). It incorporates not only the listings from the West German libraries already catalogued for RISM A/II, but also the incipits from many early thematic catalogues, published and unpublished.[10] In addition, close contact is maintained with other national RISM offices and with the RISM international centre in Kassel. Through the use of such files and through communication with other centres, it has been possible to minimize the danger of false attribution, a major pitfall when dealing with seventeenth and eighteenth-century music. A large number of anonyma have thus been identified, and many manuscripts bearing conflicting attributions in different sources have been assigned to their proper parent (in brackets, of course).

The volumes' catalogue portions are produced by photo offset of the typed catalogue cards, somewhat reduced, incipits having been hand-drawn, with text underlay where called for. Introductions, appendices and indexes, however, have been elegantly typeset. The quantity of information conveyed by each densely-packed 8 by 11½-inch page is impressive.

The third volume in the series is the *Thematischer Katalog der Musikhandschriften der Fürstlich Oettingen-Wallerstein'-schen Bibliothek Schloss Harburg* (Munich, Henle, 1976). It is edited by Gertraut Haberkamp, head of the West German

RISM office, and contains a splendid historical essay on the two-hundred years of the Schloss Harburg collection by its curator, Volker von Volckamer. The collection contains entries for 1,700 manuscripts including rare works of Leopold Mozart, a feast of Haydniana, many works, including unica, by composers from Salzburg, Vienna, Munich, Mannheim and the Oettingen-Wallerstein court.

The overall organization of this model catalogue is generally similar to that of the others in the series. Here, the introduction is followed by nine eighteenth-century music lists from the Oettingen-Wallerstein archives, including one thematic index of a choral director's library dated 1745, an auction list from 1791, three Nachlass inventories, and an index of horn music from 1858 (including 22 double concertos).

The thematic catalogue itself is divided into two parts: individual authors (pp 3-218), and anonyma and collections (pp 218-243). Each entry 'gets it all', including the thirty items on the RISM A/II checklist (in a somewhat different order) and several others such as both the treble *and* bass incipits; extensive bibliographical references; etc.

The invaluable scholarly apparatus of over fifty pages which follows includes:

> Copyists (with a glossary of identified ones and numbered anonymi).
>
> Indexes of frequently-encountered papermills, with dates of their watermarks. Index of names, persons and initials found in the numbered list of watermarks that follows.
>
> 235 watermark descriptions with identification by papermill, etc, and approximate dates.
>
> Watermark reproductions for those not previously reproduced in the KBM series.
>
> Summary list (non-thematic) of some 650 printed editions

in the Schloss Harburg library, with their call numbers. All of these works have been reported in volumes of RISM A/I.

Bibliography of catalogues and worklists, and of other literature.

Index of titles and first lines. Titles include genres very usefully subdivided by key and composer.

Index of names.

What other kinds of data might have been included in this catalogue? One could argue, for example, that the presence of single-staff incipits for *all* movements of an instrumental work or for all numbers of an operatic score, would have been more useful than double-stave incipits for the opening movement or number only. The editors felt, however, that the inclusion of the bass voice in the incipits of the opening movements was invaluable for the identification of anonyma and that incipits for the other movements could be left for individual composer catalogues. For the latter reason also, the editors decided not to go to the immense trouble of counting measures for each work or movement. Less defensible, however, is the omission of incipits for the allegros of movements beginning with a slow introduction.

Since this volume is entitled 'Thematic catalogue of the manuscripts of . . .,' it should not be criticized for omitting the incipits for its 650 printed editions listed in summary form (readers are referred to non-thematic RISM A/I for further details). However, as will be discussed below, the ideal library catalogue would have included such incipits, in coded form if necessary, *especially* in view of their unavailability in A/I.

Catalogue III

Our final example is a union catalogue on microfiche produced entirely by computer and entitled 'Musicat 1978: Catalogue of pre/1800 music manuscripts in libraries in Denmark: the Danish contribution to RISM'. It was compiled by Nanna Schiødt, who has been in charge of RISM manuscript cataloguing in Denmark, and Sybille Reventlow. It was 'published' by the Royal Danish library. The Danish RISM committee was responsible for the overall operation. Programming and technical procedures were developed at the Northern European University Computing Centre.

The catalogue includes 4,000 entries, or virtually all the music manuscripts from the tenth through the eighteenth centuries that have survived in Danish libraries.[11] It is presented on twenty microfiches and accompanied by a forty-page guide in pamphlet form prepared by the two compilers. The text (in Danish, English, and German) gives the format used for the entries, lists the libraries inventoried and shows how the 'Plaine and easie code' used for musical incipits can readily be retranslated into ordinary notation. Numerous helpful illustrations are included. The guide, entitled 'The Danish RISM Catalogue; Manuscripts; an introduction', also explains that the catalogue is really three catalogues, each with the same entries arranged by composer, library, and genre; there are two indexes, one of musical incipits arranged alphabetically by pitches, the other of text incipits.

This, the first thematic catalogue ever to be published in microfiche, is remarkable for a number of reasons. To begin with, although microforms have been with us for many years, one does not easily overcome the astonishment at finding a catalogue of over 4,000 items and 3,000 pages taking up a space that totals four inches in height, six inches in width, and one-eighth of an inch in thickness (4 x 6 x ⅛ inches). To look at it another way, the total space equals three cubic inches. Furthermore, microfiche are easy to store in a file drawer and, once one gets used to them, easy to consult.

The main (composer) catalogue with its 4,000 manuscripts

requires six microfiches, as do the other two catalogues; all three provide complete data for each entry, a luxury that the compactness of microfiche publication makes possible; the two incipit indexes require one fiche each. In addition, in the lower right hand corner of each fiche there is an index of its contents.

Secondly, the method of recording the data for this catalogue was unusually efficient for a computer project, since it was a one-step operation. The information was input directly from the manuscripts themselves into a computer terminal located in the Music Department of the Royal Library. No intermediary data-gathering form needed to be filled out, thus removing a major source of error. The terminal was also used to correct or update the data base, either at the input stage or at any time thereafter. Manuscripts from other libraries were usually brought to the Royal Library for cataloguing.

Thirdly, the text incipits in the catalogue output were located immediately below the music incipits, given in 'Plaine and easie code.' By adding slashes (/) to indicate bar lines in the text incipit and hyphens to show when a different pitch is used for a new syllable, a quite accurate text underlay can be recorded.

The scheme for each entry is clear and concise; it contains only twenty items, and these are often less detailed than in the two catalogues previously discussed. It does not include, for example, references to watermarks, to other RISM series, to non-standardized names of composers, etc (see *Fontes artis musicae* xxiii 1976, 162).

The future

Before proceeding to the discussion of the future of music library cataloguing, both conventional and computerized, I should like to make a series of general observations on the problems of bibliographic control of music sources. I shall focus on manuscript sources from 1600 to 1800 and printed music to 1800, since the methods for the bibliographic control of mediaeval and renaissance manuscript sources are relatively well developed.

1 The ideal thematic library catalogue provides the researcher with all the essential elements of identification, source description and reference that would enable him to proceed directly to subsequent musicological processes, such as source concordance, analysis, critical evaluation and finally the synthesis or the writing of history. (There is no implication of scholarly hierarchy here. The bibliographer, the analyst, the critic and the chronicler are equally important; indeed, they may all be combined in the same person.) I subscribe to the principle that it usually makes more sense for a bibliographical scholar to do the primary source research for an entire library or collection, than for dozens of researchers to work independently, risking duplication of effort and repetition of mistakes. It is more efficient for the trained bibliographer or bibliographic team to amass the incipit files and accompanying documentation in order to ensure proper dating, attribution, identification of copyists, printers, engravers, watermarks, papermills, etc, especially since problems of dating and attribution are often common to many composers and to complete repertories. To paraphrase a half-remembered adage, a bibliographer should 'Do it once, do it right, get it all'.

2 Identification of a musical work is the thematic catalogue's most important function. The key to identification is the musical incipit. As I have stated elsewhere:

> A musical work, printed or manuscript, may be identified by composer, title, opus number, key, instrumentation,

movement headings, first line of text, date, publisher, dedicatee, plate number, etc. No one of these elements, indeed no combination of these, can provide as certain an identification as an incipit. . . . The incipit rarely leads one astray. Even transposed works can be readily identified in properly organized incipit files. In dealing with anonyma and with works of disputed authorship, the incipit becomes indispensible—as a catalogue without them will readily demonstrate. In short, the collection, classification, transposition and lexicographical ordering of the incipits into thematic catalogues has enabled scholars to solve a myriad of otherwise insoluble problems.[12]

The nature and number of the incipits provided for each work (single or multiple staff, one or all movements, etc) are a function of the cataloguing depth and not central to the issue of identification since a single incipit (ie the opening dozen notes of the principal voice) serves the purpose 99 per cent of the time (unless the principal part is missing).

3 The initial decision, made many years ago by RISM's Commission Internationale Mixte, to omit incipits from RISM A/I (printed works to 1800), was, I submit, a fundamental mistake. Because of that decision, the listings in A/I are incomplete in an essential detail and will eventually have to be redone, perhaps in another generation, or in bits and pieces, genre by genre, and composer by composer. The sad fact is that, as it stands now, there is no way of knowing that a printed edition of a work listed in A/I is the same composition as a manuscript copy listed, with incipit, in A/II. If the distinguished group of scholars then making up RISM's Commission Internationale Mixte had, at the outset, insisted on incipits for A/I, the cause of sixteenth to eighteenth-century

source research would have made a significant leap forward. It is true that requiring such added effort from collaborators all over the world would indeed have slowed things down considerably, but only in the initial stages. For the central editing office in Kassel, having a sure means of identifying the works involved, would, in the long run, have made its task infinitely easier. It is also true that to include incipits in the published A/I volumes would have added to their already high cost; but they would have been so much more useful that the difference in price would have seemed small in comparison. The contents of a *thematic* RISM A/I could have been immediately compared and cross-referenced to the in-progress thematic A/II (and to other thematic indices); a thematic A/I would have been a truly powerful research resource and would have demonstrated how the properly planned work of the few could save a vast amount of labour for the many.

That no reviewers and only a few individuals to my knowledge have protested about the omission of incipits from A/I may have been due to the fact that virtually every previously published library or union catalogue has not included incipits for printed sources. However, although printed works are more easily catalogued than manuscripts, title-page data, plate numbers, etc do not, in fact, always identify the specific work itself. The same trio sonata in D major may be published many times by various publishers, in different cities, under different composers' names, with different opus numbers, different plate numbers, etc. Nor does the title-page information suffice to differentiate a printed edition from manuscript copies of similar works; a composer may have written several different trio sonatas in D major, some even with the same sequence of movements.

Furthermore, there is no logical basis or musicological justification for the tradition of providing thematic catalogue incipits only for manuscripts, or even worse, only for anonymous manuscripts. Many printed editions from 1501 to 1800 have survived in very few copies, some in only a single copy, or even a single part from a single set of parts. There are often no extant manuscripts paralleling surviving printed works. Often also, it is the printed edition rather than the manuscript copy that is the primary source.

Thus, print and manuscript must be considered, initially at least, as equal pieces of historical evidence. And even when three, five or seventeen examples of a printed work are to be found scattered throughout Europe, what is the rationale for treating the print and manuscript differently in so essential an identifying element as the incipit? The print may be as difficult to get to and consult as the manuscript copy.

4 If one accepts the premise that incipits are essential to proper identification, one must reject the argument that they are too time-consuming to obtain and too costly to produce. Publishers will have to learn that their inclusion is simply non-negotiable. For very large projects, and only as a last resort, the incipit may be presented in coded form, which requires only the addition of a single line of type for each work. Coded incipits using numbers and letters have been successfully employed in both published volumes and computer data banks. As one who has long been associated with the 'Plaine and easie code' 'now used for the inputting of RISM A/II and other projects, I much prefer standard notation for thematic catalogues. When all else fails, however, the coded incipit is better than none, especially since it can also be used to create supplementary automated indexes, for checking duplications, for identifying anonyma, for the printing out by photo-composition of conventional notation.

5 If I appear to be labouring the incipit issue over much, it is because many scholars are not yet convinced of its importance.

Indeed, the recently constituted Advisory Research Commission (ARC) of RISM, which was responsible for the final establishment of cataloguing guidelines for A/II, originally decided to do without incipits because they were 'impractical'. This decision was made in part on the old grounds of the difficulties in both securing and publishing incipits and in part because several major countries (eg France, United Kingdom, USA) had already completed their cataloguing for A/I and A/II without them, and they would not, it was thought then, be able to retrace their steps. Fortunately, this decision was reversed; steps are being retraced; A/II will have incipits. To do otherwise would have been disastrous.

The music library catalogue of the future, when dealing with early sources both printed and manuscript, should omit music incipits *only* for works of Bach, Haydn, Mozart, Beethoven; these must be identified by catalogue numbers in Schmieder, Hoboken, Köchel and Kinsky.

A thematic catalogue should be a bibliographic tool rather than a bibliophilic model. It may therefore be published by photo-offset from typed catalogue cards with hand-drawn incipits saving the cost of typesetting and engraving, using the funds saved to prepare and print vital appendices and indexes. This approach was splendidly demonstrated by the Schloss Harburg catalogue. The scheme it employs for organizing information may be considered (with the addition of themes for printed works and the RISM A/II numerical system for indicating instrumentation) a model for catalogues of individual libraries produced by conventional means.

Modern technologies, however, offer many new and quite fantastic possibilities, only a few of which have been seen in the two RISM catalogues examined here. The use of new methods of storage, access, and display will be essential if we are to achieve bibliographic control over manuscript and printed sources that may number several million. Some of these methods are already with us. As Dorfmüller put it, in his introduction to the Langenburg catalogue, 'We envisage RISM A/II not necessarily as a fixed publication or an A-Z series (like A/I) but as a flexible information system. . . [which could produce] short title catalogues and indices of the complete material or the holding of individual countries or other units. . . [It could provide] lists compiled in response to specific questions relating to the processed catalogue.'

Other methods hold even greater promise. To mention one soon to be commercially available: the twelve-inch video disc (equal in size to a sound recording) can store 54,000 frames per side in colour or black and white (text, music, drawings, paintings, films, etc). A conventional colour television screen is employed for display and the user can call up and 'freeze' any individual frame instantly. The disc which stores the information digitally is read by a laser beam or (in a competing system) by a stylus. One can hardly imagine what such computerized systems will do to the world of information storage and of libraries, let alone that of music library cataloguing.

The cataloguing of two to three million manuscripts in the kind of depth outlined in the RISM A/II checklist is a monumental *human* task. Utopian as it may seem, the task is slowly being accomplished, library by library, region by region, country by country, by teams of RISM cataloguers all over the world. Great strides have been made, only very recently, in the cataloguing of the manuscripts in Spain and Italy, countries where RISM had previously made few inroads. By contrast, in the United Kingdom and the United States, where RISM A/II cataloguing was 'completed' several years ago without incipits, recataloguing in full is now being begun. In several smaller countries, such as Denmark and Sweden, work has been completed in accordance with current RISM guidelines. In some countries with very extensive holdings, such as Germany, Austria and Czechoslovakia, the larger part of the job has already been accomplished although much is still to be done.

Computer input and storage of so vast a body of data is almost impossible to contemplate. The dimension of this task is such that if one were to publish RISM A/II in A/I sized pages, and include all the information called for in the A/II checklist for each manuscript, well over a thousand volumes would be required. Perhaps twenty-five pages would be required for the many eighteenth-century copies of a single Haydn quartet, fifty pages for the extant copies of *La serva padrona*.

The RISM central office, which now has a modest sized computer on its Kassel premises, is perfecting the necessary programmes and testing them on the full catalogues of several small collections from different countries. It has yet to come to grips with the fact that it must deal with an oceanic quantity of data and that some means of operation other than full inputting must be sought.

One solution is fully to catalogue the holdings of all libraries and publish them individually, with or without computer, and either in book or microfiche form. Indeed we seem to be moving in that direction with the several large thematic cataloguing series now under way. This does not solve the problem of the composite RISM A/II catalogue as originally envisaged, which would bring all manuscript works of a composer together in a new Quellenlexikon.

Using a different approach such as the video-disc, the equivalent of 150 normal sized volumes could be stored on a single 12-inch disc. This might mean that all the data of RISM A/II, when it is finally accumulated, could be stored in a dozen discs by video-photographing either the pages of published thematic catalogues or the catalogue cards themselves. RISM would then need to input only a composite, continually up-dated, Stylized Thematic Inventory of the contents of the video-discs. Each entry would contain a brief stylized representation of the work itself, not of any specific manuscript. And each entry would be followed by a list of library sources with, for each, the video-disc address where the full description of that manuscript may be found.

This approach would eliminate the virtually impossible job of also keyboarding in complete detail all the information found in already published volumes. Once the Thematic Inventory entry is input, new library sources with their video-disc addresses can readily be added. What I refer to as the Stylized Thematic Inventory would be limited for each entry to the four items (five for vocal works) that in my opinion are absolutely essential to the identification of a piece of music:

Composer (plus dates)

Normalized title (including standard thematic catalogue number and earliest known date)

Musical incipit

Text incipit (plus author's name when known)

Setting (voices, instruments)

Reference to each library source (and video-disc address) need mention only special information, eg score (parts are normally assumed); missing parts; conflicting title or composer's name.

All this is less utopian than it may first appear; it may indeed be the only realistic way for RISM A/II to proceed if it is ever to achieve a composite catalogue. To leave the video-disc aside for the moment, inputting only the limited information required by the Stylized Thematic Inventory brings the inputting process and data storage problem down to a manageable dimension. It would also make possible the publication of RISM A/II in a series of (conventional) volumes numbering dozens rather than many hundreds.

The Stylized Thematic Inventory would serve as a master control information bank whose data could be indexed in various ways for various purposes including the identification of anonyma and works of conflicting parentage. It could also include, for each entry, references to early thematic catalogues and to the printed editions listed in RISM A/I (thus providing thematic identification absent in A/I, at least for those printed works corresponding to the inventoried manuscripts). During this process, as more and more information is added to the data bank, a great variety of intermediary catalogues and indexes could be printed out in hard-copy or microfiche—by composer, setting, library, region or country.

With the help of automation, with growing acceptance of the view that to catalogue music once and completely is the wisest course, and with the intensification of cataloguing efforts both nationally and internationally, the future of music library thematic cataloguing should be assured.

REFERENCES

1 *Monthly musical record* lxxxiv/953, 954, 1954, 10-13, 39-46.
2 See *Thematic catalogues in music* New York 1970, which is prefaced by an essay entitled 'On the definitions, history, functions, historiography, and future of the thematic catalogue'. Alec King's scheme is discussed on pp xvii-xviii; in footnote 9 one reads 'Mr. King's admirable essay has been a source of inspiration to my own. . .'
3 Several paragraphs from this section and a later section have been quoted or paraphrased from the author's review of the first three volumes of the *Kataloge bayerischer Musiksammlungen*, which is scheduled to appear in the Fall 1979 issue of the *Journal of the American Musicological Society*.

4 The four that come to mind are all very modest in incipit coverage compared to Kade: the appendix of 50 anonymous masses to E de Coussemaker *Notice sur les collections musicales de la Bibliothèque de Cambrai* Paris, 1843; F X Haberl *Bibliographischer und thematischer Musikkatalog des Päpstlichen Kapellarchivs zu Rom* Leipzig, 1888; J Richter *Katalog der Musik-Sammlung auf der Universitäts-Bibliothek in Basel* Leipzig, 1892; R Jacobs and R Eitner *Thematischer Katalog der von Thulemeir'schen Musikalien-Sammlung in der Bibliothek des Joachimsthal'schen Gymnasiums zu Berlin* Berlin, 1899.

5 The author, in collaboration with Gertraut Haberkamp of the Bayerische Staatsbibliothek, is preparing a 'composite thematic catalogue of early thematic catalogues to 1830'. It will include incipits from all published and manuscript catalogues, excluding those of individual composers.

6 See *Thematic catalogues in music* xxi-xxv, 'Appendix A: Manuscript thematic catalogues before 1830' and the description of the contents of these catalogues given in the body of the volume.

7 Among these rare—and usually not very comprehensive—exceptions are: J Ecorcheville *Catalogue du fonds de musique ancienne de la Bibliothèque Nationale* Paris, 1910-14, which, useful as it is, only goes up to 1750 and provides incipits only for manuscripts; R M Haas *Die Estensischen Musikalien; thematisches Verzeichnis mit Einleitung* Regensburg, 1927; K E Roediger *Die geistlichen Musikhandschriften der Universitäts-Bibliothek Jena* Jena, 1935; F Welter *Katalog der Musikalien der Ratsbücherei Lüneberg* Lippstadt, 1950; and E Refardt *Thematischer Katalog der Instrumentalmusik des 18. Jahrhunderts in den Handschriften der Universitätsbibliothek Basel* Bern, 1957.

8 For example: J M Llorens *Capellae Sixtinae codices, musicis notis instructi sive manu scripti sive praelo excussi* Città del Vaticano, 1960; G Walter *Katalog der gedruckten und handschriftlichen Musikalien des 17. bis. 19. Jahrhunderts im Besitz der Allgemeinen Musikgessellschaft Zürich* Zurich, 1960; K Hortschansky *Katalog der Kieler Musiksammlungen* Kassel, 1963; G Göller *Die Leiblsche Sammlung. Katalog der Musikalien der Kölner Domcapelle* Köln, 1964; B Ormisová-Záhumenská *Súpis Hudobnín z bývalého promonštrátskeho kláštora v Jasove. I. Zbierka z bývalého jezuitského kostola sv. Trojice v Košiciach* Martin, 1967; and the Friedrich Lippmann, Ludwig Finscher, Hubert Unverricht inventories of the manuscripts in the Biblioteca Doria Pamphilj in Rome, in *Analecta musicologica* v, vii, ix 1968-70.

9 Representative catalogues published individually in the 1970s include: G Barblan *Musiche della Cappella di S. Barbara in Mantova* Florence, 1972; I Bittman *Catalogue of Giedde's music collection in the Royal Library of Copenhagen* Egtved, 1976 and Robert Murányi's catalogue of the Bartfa collection in the Hungarian National Library in Budapest.

10 Other RISM centres (eg Prague and Vienna) have larger incipit files, but the one of comparable cross-indexing effectiveness is that established in the library of the Kungliga Musikaliska Academien in Stockholm by the late Cari Johansson.

11 One sizeable group of works, the Giedde Collection of the Royal Library, was omitted because a detailed thematic catalogue has just been published; data from this collection and a few other omitted items such as instrumental parts from operas will eventually be added to the data base.

12 See *Thematic catalogues in music* vii-viii.

PROBLEMS IN TEACHING
THE BIBLIOGRAPHY OF MUSIC

BRIAN REDFERN

The training and education of potential music librarians in the United Kingdom is largely carried out at the full-time library schools. There are no specialist courses as such, as it is rightly felt that in this country it is inappropriate to train people to be limited to being specialist librarians of whatever kind—music, children's, law, etc.[1] They are best trained to be librarians, as they will then have a range of potential posts within their grasp, whereas to be a specialist would be to limit opportunities and, frequently, salary. This means that any studies which concentrate on music librarianship and bibliography have to be seen within the framework of a course as a whole. Therefore the student who elects to take music bibliography will already have studied or be studying contemporaneously the subject of general bibliography. This is entirely appropriate, as many answers to enquiries, whether generated by librarians or readers, can be found more easily in general rather than special sources. For example at the present time, while it is by no means perfect, the *British national bibliography* gives better current coverage of new books on music than the *British catalogue of music*, and there may be better introductory articles on musical topics in the *Encyclopaedia Britannica* than those to be found in *Grove's Dictionary of music and musicians*.

This last example poses one of the major problems encountered in the teaching of music bibliography, because this kind of knowledge is unlikely to be significantly acquired in any other way than by actually working in a library with the materials over a long period of time. It is only in handling reference and bibliographical works daily that a librarian can build up awareness of the patterns of knowledge contained in them, their weaknesses and their strengths. However much library schools attempt to recreate the working situation in practical exercises, these remain artificial and will be seen as such by students, some of whom will not find their minds fully engaged as a result.

The library schools in this country were established in the late 1940s to cope mainly with the immediate problem of training those returning from the armed forces. They were very much the brain child of Lionel McColvin, who had suggested in his *Report on the public library system of Great Britain*[2] that, if created, they could be a major force in the development of library services. He had the example of the impact made by the school at University College, London, to strengthen his case. This had been established in 1919 and, although the number of students attending had been small in comparison with those qualifying by part-time study, the impression made by the school had been significant. That McColvin was to a very great extent correct is evidenced by the impressive growth of library services in the past thirty years, due in no small measure to the impact of the schools. It is easy for scoffers to be gloomy about the current situation during this period of nil economic growth, but there is no reasonable doubt that librarians are better educated and trained now than they were before the last war.

Librarianship is now a very attractive career, particularly for postgraduate students, and many excellent people are coming from the universities. It is a major tragedy that at this time the Department of Education and Science has chosen to cut back the number of postgraduate bursaries. The decision is an example both of central government folly and shortsightedness and of the kind of external influence on courses over which the library schools have little control.

One major problem which affects the teaching of music

bibliography is the lack of recent practical experience—of actually handling enquiries in a library—from which many library school lecturers suffer. As has already been said, knowledge of materials develops better in real situations. Without such contact, memory can fade and it is not easy to keep fully aware of current new material. The library profession must give attention to this problem and try to work out an acceptable way for there to be interchange of staffs on a regular basis between library schools and libraries. Both will benefit. There are difficulties such as salary differentials and superannuation payments, but these must surely be resolved in the interests of common sense.

However, these are really general questions which affect all subjects to a greater or lesser degree. The particular concern here is not the political arguments which have been touched on above, but the very practical aspects of how music bibliography can best be taught and the problems which arise when attempting to achieve that end.

Sharon L Paugh and Guy A Marco have recently examined the problem in the United States.[3] The inevitable questionnaire was sent off and from their replies they came to the rather gloomy conclusion that, with most lecturers 'admitting to lecturing and calling for oral reports on various books' there was in such methods 'a combined approach that must deaden many young hearts'. It is probable that a similar investigation here would produce the same response. It is almost alarming for a British library school lecturer to discover that there appear to be few really fresh ideas on teaching methods even in the United States. It might be appropriate for the International Association of Music Libraries (IAML) (UK) to carry out such a survey here. Papers presented at the 1976 IAML conference in Bergen on the training and education of music libraries in various countries[4] reveal very similar approaches whenever the presenter touches on the teaching of music bibliography.

However, the largest and most important comment comes from the United States again, in the form of a statement prepared by the Committee on Professional Education of the Music Library Association (MLA).[5] This is a daunting effort which in its coverage and demands has produced some rather abrasive comments here. But, though it has to be recognized that such a large and comprehensive syllabus for the training of music librarians could never be introduced into this country while the present general approach to library education prevails, it must equally be acknowledged that music librarians do need to have the kind of knowledge that is set out in the MLA statement. Fortunately, there are possible alternative ways of acquiring this knowledge. These ways will involve close co-operation between library schools and music libraries, with the processes of education and training taking many years. Most will be done in libraries, but the library schools should provide the basic education and training and the opportunity for regular refreshment through short courses, study seminars and work for higher degrees. The recognition of the necessity for this type of close and carefully planned co-operation is a first step towards solving some of the problems encountered in teaching music bibliography, many of which are implicit in the MLA statement.

1 Problems arising from enquiries.

It has become a feature of the teaching of general and subject bibliography in some schools that much emphasis is placed on enquirers and the kind of questions they are likely to ask.[6] Indeed it is not uncommon in some subjects to spend a whole term at least on a careful study of this area, in the belief that once a logical pattern of enquiry has been worked out it is possible to fit the profiles of readers and their enquiries against the available resources, see where the strengths and weaknesses of the existing literature of a subject lie, and begin to formulate ideas on how the relationships between enquiries and sources can be improved. This is not to suggest that it is easy to establish a pattern for enquiries, but that such a process will help students to understand ways of informing themselves as librarians about the nature of enquiries and show that, even in a seemingly chaotic situation, there are trends and patterns of behaviour which enable them to move towards a clearer understanding of how enquiries can be answered.

The use of this technique has been most successful in subjects like sociology. In subjects like music there is a tendency to take a fairly simple view based on the assumption that the needs of a viola player, a conductor, a piano teacher or a soprano can be fairly clearly defined. Maureen Long's *Report*[7] revealed that in fact the demands made on music libraries were more complex than was thought and that unhappily many of them were not being satisfied. She showed moreover that, while both public and academic library services to musicians and listeners in some areas of the country were very good and had developed considerably since the war, there were still some very grey, indeed black, areas of the country. Unfortunately her full report was not published for fear of repercussions, but the edited version gave a clear indication as to the value of such surveys in demonstrating weaknesses in stock and services. There is need now for a further Long report, but there is also much to be said for a local survey of users' needs and an attempt to recast the service as far as possible to meet revealed trends in demand. Much of this can of course be done by the attentive ear, and academic librarians can build a profile of each user, so that appropriate new publications can be signalled. There is a tendency to ridicule surveys, but provided they are handled properly they can be of immense value[8]. The music librarian will find reports on the musical life of the country completed for other interested groups[9] extremely valuable.

The problems of teaching this aspect of music bibliography spring mainly from a shortage of time and the small part which this subject plays in most studies at present. It is usual for survey techniques to have been examined in general studies such as management. What has to be demonstrated is the validity for music of such exercises. Attention can be drawn to published examples which exist, and the Long report is invaluable here. But this means either a lecture or a handout, neither of which is a particularly effective way of presenting information. Most people shut off mentally very soon after a lecture has started; they may take notes but there is no guarantee they will be the right notes. Too many handouts tend to stay in the students' briefcase unread, sometimes because the number issued by staff is overwhelming. The most useful exercise would be for students themselves to produce a profile of a musical community and its library needs. This is a valuable area for potential co-operation between libraries and schools, provided always that the catchment area is small and the objectives limited, eg a survey of the total musical requirements of viola students in an academy. Such exercises have been completed jointly by a number of libraries and schools in recent years and have proved of benefit to all concerned. They obviously need very careful planning and avoidance of clashes with other subjects' teaching time. Up to now they have not, so far as is known, dealt with music. This is a pity, since for students the subject would be brought alive, as they would then have an opportunity to meet musicians or listeners and hear what each of them wanted in the way of bibliographical services.

They would also learn, most usefully, that musicians cannot

be categorized too easily. Library students tend to be very conservative, in spite of recent indicators of a contrary view, and to favour the tidy rule or idea which can be noted, learned and re-presented as part of an exam answer. There is value in any exercise which reminds them that the world is not a neat and orderly place, in which readers fall into neat little boxes which can be matched with equally neat subjects on the shelves. It is the serious desire to control their study material which makes students put on blinkers and categorize too narrowly. It is a useful shock to discover that the key-board continuo player in a baroque ensemble is also absorbed in rock music and thinks the local library's collection in both subjects 'is pretty poor', that conductors and opera singers sometimes borrow recordings from libraries to learn new pieces quickly and that students are not using the college library because they have not been told about its range of services.

2 Problems inherent in the materials.

This is the real core of the problem. Half an hour spent with Vincent Duckles's invaluable guide[10] will give some grasp of the range of material to be examined. Even John Davies's more conversational approach[11] can be daunting in the extent of knowledge easily won which it implies. The latest survey of music materials by Guy Marco[12] looks likely to be more extensive than either. To expect students to gain a knowledge of all the items covered by these invaluable guides is obviously nonsensical. It is to be hoped that the days are gone when student librarians are expected to learn such details by rote, long lists of titles being read out by a lecturer who would comment briefly on the essential features of each. Taking the exams successfully was more a lottery than an educational process, as students tried to guess by careful examination of previous years' papers which reference books would be required for their turn at the dice. It was not unknown for weaker students to ignore *The new Oxford history of music* and other important histories of music because a question had been set on them the previous year, thereby supposedly increasing their chances of success but reducing their potentiality as librarians. Ignorance of *MGG, Grove, BUCEM* etc could more often be laid at the door of the exam system than attributed to any other cause.

However, gradually, under the influence particularly of Ronald Staveley[13], who worked quietly at his own particular miracle, changes in the system were made and it was seen that there was much more value in the study of the nature of bibliography and the categories into which its resources could be grouped. Once this was done it was possible to take the kinds of enquiry and see which category of material would probably provide the answer to which kind of question.

The literature which builds up around composers' lives and works can be used to illustrate the difference. The older method required students to study the literature associated with all the major (and even the not so important) composers, because they had no idea about which composer they might be asked in the exam. The new approach, which has been used successfully in several schools for over a decade, requires them to examine one composer's works and the associated literature in depth. The composer has to be selected with some care as there has to be a considerable literature available; thus Tchaikovsky is not a possible choice, however popular he may be as a musician. The best are people like Bach, Handel, Mozart, Haydn, Beethoven, Schubert etc. Of the modern composers Bartók and Schoenberg seem to have generated the most literature so far. It is interesting to speculate on the absence of French and Italian names, although in recent years Verdi's documentation has increased rapidly. Good students can be allowed to study lesser composers (purely in the bibliographical sense!) in the hope that comparisons may be made and questions asked about the gaps in their documentation.

The first part of the exercise, which ideally extends over three terms and is completed concurrently with other work, is to find out about the composer, how he is treated in general and special encyclopaedias, histories, etc, what music he wrote etc. In the second term a list of all the items associated with him is produced and arranged into categories such as popular biographies, books for children, reminiscences of friends, documentary and/or picture biographies, thematic catalogues, publishers' lists, analyses, popular guides to the music, collected editions, Urtext editions, recordings, discographies etc. This list is neither exhaustive nor arranged in any order; it merely demonstrates the kind of categories discussed. It is the responsibility of the student to produce an exhaustive list of categories, to suggest the kind of questions each might answer and to support each category with examples from the literature associated with the selected composer. This work occupies the third term. On completion the study has enabled several things to be done: firstly, all kinds of bibliographies and reference works will have been searched for information about the composer; secondly, several libraries will have been visited and their catalogues used and shelf arrangement tested; thirdly, the student will have the satisfaction of having completed a major piece of work demanding the qualities of search, concentration, attention to detail and accuracy which a professional bibliographer must have; finally, the knowledge about one composer's literature can be used as a key to answer enquiries about other composers. Thus, if it is established that the identity of one of Bach's works can be substantiated by reference to Schmieder's thematic catalogue it is reasonable to suppose that Burghauser's similar study of Dvořák's music will provide the same answer for Dvořák.

A sleight of hand has been accomplished here. Students have been given the impression that they have acquired the same knowledge which earlier students achieved by rote learning of long lists. They have not. They have been given something rather better, as they have acquired a knowledge of the structure of bibliographical work associated with composers and the ability to apply that knowledge in any comparable situation. It is not only a better and more interesting way to acquire knowledge, but also provides a stimulus to further study. The same technique can be applied, though not quite so successfully, to subjects like jazz, folk and rock music. It can certainly be applied to the great artists of these styles of music, each of whom rapidly attracts an impressive literature. Here students can be brought to understand the difficulties of acquiring ephemeral literature and the need to be able to tap unfamiliar sources. Explorations of the recording industry can be included, and by practical experience of trying to acquire information students can be made aware of the lack of discographical control of important styles of music.

Nevertheless it has to be admitted that the fundamental problem still remains. The literature about music is vast and students still leave library school knowing only a fraction of it. It is, perhaps, strange that music has generated so many words about itself when its apologists claim that it has a power of speech beyond words! It can be accepted that a fairly high proportion of this material does not merit retention in the memory, but even so there remains a mass of reference sources and monograph studies of sufficient merit for an employing librarian to expect their names to bring a glimmer of recognition in students' eyes when they begin their first employment after library school. Thus the old battle is joined and lecturers are chastised because students do not know Altmann. They know Farish, but then the library may not have that. Perhaps the librarian might be encouraged to acquire it by the students' comments on its value. At the same time the students might be taught about Altmann and have its particular virtues demonstrated. The point at issue here is not really the failure of the library school to provide adequate teaching, but the misunderstanding of the learning process which must be attributed to many librarians.

The period at library school, which is at most four years, is in reality a very small part of a librarian's total career of about forty years. As has already been suggested, the learning process must continue through the whole of a career and therefore it has to be accepted that libraries have probably a more important rôle than the schools in the education and training of librarians. They must build on the basis established by the schools and, particularly in the early career years, there must be a carefully planned training programme which makes full use of all a library's resources and widens young librarians' knowledge of bibliographical materials. The acquiring of this knowledge cannot be left to chance. The best libraries already have such training programmes and in addition frequently send their staff on refresher courses arranged by the schools. Only on such a basis of concerted effort can British music librarians hope to train new entrants to the standard implied by the MLA syllabus.

There are of course many other ways of teaching music bibliography; the approach by composer study has been used only as an example. That method is perhaps more appropriate for the two-year non-graduate and three or four-year undergraduate courses, because of the time involved. For the postgraduate one-year course it has proved better to ask students to complete a bibliography of a very narrow topic within the subject of music. Examples are the effect of Nazism on music in Germany, music in the Vauxhall gardens in the eighteenth century, the Victorian piano makers, chamber music of the Second Viennese School of composers etc. The chosen topic must be small enough to produce a total of between thirty and fifty items and, to achieve this, can be further limited in various ways, such as by language to books in English, by date to publications issued since 1945 etc. The final product should also contain examples of different kinds of materials, eg monographs, periodicals, theses, recordings, etc. Each item must be correctly catalogued and a number of them annotated and abstracted. In addition there must be an introduction, a sample index and a working report showing clearly the steps by which the work has been done. Once again it means a variety of tools will have been handled and knowledge about them gained. The satisfaction level for the student is apparently fairly high, particularly because the work is complete in itself and so far as can be reasonably ascertained no one has ever done it before. The procedures, information and knowledge gained can be applied to other topics. In fact it is possible for students to find themselves in their first appointment after library school doing precisely the same kind of work for readers. Perhaps the final proof of these two methods having aroused the interest of students is in the care which is generally lavished on the presentation of their work for examination.

They are of great value therefore, for, as Paugh and Marco [3] suggest, a lecture is not a very stimulating method of presenting such material. Nor, as they quite rightly comment, is a request for oral reports on titles which have been examined. Bibliographies of music are not very exciting viewed on their own; they only really stimulate interest when examined in a quest for knowledge. Nevertheless, such is the time factor in most courses that some lectures and comparison seminars have to be included in order to draw students' attention to some of the tools which they will use in their own work. These are best presented by trying to convey some impression of the current situation as far as users are concerned, the kind of information they might want from the particular category of materials being examined and how the existing sources can be used to supply the information. This enables attention to be drawn to gaps in overall coverage, eg the lack of a national discography and the consequences, the fact that information supplied is not always accurate and needs to be checked in more than one source if possible, and that other libraries etc are valuable when the printed sources prove fallible.

Most libraries depend on public funds for their finance, and it seems likely that, whatever the political persuasion of the government, these are going to be severely restricted in the years ahead. It is important therefore that the librarians of the future should be stimulated to use their ingenuity to find answers to questions presented to them, as there is no doubt that the demand for a high level of service will continue alongside the demand for a restriction in funds. It follows therefore that methods of teaching and presentation of subjects like music bibliography must be constantly examined, so that students are stimulated to broaden and deepen their knowledge not only of users and materials, but also of techniques and methods of finding answers. The problem then is that library schools also depend on public funds and are being similarly restricted. Nevertheless, such is human ingenuity that faith remains that solutions will be found. The situation is difficult and calls for the maximum co-operation, which can best be provided within the framework of IAML, where so much has already been achieved.

REFERENCES

1 B Redfern 'The education of music librarians in the United Kingdom' *Fontes artis musicae* xxv 1978, 217-219.

2 L R McColvin *The public library system of Great Britain. A report on its present condition with proposals for post-war re-organisation* London, 1942, 182-189.

3 S L Paugh and G Marco 'The music bibliography course : status and quo' *Notes* xxx 1973, 260-262.

4 Several reports from the Bergen conference have appeared in *Fontes* since 1977, eg H Bruhns and B Christiansen 'Music library education in Denmark' *Fontes artis musicae* xxv 1978, 142-145.

5 'Qualifications of a music librarian' *Journal of education for librarianship* xv 1974, 53-59.

6 C D Needham 'The design of undergraduate courses' *Curriculum development in librarianship and information science* London, 1978, 7-27.

7 M W Long *Musicians and libraries in the United Kingdom* London, 1972.

8 L A Martin 'User studies and library planning' *Library trends* xxiv 1976, 483-496.

9 *A report on orchestral resources in Great Britain* London, 1970.

10 V Duckles *Music reference and research materials* 3rd ed New York, 1974.

11 J H Davies *Musicalia* 2nd ed London, 1969.

12 G Marco *Information on music: a handbook of reference sources in European languages* Littleton, Colorado, 1975-   , in progress. 6 volumes.

13 R Staveley *Notes on subject bibliography* London, 1962.